FIELDS OF FAITH

How will the study of theology and the religions in higher education be shaped in the coming century? This book offers several different perspectives on this field of study with suggestions for a future in which theology and religious studies are pursued together. There are examples of the interplay of theology and religious studies with reference to a range of topics: God, love, scripture, worship, argument, reconciliation, friendship and justice. The contributors practise different disciplines within the field, often in combination, covering theology, philosophy, history, phenomenology, literary studies, hermeneutics, politics, ethics and law. Their specialisms embrace Judaism, Christianity, Islam and Indian religions, with particular focus on the field in Europe, the US and South Africa. Recognising the significance of the religions and of higher education, the book explores what best practice can be adopted to fulfil responsibilities towards academic disciplines, the religions and the societies of which they are part.

FIELDS OF FAITH

*Theology and Religious Studies for the
Twenty-First Century*

EDITED BY

DAVID F. FORD, BEN QUASH AND
JANET MARTIN SOSKICE

PUBLISHED BY THE PRESS SYNDICATE OF THE UNIVERSITY OF CAMBRIDGE
The Pitt Building, Trumpington Street, Cambridge, United Kingdom

CAMBRIDGE UNIVERSITY PRESS
The Edinburgh Building, Cambridge CB2 2RU, UK
40 West 20th Street, New York NY 10011–4211, USA
477 Williamstown Road, Port Melbourne, VIC 3207, Australia
Ruiz de Alarcón 13, 28014 Madrid, Spain
Dock House, The Waterfront, Cape Town 8001, South Africa

http://www.cambridge.org

First published 2005

Printed in the United Kingdom at the University Press, Cambridge

Typeface Adobe Garamond 11/12.5 pt.   *System* LATEX 2ε   [TB]

A catalogue record for this book is available from the British Library

Library of Congress Cataloguing in Publication data
Fields of faith : theology and religious studies for the twenty-first century / edited by David F. Ford,
Ben Quash, and Janet Martin Soskice.
p.   cm.
Includes bibliographical references and index.
ISBN 0 521 84737 0
1. Religion–Study and teaching (Higher)   2. Theology–Study and teaching (Higher)
I. Ford, David, 1948-   II. Quash, Ben.   III. Soskice, Janet Martin.
BL41.F53   2004
200′.71′1 – dc22   2004054643

ISBN 0 521 84737 0 hardback

This book is dedicated to
Nicholas Lash
Norris-Hulse Professor of Divinity
in the University of Cambridge
1978–1999
in honour of his immense contribution
to philosophical theology,
to the whole field of theology and religious studies,
to the University of Cambridge and in particular its Faculty of Divinity,
to the Catholic Church, other Churches, and other religious traditions,
with great gratitude from
his many friends and colleagues,
among them the contributors to this book.

Contents

Notes on contributors

NICHOLAS ADAMS is Lecturer in Systematic Theology and Theological Ethics, New College, University of Edinburgh. His research is at the interface between doctrine and ethics, with special interests in eschatology and in the influence of German philosophy on theology.

MICHAEL J. BUCKLEY S.J. is Professor of Theology at Boston College. He is the author of numerous articles and books in systematic theology, philosophy, spirituality, science and theology, and the history of ideas including *At the Origins of Modern Atheism* (1987), and *The Catholic University as Promise and Project* (1999).

SARAH COAKLEY is Edward Mallinckrodt Professor of Divinity at the Divinity School, Harvard University. She is primarily a systematic theologian and philosopher of religion, but her teaching also includes topics in feminist theory and theology, patristic thought, and applied theology. Her books include *Religion and the Body* (1997), *Powers and Submissions: Spirituality, Philosophy and Gender* (2002) and *Re-Thinking Gregory of Nyssa* (ed., 2003). Professor Coakley is an ordained priest of the Church of England.

OLIVER DAVIES is Professor of Theology, King's College, University of London. He is also a visiting fellow at the Centre for the Study of Christianity and Culture at Regent's Park College, University of Oxford. He is co-editor with Denys Turner of *Silence and the Word* (2002) and author of *A Theology of Compassion* (2001) and *The Creativity of God* (2004).

EAMON DUFFY is Professor of the History of Christianity at the University of Cambridge. His research interests include the iconography and history of medieval Christian art, and popular religion in the Middle Ages and Reformation. His books include *The Stripping of the Altars* (1992), *Saints and Sinners: A History of the Popes* (2002) and *The Voices of Morebath: Reformation and Rebellion in an English Village* (2003).

GAVIN FLOOD is Professor of Religious Studies at the University of Stirling. His main work has been on South Asian traditions, particularly Hindu Tantra, and he has research interests in textuality, phenomenology, asceticism, and theory and method in the study of religion. His publications include *An Introduction to Hinduism* (1996) and *The Blackwell Companion to Hinduism* (ed., 2003).

DAVID F. FORD is Regius Professor of Divinity at the University of Cambridge and a Fellow of Selwyn College, Cambridge. He is Chairman of the management committee of the Centre for Advanced Religious and Theological Studies and Director of the Cambridge Interfaith Programme. His many publications include *Theology: A Very Short Introduction* (1999) and *Self and Salvation* (1999).

JOHN W. DE GRUCHY is Professor Emeritus of Christian Studies at the University of Cape Town. His published works include *Reconciliation: Restoring Justice* (2003), *Christianity, Art and Transformation* (2001) and *The Cambridge Companion to Dietrich Bonhoeffer* (1999).

JULIUS LIPNER is Professor of Hinduism and the Comparative Study of Religion at the University of Cambridge. His research interests include the classical Vedanta, truth and inter-religious dialogue and nineteenth-century Bengal. His publications include *Hindus: Their Religious Beliefs and Practices* (1994).

MALEIHA MALIK is a lecturer at the School of Law, King's College, London. She specialises in tort, jurisprudence, and anti-discrimination law. Her recent publications include 'Faith and the State of Jurisprudence', in *Faith in Law: Essays in Legal Theory*, ed. S. Douglas Scott et al. (2000).

PETER OCHS is the Edgar M. Bronfman Professor of Modern Judaic Studies at the University of Virginia and cofounder of the Society for Scriptural Reasoning and the Society for Textual Reasoning. He is the author of *Peirce, Pragmatism and the Logic of Scripture* (1998), and an editor of *Christianity in Jewish Terms* (2000).

BEN QUASH is Dean and Fellow of Peterhouse and lectures at the Faculty of Divinity, University of Cambridge, where he is also Convenor of the Cambridge Interfaith Programme. He has a particular interest in the nineteenth-century background to modern theology, twentieth-century

Catholic and Protestant thought, philosophical theology, ethics, and the use and interpretation of the Bible both within and across religious traditions.

JANET MARTIN SOSKICE is Reader in Philosophical Theology at the University of Cambridge and Fellow and Director of Studies at Jesus College, Cambridge. She has research interests in the symbolics of gender, and in the Divine names. Her publications include *Metaphor and Religious Language* (1984), *Medicine and Moral Reasoning* (ed. with Gillett and Fulford, 1994), and *Feminism and Theology* (ed. with Diana Lipton, 2003).

DENYS TURNER is Norris-Hulse Professor of Divinity at the University of Cambridge. His research interests are high and late medieval mystical theologies, Denys the Carthusian and God. He is the author of *Marxism and Christianity* (1983), *The Darkness of God* (1995) and *Faith Seeking* (2002) and co-editor of *Silence and the Word* (2002) with Oliver Davies.

ROWAN WILLIAMS, Archbishop of Canterbury, has written a number of books on the history of theology and spirituality and published collections of articles and sermons. He has been involved in various commissions on theology and theological education, was a member of the Church Schools Review Group led by Lord Dearing, and chaired the group that produced the report *Wales: a Moral Society?* His recent publications include: *On Christian Theology* (2000), *Writing in the Dust: Reflections on 11th September and Its Aftermath* (2002) and *Anglican Identities* (2004).

Introduction

David F. Ford

How is the study of theology and religions in higher education to be shaped in the coming century? There is obviously no single answer to that question. Empirically, there will of course continue to be great diversity in the ways the field is formed, some of which do not accept that theology and the study of religions should be institutionally connected. This diversity is rooted in different histories, interests, commitments and visions, but there is little enough literature that engages with these in order to shape a fruitful future for the field. The lack is especially serious in relation to those settings where theology and religious studies go together, the number and vitality of which increased in the last quarter of the twentieth century.

The contributors to this book examine that togetherness from various angles with a view to the future. They do this in Part I by giving accounts of the field and making suggestions about its future; and then in Part II by 'performing' the interplay of theology and religious studies. In this part the claim that the two should come together is supported by showing in practice that the treatment of significant topics benefits from their interplay. In conclusion, there is a response to the book based on some intensive discussion between an editor, a contributor, and a participant in the consultation that was part of the book's genesis.

The aim of the book is therefore to conceptualise, exemplify and reflect upon the study of theology and religions, with a special concern for the interaction of two dimensions of the field that are often separated institutionally. It is conceived not only in relation to those settings where theology and religious studies already come together, but also to those where there is a more single-minded focus on either 'theology' or 'religious studies'. As decisions are taken about course topics, contents and methods, and about institutional policies in teaching, research and staffing, it can be of considerable importance whether a basic commitment to theology is open to contributions from religious studies or a religious studies tradition is hospitable to theology. For those academics who are working in the field, or are trying to orient themselves early in their careers, the horizon within which they see their specialism can help shape their research, teaching and career decisions.

Yet the shaping of this field has implications far beyond the academy. The contributions in Part II especially show this. Under the heading of 'Understanding Faith' a series of basic questions is explored. What if modern notions of 'religion' and 'mysticism' are shown to be untenable by a critique that draws simultaneously on phenomenology of religion and theology? (Williams) If love is a widespread human phenomenon worthy of academic and theological attention, how can Theology and Religious Studies do justice to it in the context of a secular university? (Lipner) Lipner's questions about religious studies, descriptive theology and performative theology are strikingly addressed by Ochs in his discussion of Jewish study of scripture and Talmud after the Shoah, of the University of Virginia's model of 'religious studies as comparative traditions', and of 'theological studies as scriptural reasoning' in engagement with Jewish, Christian and Muslim scriptures. Ochs even offers four basic rules for the peaceful co-existence of theology and religious studies. The fourth contribution in this part shifts the focus to worship: how would hundreds of millions of Christians be worshipping today if Jungmann's tendentious account of liturgical development had been less influential? (Duffy)

'The Practice of Justice and Love' raises a further four radical questions. What if academic argument were to serve the task of learning a wisdom for living? (Adams) What can a divided, multi-racial and multi-faith society such as South Africa's learn from academic contributions that help religious communities not only to understand each other but also to engage in critical and constructive research, teaching and dialogues with a view to a better common future? (de Gruchy) What if a Jewish conception of friendship with God and other people were to be practised more widely in the academy and elsewhere? (Soskice) Her analysis of Western Christian traditions on friendship (including a *jeu d'esprit* on gender) is Christian theology done in the formative presence of another faith and resonates with Ochs on comparative traditions and scriptural reasoning. Finally, how is a minority religious community to relate its understanding and practice concerning justice to the public institutions and debates of a liberal Western democracy? (Malik) The mutual inextricability of elements that are often ascribed either to theology or to religious studies is especially demonstrated in such practical implications for worldviews, politics, the life of religious communities and personal relationships.

Through these chapters elements that are often ascribed in binary fashion either to theology or to religious studies are found to be mutually inextricable. The artificiality and even destructiveness of separating the two is especially clear when the large, deep questions are tackled and there is a need to draw on all relevant resources to do justice to them. Philosophy, history, phenomenology, literary studies, hermeneutics, semiotics, liturgiology, politics, ethics and law are all in play. They are employed very differently, but they are not self-enclosed: they are in dialogue with each other and also allow for theological questioning and answering.

This complex set of interactions requires the sort of theology, history, philosophy, 'thick description' and fresh conceptualising that Part I brings to bear on the field. The overall intention is not to propose a general framework for the field that might be universally applied. It is rather an attempt to articulate and debate the wisdom that has been learnt in particular traditions, institutions and conversations under specific historical influences and constraints. This family of understandings, together with critical questions about it, is shared in the hope that others in their settings might have something to learn from it, and that the interplay of theology and religious studies might be more widely accepted as deserving to be a major contributor to the future of the field.

The contributors' particularity and the refusal to offer generalised prescriptions for all contexts is reflected in the specificity of the book's origins. Britain is the country in which the institutional association of Theology and Religious Studies in universities is most common. Most of the authors are based in British universities (though some have origins in Ireland, North America and South Asia), but there are also contributions from universities in the US and South Africa, in both of which there have been developments that combine Theology with Religious Studies. In addition, part of the process that generated the book was a four-day consultation on 'The Future of the Study of Theology and Religions'. There, initial drafts of some of the chapters were intensively discussed by a group of sixty invited academics, who greatly expanded the religious, disciplinary, institutional and geographical range of the input.

In British universities, for reasons largely to do with history and the religious makeup of the country, there is more study of Christianity than of other religions. This local characteristic is also reflected in the book. Eight authors of chapters specialise in areas related to Christianity, two in Indian religions, one in Judaism and one in Islam.

Within Britain, the largest single group of contributors (the editors and three others) is from the University of Cambridge. The consultation mentioned above was preceded by two years of preparatory discussion during which senior seminars of the Cambridge Faculty of Divinity (covering the religious traditions of Christianity, Judaism, Islam, Hinduism and Buddhism, and also the study of religions by the human sciences) engaged with questions relating to the future of their field. Many of the sessions drew together seminars specialising in different areas in order to do justice to the interdisciplinary nature of the field. In the last quarter of the twentieth century the Cambridge Faculty had gone beyond its traditional study of Christianity to include other religious traditions in its curriculum and call its main degree course 'Theology and Religious Studies'. The seminar discussions that contributed to this book took place as the pace and range of the Faculty's development accelerated, embracing a Centre for Advanced Religious and Theological Studies, new posts, a revised curriculum, the construction of a Faculty building, and new forms of collaboration with the expanding Cambridge Theological Federation (Anglican, Methodist, Roman Catholic, Orthodox, United Reformed, and a Centre for Jewish–Christian Relations). This meant that ideas about the nature of the field and its future were being applied and tested in practical ways that involved not only the University and its disciplines but also many religious communities and a range of other constituencies that were concerned with research projects or with funding.

Finally, and most important of all in the genesis of this book, there has been one particular person, Nicholas Lash, the Norris-Hulse Professor of Divinity in the University of Cambridge from 1978 till 1999. While playing a leading role in national and international theology and philosophy of religion he was also pivotal over many years in the development of the Cambridge Faculty of Divinity described above. He succeeded in his chair one of the towering figures of British philosophical theology, Donald MacKinnon. Like MacKinnon, Lash succeeded both in sustaining a lively engagement with the tradition of analytical philosophy and at the same time in cultivating a rich – and often sharply critical – theological, literary and political sensibility. Lash also developed his own distinctive theological thrust, indebted to Aquinas, Schleiermacher, Lonergan, Rahner, and perhaps above all to John Henry Newman. He helped to make England a leading centre for lay Roman Catholic theology, and himself played a vital role as its most distinguished academic and arbiter of intellectual quality. His most recent major work, *The Beginning and the End of 'Religion'*,[1] could be read as offering the historical, philosophical and theological rationale for

---

[1] Cambridge: Cambridge University Press, 1996.

the claim that in university settings both Theology and Religious Studies flourish best together. In place of the Enlightenment's 'neutral ground' it cultivates the 'mutual ground' of particular traditions in deep engagement with each other.

It was this book that inspired the thought that the appropriate way to mark Nicholas Lash's retirement would be to do some serious collaborative thinking about the field of theology and religious studies. Those of us in the Faculty who came together to plan the process of seminars, consultation and the present book did not, however, want to deprive ourselves of Nicholas's contribution to our discussions. So we shared our intentions with him and have had the benefit of his participation, especially in the consultation. We dedicate the result to him, with great gratitude for a lifetime's achievement, and in the hope that the fruits of his retirement will contribute yet further to the field.

In his Teape Lectures, delivered in India in 1994, he suggested that 'we should understand the great traditions as schools whose pedagogy serves to wean us from idolatry'.[2] He drew deeply on the Abrahamic and Indian religious traditions to evoke the purification of desire and the disciplines of adoration, affirmation and negation that are part of that schooling. In the last lecture he daringly explored affinities between Brahman and the Trinity under the heading of 'reality, wisdom and delight', and the culminating section of that lecture was entitled 'In Quest of Wisdom'. In it he recalled an earlier remark about the crisis of our time being characterised by the extent to which our ingenuity has outstripped our wisdom. It is a diagnosis that may seem uncomfortably appropriate to the field of theology and religious studies, with its ramifying ingenuity in methods, critiques, constructions and deconstructions. He continues: 'It would therefore seem that those of us who live, work, and think within the ancient schools of wisdom that we call "religions" bear heavy burdens of responsibility to the wider culture.'[3] Perhaps the most fundamental challenge for those of us in the field of theology and religious studies is to let our passion for wisdom outstrip our ingenuity in the interests of fulfilling responsibilities towards our world.

[2] Ibid., p. 60.   [3] Ibid., p. 71.

PART I

The End of the Enlightenment's Neutral Ground

CHAPTER I

The study of religion and the rise of atheism: conflict or confirmation?

Michael J. Buckley S.J.

INTRODUCTION TO THE QUESTION

'Religion' and 'theology' are not terms with fixed meanings and invariant applications. They are rather topics or commonplaces – not in the sense of the familiar and the trite, but in the classical sense of linguistic variables, terms ambiguous and capacious enough to house a vast diversity of meanings, arguments, and referents.[1] The interconnection of such topics constitutes neither a determined problem nor an exact proposition. It constitutes what John Dewey called 'a problematic situation', an indeterminate area out of which problems and their resolutions can emerge only if these ambiguous terms are given specific meanings and definite applications within particular inquiries.[2] Recognising the ambiguity of both 'religion' and 'theology', this paper proposes to obtain a greater purchase on the problematic situation they together delimit, first, by offering a few precisions on 'religion' as its meaning developed through history to reach its generic consensus in late modernity; and then, by exploring how the scientific study of religion, so understood, came to engage one of the arguments of modern theology: the existence or non-existence of God.

In a remarkable review of the scientific study of religion over a fifty-year period, Mircea Eliade provides a benchmark for this project by selecting 1912 as a date of particular consequence.[3] That year, five stars rose in the firmament. Émile Durkheim published his *Formes élémentaires de la vie religieuse*. Sigmund Freud 'was correcting the proofs of *Totem und Tabu*, to be issued in book form the following year', and Carl Jung was publishing his

---

[1] See Richard P. McKeon, 'Creativity, and the Commonplace', in Mark Backman, ed., *Rhetoric: Essays in Invention and Discovery* (Woodbridge, CT: Ox Bow Press, 1987), pp. 25–36. For commonplaces as linguistic variables, see Aristotle, *Topics*, 1.13–18, 105a20–108a36; *Rhetoric* 1.2.1358a10–35; 2.23.1398a27–8.

[2] See John Dewey, *Logic: The Theory of Inquiry* (New York: Holt, Rinehart and Winston), pp. 105–8.

[3] Mircea Eliade, 'The History of Religions in Retrospect: 1912 and After', in *The Quest: History and Meaning in Religion* (Chicago: University of Chicago Press, 1969), pp. 12–36.

Wandlungen und Symbole der Libido. Raffaele Pettazoni's first monograph, *La religione primitiva in Sardegna,* appeared that same year, and Wilhelm Schmidt completed the first of the twelve volumes in his monumental study *Der Ursprung der Gottesidee.*

In these five works, four very different methodologies advanced towards greater academic acceptance and influential presence in the scientific study of religion: the sociological, the psychological, the ethnological and the historical. Eliade paints all this in broad brush strokes, depicting the intrinsic value and perduring authority of each of his chosen authors. What he does not examine or evaluate, however, forms the interest of this essay. For these seminal and even paradigmatic studies from the early twentieth century bore witness, in all of their diversity of methods, to an agreement and a controversy about religion: an agreement about the genus that 'religion' had become over the centuries, and a controversy over the collateral that religion so understood would offer to belief and unbelief.

RELIGION: FROM VIRTUE TO CATEGORY
OF 'THINGS'[4]

To chart something of the lengthy journey by which 'religion' reached its generic and accepted understanding by 1912, this essay proposes – as they do on the Mississippi – to take three soundings. It will drop a plumb line into the medieval controversies of Thomas Aquinas; then, gauge the modification of that tradition in the heady days of Baroque scholasticism; and finally allow Eliade's Five to exemplify the 'religion' secured by late modernity. Such discrete measurements might supplement, rather than repeat, the magisterial studies of such scholars as Wilfred Cantwell Smith and Peter Harrison.

For Thomas Aquinas, '*religio*' – irrespective of how one comes down on its etymology – 'properly denotes or implies a relationship to God (*proprie importat ordinem ad Deum*)'.[5] More specifically, it designates a habit or a virtue by which one gives God what is due to God, and in this way lives 'in an appropriate relationship with God'.[6] But since it is impossible to render to God all that is owed to the divine goodness, religion always limps. Religion is like justice in that it renders to another what is his or her due. Because of its inherent inadequacy, however, it does not simply identify

---

[4] For the history of 'religion', see Wilfred Cantwell Smith, *The Meaning and End of Religion* (Minneapolis: Fortress Press, 1991), pp. 15–50.
[5] *Summa theologiae* 2-2.81.1.   [6] Ibid., 2-2.81.2.

with justice, but is a virtue joined to justice, i.e., a potential part of justice.[7] God enters into the constitution of religion not as its direct object, not that to which it immediately attends, but as the end or purpose of what *religio* does properly attend to, i.e., any human action or thing that embodies the worship and service of God. Such practices could be external activities like public adoration or sacrifice or vowing or, more importantly and primarily, internal actions such as devotion and prayer.[8] These individual or social actions and cultic units are not religion; they are the acts and objects of religion. They look to God; religion looks to them. Thus *religio* is a moral rather than a theological virtue, taking such human acts and practices as its direct object.[9]

For this reason, unlike the use of this term in the English Enlightenment, religion could never substitute in Aquinas for faith, though to be 'true religion' it had to be grounded on true faith.[10] But religion was comprehensive; it could command the acts of all the virtues and human activities insofar as they were directed to the service and honour of God.[11] William T. Cavanaugh narrows the range and acts of religion considerably by maintaining that *religio* for St Thomas 'presupposes a context of ecclesial practices which are both communal and particular to the Christian Church'. It certainly includes these practices, but there is no justification for limiting *religio* in this fashion. *Religio* can command a single and private act of worship or service as well as a communal one. Cavanaugh further and needlessly insists that 'religion refers specifically to the liturgical practices of the Church'.[12] Again these are certainly included in Aquinas's *religio*,

---

[7] Ibid., 2-2.80.prol and art. 1; 81.5.ad 3.

[8] Ibid., 2-2.81.1.ad 1; 81.4. ad 4; 81.7: 'Mens autem humana indiget ad hoc quod conjungatur Deo, sensibilium manuductione … Et ideo in divino cultu necesse est aliquibus corporalibus uti, ut eis quasi signis quibusdam mens hominis excitetur ad spirituales actus quibus Deo conjungitur. Et ideo religio habet quidem interiores actus *quasi principales et per se ad religionem pertinentes*, exteriores vero actus quasi secundarios et ad interiores actus ordinatos.' (Emphasis added.)

[9] Ibid., 2-2.81.5. See *In Boeth. De Trinitate* 3.2: 'Ipsa tamen religio non est virtus theologica: habet enim pro materia quasi omnes actus, ut fidei, vel virtutis alterius, quos Deo tamquam debitos offert; sed Deum habet pro fine. Colere enim Deum est hujusmodi actus ut Deo debitos offerre.'

[10] Peter Harrison, *'Religion' and the religions in the English Enlightenment* (Cambridge: Cambridge University Press, 1990), pp. 61ff. See *In Boeth. De Trinitate* 3.2: '… actus fidei pertinet quidem materialiter ad religionem, sicut et aliarum virtutum, et magis in quantum fidei actus est primus motus mentis in Deum; sed formaliter a religione distinguitur, utpote aliam rationem objecti considerans. Convenit etiam fides cum religione praeter hoc, inquantum fides est religionis causa et principium. Non enim aliquis eligeret cultum Deo exhibere, nisi fide teneret Deum esse creatorem, gubernatorem et remuneratorem humanorum actuum.'

[11] *Summa theologiae* 2-2.186.1.ad 2; 81.1.ad 1. See *In Boeth. De Trinitate* 3.2: 'Sic ergo omnes actus quibus se homo subjicit Deo, sive sint mentis, sive corporis ad religionem pertinent.' And even further: 'et sic diligenter consideranti apparet omnem actum bonum ad religionem pertinere.'

[12] William T. Cavanaugh, 'The Wars of Religion and the Rise of the State', *Modern Theology* 11/4 (October 1995), pp. 403–4. For the sweeping character of Aquinas's understanding of *religio*, see

but by no means exhaustive of it. Aquinas, relying explicitly upon Cicero, is far more generous in the inclusion he gives to *religio*. It can be pagan or Christian, private or social, as long as it directs one to the service and reverence of God.

By the same act, a human being both serves and worships God. For worship looks to the excellence of God, to which reverence is due. Service, however, looks to the subjection of the human person, who by reason of his condition is obliged to give reverence to God. To these two acts belong all the acts that are attributed to religion, because through all of them the human being acknowledges the divine excellence and his subjection to God, either by offering something to God or also by accepting something divine'.[13]

This is far more sweeping than Christian liturgical practices and specific symbols and beliefs and is not constrained into the public/private distinction. *Religio* looks to all of the acts by which God is served and worshipped as '*principium creationis et gubernationis rerum*', whether Christian or not.[14]

For Aquinas, *pace* Wilfred Cantwell Smith, this virtue constituted the fundamental meaning of *religio* – a good habit, not 'an activity of the soul' and not just a 'prompting', but a developed capacity and inclination.[15] What is astonishing to record is the close conjunction that Aquinas draws between *religio* and *sanctitas* – in light of the role that 'the sacred' will play later in the works of Durkheim and Eliade. *Sanctitas* and *religio* differ not in essence but only in their grammar, as one might here translate *ratione*. *Religio* (*dicitur*) is said to look to all of the acts by which God is served and worshipped as '*principium creationis et gubernationis rerum*' whether Christian or not, while sanctity (*dicitur*) bespeaks not only divine worship but 'the work of all of the virtues or all good works by which the human person disposes herself for divine worship.'[16]

It is here that institution entered into the ambit of Thomistic '*religio*.' Those who dedicate their entire lives to this divine service are called *religiosi*, and their groupings and communities became 'religious orders' or

---

2-2.81.4. ad 2: 'Omnia, secundum quod in gloriam Dei fiunt, pertinent ad religionem, non quasi ad elicientem sed quasi ad imperantem; illa autem pertinent ad religionem elicientem quae secundum rationem sua speciei pertinent ad reverentiam Dei.'

[13] *Summa theologiae* 2-2.81.3.ad 2: 'Eodem actu homo servit Deo et colit ipsum; nam cultus respicit Dei excellentiam, cui reverentia debetur; servitus autem respicit subjectionem hominis, qui ex sua conditione obligatur ad exhibendam reverentiam Deo. Et ad haec duo pertinent omnes actus qui religioni attribuuntur, quia per omnes homo protestatur divinam excellentiam et subjectionem sui ad Deum, vel exhibendo aliquid ei, vel etiam assumendo aliquid divinum.'

[14] Ibid., 2-2.81.3.

[15] See Smith, *Meaning and End of Religion*, p. 32. See *In Boeth. De Trinitate* 3.2: 'religio est specialis virtus, in actibus omnium virtutem specialem rationem objecti considerans, scilicet Deo debitum.'

[16] *Summa theologiae* 2-2.81.3.

'*religions*'.[17] 'Religion' not only denoted a virtue, but also the 'status' of those whose vows were specified by that virtue.

In the thirteenth century, *religio* combined into a phrase that bespoke an Augustinian rather than a Ciceronian heritage. At least sixty-eight times, Aquinas, following a lead taken from Augustine, joined *christiana* with *religio*. Indeed, he made the avowed purpose of the *Summa theologiae* 'to treat those things that pertain to Christian *religio* in the manner that would be appropriate to the instruction of beginners'.[18] But what was meant by this *christiana religio* was not the institution and the set of characteristic beliefs, symbols, or ceremonial practices of the Church, as it is so often interpreted, but rather something much closer to what one would today call Christian piety or devotion. Aquinas, of course, specified 'piety' quite differently, but *religio* remained a virtue that would govern and be expressed in practices and devotions. For Aquinas, these latter were not religion, either severally or collectively; they were the objects of religion. With such an understanding, it could make perfect sense to assert that 'the highest reaches of Christian religion consist in mercy in so far as one is speaking of exterior works; but the interior affection of charity, whereby we are united with God, takes precedence over love and mercy towards our neighbor'.[19] Aquinas never gives any indication that Christianity is one institutional religion out of many, that religion was a genus specified into various communities of different beliefs, practices and traditions. In fact he never groups *religio* with other traditions such as the Jewish, Muslim or pagan.

In this understanding of 'religion', John Calvin and Huldreich Zwingli seem much closer to Aquinas. When Zwingli titled his book, *De vera et falsa religione commentarius*, he was not distinguishing between two communities with their characteristic and divergent beliefs, symbols and practices. He differentiated, as had Lactantius before him, between two different attitudes towards worship.[20] True religion is that piety or reverence that emerges from the comprehensive entrustment of oneself to the true God in faith; false religion occurs when this reverence is given to anything other than God.[21] When John Calvin published *Christianae religionis institutio* in 1536, he was writing not about 'the' Christian religion – one denomination

---

[17] Ibid., 2.81.1.ad 5 and 2-2.186.1.ad 2.

[18] Ibid., Prologue: '. . . ea quae ad Christianam religionem pertinent eo modo tradere secundum quod congruit ad eruditionem incipientium.'

[19] Ibid., 2-2.30.4.ad 2: '. . . summa religionis Christianae in misericordia consistit quantum ad exteriora opera, interior tamen affectio caritatis, qua conjungimur deo, praeponderat et dilectioni et misericordiae in proximos.'

[20] Smith, *Meaning and End of Religion*, pp. 27–8.

[21] Ibid., pp. 35–6, 224 n. 83, 84. For the meaning of *vera religio* in Aquinas, see 2-2.81.3.sc.

among many other religious bodies – but about Christian piety. It was
not until the nineteenth century that translations placed a definite article
before the adjective 'Christian' and brought John Calvin into the more
contemporary understanding of 'religion', one that he had never actually
shared.[22]

This basic understanding of 'religion' allowed Schleiermacher to move
consistently from a defence of religion as the intuition and feeling of the
infinite in his youthful *Über der Religion* to the *Glaubenslehre* in which
the foundational concept is piety (*Frömmigkeit*) or the feeling of absolute
dependence. The intuition and feeling of the first identified with the piety
of the second, and he was at pains to advance this understanding against the
false attribution of religion to external forms, symbols and propositional
beliefs. Kant equated his *Religion within the Limits of Reason Alone* with a
fundamental and habitual ethical orientation towards duty.

One can register the beginnings of a radical change in *religio*, however, by
taking a second sounding, this time among theologians of the sixteenth and
seventeenth centuries and specifically as it was bodied forth in the massively
influential textbooks of Francisco Suarez. *De virtute et statu religionis* (1608–
9) continued much of the Thomistic tradition, with *religio* a moral virtue,
realised in the vowed 'religious' state and sometimes modified by *christiana*
to indicate the fundamental habit of Christian worship and service of God
founded upon Christian faith.[23] But here one can discover also the subtle
beginnings of what will become a sea change. For Suarez contended that
the term *religio* – like '*fides*' and '*votum*' – was legitimately and 'customarily
applied (*tribui solere*) not only to internal affect, but also to the *external
actions* and, indeed, to the *things* (*rebus*) by which God was worshipped
as also to the *doctrina* that teaches such worship or ceremony'.[24] Religion
in this sense is no longer simply a virtue; it is also both things such as
external ritual and ceremonial objects and the teachings and the beliefs that
instruct about their appropriate use. Scripture is cited for the legitimacy

[22] Wilfred Cantwell Smith has it exactly right: 'To the author and those who first read it the title
of Zwingli's book meant, "An essay on genuine and spurious piety"; and Calvin's, something like
"Grounding in Christian piety"' (*Meaning and End of Religion*, p. 37).

[23] Francisco Suarez, S.J., 'Tractatus primus: De natura et essentia virtutis religionis', in *Opus de virtute
et statu religionis*, in *Opera omnia*, editio nova, vol. XIII (Paris: Louis Vivès, 1859), 3–76. The first
two volumes, dealing with the virtue of religion, and XIV of the *Opera omnia*, were published by
1609, while the second two volumes were published posthumously at Lyons in 1623 and 1625. See
Joseph de Guibert, S.J., *The Jesuits: Their Spiritual Doctrine and Practice: A Historical Study*, trans.
William J. Young, S.J. (St. Louis: Institute of Jesuit Sources, 1972), p. 268.

[24] Suarez, 'De natura et essentia virtutis religionis', 8a: '...advertere oportet nomen religionis non
solum interno affectui, sed etiam exterioribus actionibus, imo et rebus quibus Deus colitur, tribui
solere, atque etiam doctrinae quae talem cultum vel caeremoniam docet.'

of this extension as is Clement of Alexandria (*'religio est actio quae Deum sequitur'*), but not Aquinas or the medieval doctors.

Thus, Suarez subsumes what Aquinas had called the acts or objects of religion into religion itself, and in doing so, he opens up *religio* to the cultural and anthropological meanings and inquiries that will constitute its character in modernity. He enters this extension of the meaning of *religio* as one already in common usage. Religion's objects have come to constitute religion. Harrison would trace to the English Enlightenment the emergence of *religio* as denoting the externals of worship and practice. But this attribution should go back farther, at least to the major influence that mediated scholasticism to modern philosophy, Francisco Suarez, 'Doctor Eximius'.[25] Because of his continuous presence within the textbook tradition, Suarez exercised a profound influence on subsequent centuries.

One must note also the virtually contemporary *Natural and Moral History of the Indies* (1590) by the contentious polymath José de Acosta. Acosta took the understanding of *religio* as 'the belief system that results in ceremonial behavior', as 'that which is used (*que usan*) in their rites' by the American indigenous peoples. It was also around this period that the credal content of religion could be somewhat separated from ceremonies, and so it was emphasised that 'religion' could substitute for 'faith' and become a genus – as Jonathan Z. Smith so helpfully traces. Now religion as a generic system of beliefs and practices could break down into the constituent species of 'Christianity, Mohametanism, Judaism and Idolatry'. The palm for advancing into popular reading the plural of 'religion' in this sense, i.e., for 'religions', seems to go to the redoutable Samuel Purchas with the 1613 appearance of the first volume of *Purchas His Pilgrimage; or, Relations of the World and the Religions Observed in All Ages and Places Discovered from the Creation unto this Present . . .* In a year, following hard on its heels was Edward Brerewood's *Enquiries Touching the Diversity of Languages and Religions through the Chiefe Parts of the World* (1614).[26] Here, we are much closer to modernity.

---

[25] Armand A. Maurer, C.S.B., *Medieval Philosophy* (New York: Random House, 1962), pp. 356–7. Maurer cites Suarez's presence in the education of Descartes and among the philosophical influences on Leibniz, Schopenhauer and Christian Wolff.

[26] See Jonathan Z. Smith, 'Religion, Religions, Religious', in Mark C. Taylor, ed., *Critical Terms for Religious Studies* (Chicago: University of Chicago Press, 1998), pp. 271–2. But the older usage did not die. Even when Samuel Johnson's *Dictionary of the English Language* or the first edition of the *Encyclopædia Britannica* took up 'religion', they bespoke the reverence that was due to God or the reasonable service of God. This was to continue in some variation the differentiation that obtained since the Middle Ages between the habit of religion and the objects – ceremonials, adoration, cult, and all of the virtues that *religio* could comprehensively command 'insofar as they were directed to the service and honor of God' (*Summa theologiae* 2-2.186.1.ad 2; 81.1.ad 1.).

A third sounding can be made as we come back to Eliade's *annus mirabilis*. Durkheim and Freud, Pettazoni, Jung and Schmidt are not talking about a particular human virtue or its characteristic functions. Religion was not a virtue; it had become 'things' – many of which it used to govern – but 'things' in the sense of discrete units such as sacrifice and vows, moral practices and rituals and commitments, and also myths, beliefs and symbols indicative of or common to a particular community. Religion was a congeries of such 'things', marked by the sacred or by taboo or by the fearful. One religious system of such beliefs and practices could and should be distinguished from another; its identity required it. And the conjoined units owned as sacred or interdicting were to be distinguished from another realm of 'things', that of the profane. Like 'science' and 'art', 'religion' changed from a quality of the human being or of a community to a territory of particular things, external things that could be studied by sciences such as anthropology, sociology, psychology and ethnology to determine a specific culture or cast of human character.

Wilfred Cantwell Smith describes – will subsequently question – this understanding of religion in its new form:

It is customary nowadays to hold that there is in human life and society something distinctive called 'religion'; and that this phenomenon is found on earth at present in a variety of minor forms, chiefly among outlying or eccentric peoples, and in a half-dozen or so major forms. Each of these major forms is also called 'a religion', and each one has a name: Christianity, Buddhism, Hinduism, and so on.[27]

When one spoke of '*the* Christian religion', similarity of phrase hid the profound difference between the sense carried by 'religion' in the nineteenth century and the understanding it bore for Aquinas and Calvin, Zwingli and even Suarez. Eliade's five authors might disagree on how religion should be further specified or what was worshipped, but they would agree that they were not dealing with human qualities, but with an aggregation of particular units.

Thus, in Durkheim's logistical reading, 'although religion is a whole composed of parts – a more or less complex system of myths, dogmas, rites, and ceremonies – they operate as if it formed a kind of indivisible entity'.[28]

---

[27] Wilfred Cantwell Smith, *Meaning and End of Religion*, p. 15.
[28] Emile Durkheim, *Elementary Forms of Religious Life*, trans. Karen E. Fields (New York: Free Press, 1995), p. 33. 'At the foundation of all systems of belief and all cults, there must necessarily be a certain number of fundamental representations and a mode of ritual conduct that, despite the diversity of forms that the one and the other may have taken on, have the same objective meaning everywhere, and everywhere fulfill the same functions. It is these enduring elements that constitute what is eternal and human in religion. They are the whole objective content of the idea that is expressed when religion in general is spoken of.' Ibid., p. 4.

Durkheim's world bifurcates into the sacred and profane, and 'when a certain number of sacred things have relations of coordination and subordination with one another, so as to form a system that had a certain coherence and does not belong to any other system of the same sort, then the beliefs and the rites, taken together constitute a religion'.[29] Thus it was that 'religious phenomena fall into two basic categories: belief and rites. The first are states of opinion and consist of representations; the second are particular modes of action. Between all of these two categories of phenomena lies all that separates thinking from doing.'[30] What makes Buddhism a religion, Durkheim argued, is that 'in the absence of gods, it accepts the existence of *sacred things*, namely the four Noble Truths and the practices that are derived from them'.[31]

In *Totem and Taboo*, Freud lays out two basic components of religion, what will emerge in other works as compulsive practices whose motivations are hidden and deeply treasured beliefs about powerful realities whose justifications are equally unconscious.[32] The most primitive form of these compulsive practices lay with taboo and exogamy, while the original focus of fear and reverence was the totem.[33] For Raffaele Pettazzoni, religion was itself one component within the more general category of culture. 'Religion is historically a form of culture and cannot be understood save in the framework of that particular culture of which it is a part, and in organic association with its other forms, such as art, myth, poetry, philosophy, economic, social, and political structure.'[34] Each of these denoted a set of organically interrelated things. As one spoke of Greek art or poetry constituted by their own proper objects, so one could speak of Greek religion in contrast with other religions and of religion in general in contrast with the other territories of art, myth, poetry and philosophy.

With almost scholastic precision, Wilhelm Schmidt defined religion both as beliefs and objects. 'Subjectively, it [religion] is the knowledge and consciousness of dependence upon one or more transcendental, personal

---

[29] Ibid., p. 38.   [30] Ibid., p. 34.   [31] Ibid., p. 35 (emphasis added).

[32] Sigmund Freud, *Totem and Taboo*, trans. James Strachey, with a biographical introduction by Peter Gay (New York: W. W. Norton, 1989), pp. 36–7, 109–10; 97ff.

[33] 'Obsessive Actions and Religious Practices' (1907) had already charted the parallels between religious practices and obsessive neurosis, while *The Future of an Illusion* would point up the analogies between religious ideas and Meyert's amentia, 'a state of acute hallucinatory confusion'. Sigmund Freud, *The Future of an Illusion*, trans. James Strachey (New York: W. W. Norton, 1961), pp. 55–6, cf. esp.n. 5.

[34] Raffaele Pettazzoni, 'Introduction to the History of Greek Religion,' in his *Essays on the History of Religions*, trans. H. J. Rose (Leiden: E. J. Brill, 1954), p. 68. Ugo Bianchi points out that with *La religione primitiva in Sardegna* Pettazzoni indicates his shift from classical archaeology to the history of religions. Ugo Bianchi, 'Pettazzoni, Raffaele (1883–1959)', in Mircea Eliade, ed., *The Encyclopedia of Religion* (New York: Macmillan, 1986), vol. II, p. 261.

powers, to which man stands in a reciprocal relation. Objectively, it is the sum of the outward actions in which it is expressed and made manifest, as prayer, sacrifice, sacraments, liturgy, ascetic practices, ethical prescriptions, and so on.'[35] The insistence upon reciprocal personal relations made it necessary for Schmidt to exclude early Buddhism. Later Buddhism would make the cut because it 'has included in its wide-reaching system innumerable personal deities'.[36] Finally, in *Wandlungen und Symbole der Libido*, Carl Jung takes for granted that religion is a composite of its own set of things, in contrast with 'things of a wholly other sort than religion'. It is a world of proper religious myths, rituals, hymns, dogmas and symbols, with 'its object, original sin'.[37] These components gave religion its unique concentration and differentiation from the sets of other objects. In fact, part of the contemporary problem lies in a shift from one to the other: 'To the degree that the modern mind is passionately concerned with anything and everything rather than religion, religion and its prime object – original sin – have mostly vanished into the unconscious. That is why, today, nobody believes in either ... '[38] It is religion that presents as religious objects or symbols the transformed contents of the unconscious, transposing and transforming them into religion's own world of objects or images.[39] 'In religion, the regressive reanimation of the father-and-mother imago is organized into a system.'[40]

In this generic constitution of religion as a set of particularly designated units, contrasting with the parallel territories of art or science or even politics, religion became a subset of human culture. One studies religion in order to come to understand something about the character of human beings themselves, something about a particular human culture. Religion has become the cultural evidence for the human. Durkheim spoke for

[35] Wilhelm Schmidt, S.V.D., *The Origin and Growth of Religion: Facts and Theories*, trans. H. J. Rose (New York: Dial Press, 1931), p. 2.

[36] Ibid.

[37] *Wandlungen und Symbole der Libido* was translated as *Psychology of the Unconscious: A Study of the Transformations and Symbolisms of the Libido*, trans. Beatrice M. Hinkle (New York: Dodd, Mead and Company, 1947), p. 81. For the psychological truth of symbols and myths that are 'in actual truth ... misleading', see p. 262.

[38] C. J. Jung, *Symbols of Transformation*, Bollingen Series no. 20, trans. R. F. C. Hull (New York: Pantheon, 1956), p. 72. This is a translation of *Symbole der Wandlung* (Zurich: Rascher Verlag, 1952), which is itself a fourth revised edition of *Wandlungen und Symbole der Libido*. For this citation in the earlier work, see pp. 81–2. Jung continues: 'This disbelief in the devilishness of human nature goes hand in hand with the blank incomprehension of religion and its meaning. The *unconscious* conversion of instinctual impulses into religious activity is ethically worthless, and often no more than an hysterical outburst.'

[39] Jung, *Symbols of Transformation*, p. 59; *Psychology of the Unconscious*, pp. 72–3. See Jung's previous discussion of the writing of Miss Miller and the narrative of the Book of Job.

[40] Jung, *Psychology of the Unconscious*, p. 99. For further projections into dogma, see p. 120.

almost all when he said that this study of religious phenomena in its structures and developments is finally 'to explain a present reality that is near to
us and thus capable of affecting our ideas and actions. That reality is man.'[41]
That is the reason that Jonathan Z. Smith can say so flatly, '"Religion" is an
anthropological not a theological category' and insist that the history of
'religion' prior to the sixteenth century is irrelevant to contemporary
usage.[42] Instead of inquiry into what is an appropriate response to the creative action and reality of God, there would be arguments about the cultures
that constituted religion and its focus, whether god or gods needed to be
involved in religion at all. And this brings this essay to its second question:
how did this understanding of 'religion' enter into the atheistic discussion
of these last centuries?

ATHEISM AND THE SCIENTIFIC STUDY OF RELIGION

The proponents of the newly formulated scientific studies of religion, as
represented by Eliade's Five, were drawn into the conflict about Christian
belief, especially that about the existence of God, as each of the warring
sides looked to these studies to supply it with new resources. Max Müller,
who coined the title of the 'science of religion', claimed that the studies
of the Vedas strengthened his Christianity, while E. B. Tylor believed that
these 'scientific inquiries gave support to his personal stance of agnostic
religious skepticism'.[43] Already in 1870, Sir John Lubbock (Lord Avebury)
had brought out *The Origin of Civilization and the First Condition of Man*,
proposing atheism as the initial and most primitive stage of religious belief
and supplying this stage as an aboriginal prologue to Auguste Comte's
famous triad. Appealing to the religious culture found among primitives,
Lubbock found this *Uratheismus* not in an explicit denial of the reality of
any god, but in the absence within these earliest cultures of all religion.[44]

---

[41] Durkheim, *Elementary Forms*, p. 1. Durkheim strongly advances the position that all religions are
founded on the reality of the human. 'Even the most bizarre or barbarous rites and the strangest
myths translate some human need and some aspect of life, whether social or individual.' Ibid., p. 2.

[42] Jonathan Z. Smith, 'Religion, Religions, Religious', p. 269. These settlements made in the generic
notion of religion, as represented by Eliade's five figures, had been secured comfortably by the turn
of the century and have had their own pervasive and substantial presence within contemporary
theological discourse. One has only to read, for example, the *Nature of Doctrine: Religion and
Theology in a Postliberal Age* by the distinguished theologian, Professor George Lindbeck, one of
the most influential works in theology to appear in the 1980s, to find religion specified by three
different kinds of 'things': propositional statements and beliefs, symbols and feelings, terms and the
grammar for their use and practice.

[43] Daniel L. Pals, *Seven Theories of Religion* (New York: Oxford University Press, 1996), p. 8.

[44] Schmidt, *Origin and Growth of Religion*, pp. 58–9. Lubbock enlarged Comte's triad generously by
such additions as fetishism, totemism, shamanism and anthropomorphism.

This was to counter the earlier assertion of major figures from the German Enlightenment, such as Herder and Lessing, that religion constituted a universal constituent of the human spirit, and, more recently, the claim of Christopher Meiners's *Allgemeine Kritische Geschichte der Religion* (1806–7) that 'no people has ever existed without a religion'. Meiners was one of the first modern writers to make such an assertion.[45] By 1912, the lists were drawn. How one analysed religion had come to affect heavily the credibility of theistic convictions. How was this analysis to be done? Religion was no longer a subset of virtue, but of culture, and, as a subset of culture, it was to be studied according to the path mapped out by the exemplary studies of culture. It was to busy itself with origins. Eliade recognised that during the latter half of the nineteenth century:

all Western historiography was obsessed with the quest of *origins*... Great scholars wrote about the origin of language, of human societies, of art, of institutions, of the Indo-Aryan races, and so on ... this search for the origins of human institutions and cultural creations prolongs and completes the naturalist's quest for the origin of species, the biologist's dream of grasping the origin of life, the geologist's and the astronomer's endeavor to understand the origin of the Earth and the Universe.[46]

This focus upon origins was something of a departure from an eighteenth-century past. In his *Natural History of Religion*, for example, David Hume had divided the inquiry into religion between two distinct questions: what are the *foundations in reason* of religion, and what is the *origin* of religion in human nature?[47] The nineteenth century collapsed these questions into one, and the truth about religion was to be found in its origins.

So Durkheim attempted an understanding of contemporary religions by 'tracing historically the manner in which they have gradually taken shape'.[48] Origins would explain present reality. The real is not only the underlying; it is the antecedent, and the primitive was symptomatic of the prehistoric. So to understand religion 'we must begin by going back to its simplest and most primitive form'.[49] Hence Durkheim concentrates upon the elementary forms of religion. The findings here will determine the character of everything else:

---

[45] See Seymour Cain, 'The Study of Religion: History of Study', in Eliade, ed., *The Encyclopedia of Religion* vol. XIV, pp. 65–6. Cain writes that Meiners was one of the first modern writers to make this assertion, see p. 65. Christoph Meiners, *Allgemeine Kritische Geschichte der Religion* (Hanover: Helwing, 1806–7), 2 vols.

[46] Mircea Eliade, 'The Quest for the "Origins" of Religion', in *The Quest*, pp. 37–53.

[47] David Hume, *The Natural History of Religion*, ed. H. E. Root (Stanford: Stanford University Press, 1957), 'Author's Introduction', p. 21.

[48] Durkheim, *Elementary Forms*, p. 3.   [49] Ibid.

Although religion is a whole composed of parts – a more or less complex system of myths, dogmas, rites, and ceremonies – they operate as if it formed a kind of indivisible entity. Since a whole can be defined only in relationship to the parts that comprise it, a better method is to try to characterize the *elementary phenomena from which any religion results*, and then characterize the system produced by their union.[50]

The elementary was that from which religion results. Freud also believed – with some reserve – that one could get to the prehistoric by a study of primitives, seeing in them 'a well-preserved picture of an early stage of our own development'.[51] Freud would rely upon studies done on the aborigines of Australia, and, like *The Elementary Forms of Religious Life*, *Totem and Taboo* would assert that 'it is highly doubtful whether any religion, in the shape of *a worship of higher beings*, can be attributed to them'.[52] Both Durkheim and Freud assert the worship of the totem as primordial and seminal of all religion.[53] Durkheim is content to establish this as fact and to recognise its origins as a surrogate for clan and community. Freud pushes beyond these findings of what he called 'social anthropology', back to Oedipal longings and the murder of the primal father. For psychoanalysis of the origins has shown that 'at bottom God is nothing other than an exalted father . . . Thus, while the totem may be the *first* form of father-surrogate, the god will be a later one.'[54]

Jung's *Wandlungen und Symbole der Libido* also locates the origins of divinity within the projecting human subject: 'Psychologically understood, the divinity is nothing else than a projected complex of representations which is accentuated in feeling according to the degree of religiousness of the individual, so God is to be considered as the representative of a certain sum of energy (libido).'[55] At this stage of the development of Jung's psychological inquiries, God is the construction of the libido, fixed upon

---

[50] Ibid., pp. 33–4 (emphasis added). This determines the decision of Durkheim to focus upon primitive religions, specifically those of Australia, 'because the facts are simpler, the relations between them are more apparent'.

[51] Freud, *Totem and Taboo*, p. 3. One must, however, recognise that at least theoretically Freud was aware that 'it is never possible to decide without hesitation how far their present-day conditions and opinions preserve the primaeval past.' Ibid., p. 128.

[52] Ibid., p. 4 (emphasis added).

[53] Ibid., p. 126. Freud accepts as his point of departure the statement of W. Wundt: 'at some time totemic culture everywhere paved the way for a more advanced civilization, and, thus, that it represents a transitional stage between the age of primitive men and the era of heroes and gods.'

[54] Freud, *Totem and Taboo*, pp. 182–3.

[55] Jung, *Psychology of the Unconscious*, p. 71. 'This energy, therefore, appears projected (metaphysically) because it works from the unconscious outwards, when it is dislodged from there, as psychoanalysis shows.'

the mother rather than the father.[56] This search for origins, thus, as in Freud or Durkheim or Jung, could counter with rival theories of origins any claimed stability of belief in what the Christian could recognise as God.

Or it could constitute a support. The affirmation of the existence of God could also search for its evidences in the practices, symbols and beliefs that make up the texture of 'religion'. Wilhelm Schmidt's *Der Ursprung der Gottesidee* took up Andrew Lang's theory of high gods, i.e., of supreme beings that predated in every primitive culture both animism and totemism:

> Comparing the primitive cultures with the later ones we may lay down the general principle that in none of the latter is the Supreme Being to be found in so clear, so definite, vivid and direct a form as among the peoples belonging to the former [i.e., to primitive cultures] ... This Supreme Being is to be found among all the peoples of the primitive culture, not indeed everywhere in the same form or the same vigor, but still everywhere prominent enough to make his dominant position indubitable.[57]

Thus an *Urmonotheismus* lies at the origins of all subsequent variations of the object of religion, a supreme being that is no more difficult for the primitive mind to infer than for it to recognise in anything made the necessity for a maker. Monotheism is at the origins, not the end, of human development. But against this primitive monotheism, Pettazoni was in 'repeated polemics' and saw monotheism emerge as a 'revolution against polytheism'.[58] Thus he identified the sky-god (Rangi) as primordial or superior in the Maori pantheon, one who stands behind and is ultimately sublimated and raised to a higher plane as Io, the uncreated beginning of all things.[59]

[56] Ibid., p. 474. 'We have learned in the course of this investigation that the part of the libido which erects religious structures is in the last analysis fixed on the mother, and really represents that tie through which we are permanently connected with our origin ... As we have seen, this libido conceals itself in countless and very heterogeneous symbols.' This reading becomes clearer when one considers the centrality that Jung, at this stage, gave to incest desires and fantasies. In women this desire shows itself in the Father-Imago, 'for the idea of the masculine creative deity is a derivation, analytically and historically psychologic of the Father-Imago and aims, above all, to replace the discarded infantile father transference in such a way that for the individual the passing from the narrow circle of the family into the wider circle of human society may be simpler or made easy.' Ibid., pp. 55–6.

[57] Schmidt, *Origin and Growth of Religion*, p. 257.

[58] Bianchi, 'Pettazzoni, Raffaele', vol. II, p. 262.

[59] Raffaele Pettazzoni, 'Io and Rangi', in *Essays on the History of Religions*, trans. H. J. Rose (Leiden: E. J. Brill, 1954), p. 42: 'It appears then that so lofty an attribute as omniscience also proves to be deeply rooted in the sky-natured substance of the Maori Supreme Being. On the whole it is Rangi the Sky who stands at the back of Io the Supreme Being. Lofty though the idea of Io is both in religion and speculation, its foundations lie in the nature worship of a sky-god. Io is in theory the universal cosmic principle, and as such the creator of Rangi and Papa and of the gods in the Maori pantheon. But in the last analysis Io is Rangi himself sublimated and raised to a higher plane. This substantial identity is reflected, as above shown, not only in belief, but, what is more important, in ritual and religion.' For Io as the 'uncreated beginning of all things', see p. 37.

Thus, the quest for origins awakened a question that had hitherto been unknown in the West: how necessary was 'God' or some such figure for what had come to be called 'religion'? If Western thought had disposed of the medieval virtue of religion, could one not also dispose of what had been its purpose? Both E. B. Tylor and George Frazer had found religion without god. Religion, for Tylor, was 'belief in spiritual beings', and ancient peoples reasoned to these individual spirits within each thing. Gradually 'religion' developed from animism to the gods of polytheism. Frazer began with the personal and impersonal forces conjured by magic and took from William Robertson Smith the worship of the totem as the original foundation of all religion. Religion emerged out of magic as the human means of control moved from laws of contact and imitation to pleading and vows offered to win over the supreme spirits or gods.[60] Spirits, forces, totems or gods, supreme god – the question which the inquiry into origins posed to the religious believer was far more comprehensive: did religion with its idea of god arise out of the self-revelation of god or did god arise as a cultural creation of human beings – a creation one could trace in the evolutionary progress of the idea? The pedigree of the term and the primordial character of its referent were called upon to settle the issue of the truth of fundamental theological claims. What was at the beginning became definitive.

Why? Two immediate reasons suggest themselves to explain why the origins and character of the gods told directly upon the arguments for the existence of God: the argument from universal consent and the argument from the primordial revelation described in Genesis.

Universal consent

Design in the physical universe had furnished the principal evidence for the affirmation of the existence of God by thinking men in the seventeenth and eighteenth centuries, an affirmation grounded on discoveries advanced by the greatest scientific minds of this enlightened period such as Newton and Boyle and incorporated into the pervasive physico-theologies to which all the sciences were expected to contribute. In the nineteenth century, however, this justification of religious belief was yielding to three factors: the growing autonomy of the physical sciences as insisted upon by such as Pierre Simon de Laplace; the reserve about any extension of theoretical knowledge beyond objects of possible experience with David Hume and Immanuel Kant; and – most influentially – the evolutionary etiology of what had

---

[60] Pals, *Seven Theories of Religion*, pp. 36–7.

been taken as contrived design. The patterns in nature could no longer furnish in so unchallenged a fashion the corroboration and even the warrant for grounded religious belief. Charles Darwin, as paradigmatic a figure in the late nineteenth century as Isaac Newton had been in the eighteenth, recognised that a nail had been driven into a coffin: 'The old argument from design in Nature as given by Paley, which formerly seemed to me so conclusive, fails now that the law of natural selection has been discovered.'[61]

Foundational religious reflection in the West shifted from nature to human nature, from the patterns found in one to the exigencies demanded by the other. Now God was not to explain design, but to make the ethical enterprise possible or human history intelligible. Otherwise there was only absurdity, mindless and ungrounded affirmations. To affirm the reality of God became, in Kant's formulation, a 'subjective necessity', a postulate whose denial would leave human beings with categorical commands whose attainment could only be haphazard and random. But the great classical atheists of the nineteenth century such as Feuerbach, Marx, Nietzsche and Freud, took up the argument precisely at this point, at the philosophical appeals to human nature as warrant for the affirmation of the existence of God. The case was read exactly in reverse. Not only did humanity not need God for the coherence of its development, but the progress of the human entailed the denial of God in any recognisable reading of that term. The corruption of the one became the necessary condition for the generation of the other. The ethical or social advance of humanity demanded that it claim for human beings themselves the excellence that they had historically projected onto an imaginary subject.

At the same time, in the late nineteenth century and early twentieth century, there was another shift in the focus of fundamental thinking. Major thinkers in greater numbers were looking for the foundations of all warranted assertions not so much in a prior analysis of human cognition or epistemologies or phenomenologies of spirit – a nineteenth-century enterprise that reaches for its beginning back to John Locke. Their search increasingly was turning to language and action as fundamental, to various forms of semantics and pragmatics and existentialisms that found these to be 'the house of being'. Generically, this constituted a turn to human experience in its various forms of expression as foundational, as that expression is embodied in words or in deeds. Semantics and pragmatics were increasingly seen as prior and fundamental to analyses of human consciousness and, even more, of the nature of things.

[61] Charles Darwin, *The Autobiography of Charles Darwin and Selected Letters*, ed. Francis Darwin (New York: Dover Publications, 1958), p. 63.

As John Locke had prophetically anticipated the shift of Western foundational thinking to epistemologies, so Giovanni Battista Vico had anticipated the massive shifts that would occur in the late nineteenth century from concerns about cognition as foundational to language and action. For Vico insisted that human beings can adequately know – have *scienza* about – not what confronts them in nature or in consciousness, but only what they have made.[62] Culture, then, becomes all-important – whether literary and artistic products or social and religious practices and institutions.

Thus the semantic and pragmatic turn in foundational thinking was somewhat mirrored in theological reflection by a turn towards the scientific study of religion. This turn did not counter, but transposed, the concern of the previous period for warrant either to assert or to deny the reality of a transcendent, even Christian, God.

As the nineteenth century advanced, then, the conviction was declining that either contrived designs within nature or the exigencies of human nature could ground a reasonable assertion of the reality of God. But there was still another 'topic' from which arguments for the existence of God had classically derived strength and credibility since the dawn of civilisation: the argument from the universal consent of humankind. Belief in the divine had been recognised as always and universally a part of human convictions, and this had been philosophically recognised as telling from the time of Plato's *Laws*[63] or Aristotle's *De Caelo*.[64] Like the corresponding

---

[62] Gianbattista Vico, *The New Science*, trans. Thomas Goddard Bergin and Max Harold Fisch (Ithaca: Cornell University Press, 1968). In this wider sense, *scienza nuova* embraces both philosophy and philology. See 'Introduction', F3. The philologians include grammarians, historians, and critics 'who have occupied themselves with the study of the languages and the deeds of peoples,' Book I, #138–40.

[63] Plato, *The Laws* 10.886a–888d. In Plato's *Laws*, the Athenian argues that the existence of the divine is 'the most certain of all realities', advancing stories and prayers and sacrifices as evidence against those whose 'want of faith in the stories heard so often in earliest infancy, while still at the breast, from their mothers and nurses – stories, you may say, crooned over them, in sport and in earnest, like spells – and heard again in prayers offered over sacrifices in conjunction with the spectacle which gives such intense delight to the eye and ear of children, as it is enacted at a sacrifice, the spectacle of our parents addressing their god, which assured belief in their existence, in earnest prayer and supplication for themselves and their children. Then again, at rising and setting of the sun and moon, they have heard and seen the universal prostrations and devotions of mankind, Greek and non-Greek alike, in all the various circumstances of evil fortune and good, with their implication that gods are no fictions, but the most certain of realities and their being beyond the remotest shadow of doubt.'

[64] Aristotle, *De Caelo* 1.3.270b5–8. In the problematic method of Aristotle, the same consensus, found in the usages of religion, served to confirm astronomical theories about the primary body: 'Our theory seems to confirm experience and to be confirmed by it. For all human beings have some conception of the nature of the gods, and all who believe in the existence of gods at all, whether barbarian or Greek, agree in allotting the highest place to the deity, surely because they suppose that immortal is linked with immortal and regard any other supposition as inconceivable.'

evidence from nature and human nature, universal consent would vary the-
matically as it ran through two thousand years of intellectual history in the
West.[65]

Charles Darwin maintained that by the middle of the nineteenth century,
with the demise of design and morality as bases of theistic appeal, universal
consensus was the last argument left. 'At the present day, the most usual
argument for the existence of an intelligent God is drawn from the deep
inward conviction and feelings which are experienced by most persons.'
Darwin could not share these feelings. 'It may be truly said that I am like
a man who has become colour-blind, and the universal belief by men of
the existence of redness makes my present loss of perception of not the
least value as evidence.' The issue of divine existence is joined at 'universal
belief', and Darwin is prophetic in assessing the damage that the study of
religion will work. 'This argument would be a valid one if *all men of all
races had the same inward convictions of the existence of* one God; but we
know that this is very far from being the case.'[66] That is why both sides
of this controversy looked to the emerging scientific study of religion for
resources and confirmation. Was the consensus universal and sempiternal
or was it at least primitive and prehistoric?

Fundamental revelation

There was a second reason and a more theological one why the scientific
study of religion figured critically in the rhetoric for and against atheism.
Genesis had taught that a primordial self-revelation of God took place
with the creation of humanity, a revelation believed by Christians to be
brought to its fullness finally in Jesus Christ. The various denominations
of Christian faith claimed to be responses to that revelation. Now, just
as contemporary physicists expect to find now in the cosmos the residual radiation that bespeaks the 'big bang' of some sixteen billion years
ago, so the credibility of the scriptures was to be confirmed or denied

---

[65] The argument from universal consent will vary according to the parameters offered by a particular
philosophy, but even when the doctrines and practices of the popular cults were dismissed as absurd
by, for example, the Epicureans, this school would still assert that belief in the gods has not been
established by authority, custom or law, but rests on the unanimous and abiding consensus of
humankind. The Epicureans traced this universal belief to an internal, self-justifying *prolepsis*, while
the Stoics, acknowledging its cogency and connecting it with the ritual practices of divination and
the public recognition of epiphanies, credited its origins to the self-manifestation of the internal
rationality of the universe. Even the New Academy accepted universal consensus as a tradition
within the Roman Republic. Again, religion bore to consciousness the universality of belief in the
divine, and this had stood as evidence for the affirmation of God for two millennia. For these
divergent understandings of universal consensus, see Michael J. Buckley, S. J., *Motion and Motion's
God* (Princeton: Princeton University Press, 1971), Part II, pp. 89–156.

[66] Darwin, *Autobiography*, p. 65 (emphasis added).

by what one discovered in religion's beginnings. Not that one necessarily expected to uncover primordial revelation, but at least to come upon the effects of that revelation in the history of religions. Joseph J. Baierl, the American translator of Wilhelm Schmidt, was typical of the apologists of that time:

The apologist's task is, indeed, a manifold one: to present the essence, scope, and content of primitive revelation; to show, in the light of prehistory, anthropology, and ethnology, that the earliest known men were capable of receiving such a revelation; to point out how many branches of natural science actually confirm its historicity; and, finally, to reconstruct its fate after men's fall and dispersion.

And what must Baierl's reconstruction expect to prove?

Even though the light of revelation dimmed as the race grew, and even though the darkness of paganism practically extinguished it, yet it continued to glow among those peoples who remained at the most primitive levels of culture; until at last it was entrusted to the keeping of God's chosen people, Israel, and thus became man's common heritage once more.[67]

In a very different vein, Pettazzoni finds Schmidt's *Urmonotheismus* 'a return, by a different way, to the old position of the doctrine of revelation'.[68] So the scientific study of religion, whether as resource or as threat, was inescapably drawn into the controversies about the existence of God. If the inquiry into primordial or primitive religions disclosed no presence of an *Urmonotheismus*, not only did the argument from universal consent fail, but the Judeo-Christian affirmation of a primordial revelation was read as unsustainable.

Not only were Eliade's Five inducted into these partisan conflicts, they were marked by the colours under which they enlisted. Their religious affiliations came to accredit or discredit their study of religions. Eliade noted this with Wilhelm Schmidt: 'Schmidt, though a very able scholar, was also a Catholic priest, and the scientific world suspected him of apologetic intentions.'[69] On the other hand, Gaston Richard – once the disciple Durkheim thought the best qualified to be his successor – bitterly criticized the Master for the injection of 'dogmatic atheism' into his sociology of religion. Thus:

it becomes all the more necessary to show that where religion exercises the maximum influence on society, as among primitive peoples, it manages entirely without

[67] Joseph J. Baierl, 'Introduction' to his translation of *Primitive Religion* by Wilhelm Schmidt (St. Louis, MO: Herder, 1939), p. iv. Actually this work is an amalgam of Schmidt's writings done by the translator, adapted to Baierl's series of apologetic works.

[68] Raffaele Pettazzoni, 'The Formation of Monotheism', in *Essays in the History of Religions*, p. 4.

[69] Mircea Eliade, 'The Quest for the "Origins" of Religion', pp. 45–6.

the idea of God. The essay on values gives us the last word on the religious philosophy of Durkheim but it is the task of *Les formes élémentaires* to present the
scientific proof.[70]

But no matter how differently the story of origins could have been told,
evaluated and employed, I wonder if something far more profound did not
get lost in the translation between the Middle Ages' and the contemporary
understanding and scientific study of 'religion'. And I wonder if what got
lost was 'God' – God as the purpose, and, in this way, the specification
of *religio*. Christianity believes that God gave human life not simply itself
and things created to enhance it, but God gave Himself. For Aquinas,
religion occurred as a virtue within an individual or a community when
one apperceived something of this and gave oneself to God in some way, as
through vow or sacrifice or prayer. *Religio* thus bespoke God as specifying
purpose and took its own shape from what was appropriately rendered to
God – so much so that Aquinas could say that the whole purpose of his
Summa theologiae is to treat those things that pertain to Christian religion.[71]

Much of the scientific study of religion stood religion on its head. It
turned the focus of *religio* upon human beings, with the symbols, beliefs,
practices indicating stages in their development, and with God or the gods
subsumed as yet another indicator of human culture and its evolvement.
Religion, as Jonathan Z. Smith insists, became an anthropological category.
When God is assessed primarily as one more unit within a congeries of
cultural units and criteria, the issue of atheism has already been engaged
and settled. The god that is one more thing does not exist. The god that
obtains his intrinsic interest and importance because of the light he sheds
upon human life does not exist. God is either incomprehensibly absolute in
His being and in His goodness and so adored in His self-communication,
or God is not at all. It remained only for the inherent contradiction of such
a settlement to work itself out dialectically in the explicit negation of what
had already been implicitly denied.

But a Christian theologian need not be satisfied that this is the end
of the road for theology and the scientific study of religion. Could religion – even understood as this congeries of individual units specified by the

---

[70] G. Richard, 'Dogmatic Atheism in the Sociology of Religion', in *Durkheim on Religion*: a selection
of readings with bibliography by W. S. F. Pickering (London: Routledge and Kegan Paul, 1975),
pp. 254, 270–2.
[71] *Summa theologiae* I. Prologus.

sacred – could religion not also be a productive theological category, i.e., could it not offer subject matter for inquiry that is precisely theological? Could the scientific study of religion disclose something about God, not simply about human culture? If the Christian finds, for example, the classic Pauline signs of the Spirit of God – love, joy, peace, patience, kindness, goodness, faithfulness, gentleness and self-control – is it not of theological interest to inquire what presence in this religion has fostered so sacred an atmosphere?[72] And cannot the Christ of Christianity – classically the *norma normans non normata* – illumine rather than universally be set in competition with what is discovered in the scientific study of religion? Christian theology might well attend to such a study, to seek not so much data about human culture but quite explicitly what it can learn of God.

Nostra aetate, for example, recognised that women and men have perennially questioned the various religions of the world about God, taken up with a haunting search: 'What is that ultimate and unutterable mystery which engulfs our being, and whence we take our rise, and whither our journey leads us?' From the dawn of humanity, it maintains, there has emerged 'a certain perception of that hidden power which hovers over the course of things and over the events of human life'.[73] Do Christian theologians – precisely in their recognition both of the normative character of God's revelation in Christ and also of the 'lives of these people with a profound religious sense' – have nothing to learn about God from the centuries of that experience?

Such theological attention and inquiry could well be extended to the world religions of our own time. Medieval theology could search the newly discovered books of Aristotle and Averroes and use neo-Platonic Dionysius to learn something of God. Is there nothing for us to learn about God from contemporary Islam? If in Hinduism, human beings have for millennia 'contemplated the divine mystery', does this contemplation have nothing to say to our theology – not simply to ascetical disciplines, but to what Bonaventure called our apperception of God?

One of the deleterious effects of the study of religions has been to treat these communities and traditions of wisdom and prayer as if they were univocal species of the one genus, 'religion', mutually exclusive species among which one must make a choice, territories in competition with one another. But one wonders if we have not become the victims of our

---

[72] Galatians 5: 22–23.
[73] *Declaration of the Second Vatican Council on the Relationship of the Church to Non-Christian Religions (Nostra aetate)* in *The Documents of Vatican II*, ed. Walter M. Abbott, S.J. (New York: Herder and Herder), #1, p. 661.

own language, and if even the word 'religion' is inappropriate to denote the realities or communities they name – so very different in their character as in their claims. It is not at all evident that – with appropriate modifications but without any of the artificial harmonies that bespeak a soft syncretism – one could not participate fully both in a Catholic and in a Quaker community, nor even confess oneself a Christian who has also assimilated much of the teachings of early Buddhism. The contemporary use of the word 'religion' would seem to forestall such an integration, but the early Church was able to assimilate great elements out of Neo-Platonism, Stoicism and Neo-Pythagorianism. We call these ancient traditions schools of philosophy, but I wonder whether, if we came upon them today, afresh, we would not call them religions, some even quasi-religious orders.

The word, 'religion' as we use it, may not be very helpful, introducing commonalities and disjunctions that may be unwarranted. Nevertheless, we are at present stuck with the term 'world religions'. *Nostra aetate* maintained that 'often' – I repeat the word, often – 'they reflect a ray of that Truth that enlightens all human beings'.[74] If that is the case, it is an unrealised task for contemporary theology – keeping the normativity of God's revelation in Christ – to search the 'world religions' for what they can tell us about God. Such a carefully disciplined inquiry should amplify or deepen rather than necessarily contradict what one has learned of God from Christianity. There is no time now to argue and nuance this suggestion with the distinctions it obviously cries for, but only to propose that the scientific study of religion could well call the theological enterprise to an inquiry quite different from that which obtained in the nineteenth and twentieth centuries. For, to allow the final word to Nicholas Lash: 'Every Christian, and hence every Christian theologian, is called to journey in the direction of deeper knowledge of the things of God, and the journey is a homecoming, for God is our end as well as our beginning.'[75]

[74] Ibid., 2, pp. 661–2.
[75] Nicholas Lash, *The Beginning and the End of 'Religion'* (Cambridge: Cambridge University Press, 1996), p. 5.

CHAPTER 2

Doing Theology in the university

Denys Turner

Let me be bold for the sake of brevity: I do not think there is any such discipline as 'Religious Studies'. Nor do I think that we ought to go on pretending that there is. Saying which, of course, places me at odds with the current state of academic play in the matter of curricular organisation of our subject in most universities in the United Kingdom: how we do it troubles me not a little. On the whole, in the United Kingdom we deal with this matter administratively as we deal with many other cases, by means of a sort of resolute lack of resolve, by means of a determined refusal of theoretical consistency: in short, by means of shameless fudge.

Here is the problem, put in plain terms: our subject-discipline originated as 'Theology'. And we still do something called by that name, by which we mean, most of us, something you do within, and possibly out of, a credal commitment; also for many of us theology is done in the first instance in its connections with an ecclesial community. And if we are not caused to wonder by hostile critics, we may wonder for ourselves whether a discipline so apparently in thrall to credal and ecclesial commitments can justify its place within the university. Of course in most universities it is not done in an explicitly credal spirit, because, like the rest of our colleagues in other faculties, we think of 'the academic' by way of contrast with pre-emption by an external interest, we submit to no other discipline but the common academic discipline of the university. All the same, I think at the very least we all recognise that if theology were not done in this credally and ecclesially interested spirit outside the university, there would be nothing for us to do as Theology in our own academic way within the university.

By 'Religious Studies' on the other hand we mean a theoretical discipline with no existence outside places of learning, a discipline defined not so much by its method as by its object – the religions of the world. And of course, you can engage in the study of religions with due academic objectivity and

I am grateful to my Ph.D. students, Kevin Loughton and Vittorio Montemaggi, for helpful comments on earlier drafts of this essay.

detachment, belief and disbelief in any of the religions studied being equally suspended. Now in the UK there remain a few Faculties and Departments of 'Theology', as at Oxford, at Durham and at Birmingham; and we in Cambridge teach in a quaintly named Faculty of 'Divinity'. There is also a rather larger number of Departments of 'Religious Studies', as at Lancaster, and in several new universities. But, most commonly of all, we arrange our academic affairs, with what seems to me a quite wonderful indifference to the potential for oxymoron, into Departments of 'Theology and Religious Studies', teaching with few exceptions degree courses of the same name. Then we say of the whole lot, theology and religious studies, that we engage in the *study* of them both, and with that one little word 'study', by means of its splendid vacuousness, we contrive a conceptual subterfuge of quite mystifying subtlety.

So we 'study' theology, do we? Strangely, in English, 'study' has become a word denoting a suitably academic and dispassionate mentality, though etymologically it derives from the Latin *studium* which would, on the contrary, be well translated by the word 'passion'. The Latin *studium* forms a family with *desiderium* and other words of engagement and attachment. But in English study is 'brown', what you study you disengage your passions from, and whereas it makes sense to speak of someone's 'studying' a religion dispassionately, I am not sure that I much like the idea of, in that sense, 'studying' *theology*.

Indeed, one way of distinguishing between 'theology' and 'the study of religion' is this: 'theology' is a study – of something else, say, God, or of how to talk about God, or of how God talks. And it is the study of God in the Latin sense, with passion – for to 'study' theology in the primary sense of the expression is to do theology. 'Religion', on the other hand, is not a study, though some religions are quite studious. Religion is a theorised object of study: we should not forget that, in any of its modern senses, the word 'religion' is a term of art, belonging within an explanatory hypothesis, explanatory of certain practices indeed, but not as being itself a practice. So you can study religion, in the English sense, with detachment, for the study of religion is a second-order discipline; you don't practise religion by studying it, as you practise Islam by doing Islamic theology, or practise Christianity by doing Christian theology. You can make theology into the object of a second-order study, as perhaps you do when you study the history of theology, or the sociology of theology, or conduct a philosophical critique of doctrinal statements, or whatever. But, if you do that, then, depending on how you are doing it, you are either doing theology historically or sociologically, or philosophically, or else you are engaging in the study of a religion, or a particular aspect of a religious tradition. So we are back to square one: you can do the thing and it is theology, or you can study the thing and it is anthropology or whatever, but you cannot hope to draw 'theology' and 'religious studies' into some kind of consistent conjunction by means of vacuous declamations about 'studying' both.

This is not merely carp about terms. The expression 'the study of . . .' has become one of those weasel words of a contemporary academic-bureaucratic jargon which serves mainly as a not very dense smokescreen for hiding issues we would prefer not to have to resolve. And I am not myself entirely unsympathetic to this device of methodological fudge: as a subject-discipline, placed by ancient history within the university curricula, but in recent times displaced from a central position there by rapid and radical secularisations, we gain much advantage academically from the unresolved character of these present ambiguities – that is to say, from their being, precisely, *un*resolved. At any rate, one is tempted to think so when one contemplates the excessively 'resolved' fates equally of our German colleagues confined within the narrownesses of their denominational faculties, and of our North American colleagues, whose need (it would seem) endlessly to retheorise 'religious studies' appears to be driven more by a puritanical fear of theological taint than by anything in the nature of a coherent positive intellectual project. Learning how *not* to do theology seems to me an inadequate prescription for an academic methodology, let alone for a half-interesting intellectual tradition.

That said, the complacencies of English 'fudge' seem increasingly insufficient to the case. For two reasons it seems to me that we need a more intellectually coherent account of Theology's presence in the university than we have, and neither has anything to do with the interests of the Quality Assurance Agency, which appeared to have been to require us to justify ourselves not in terms of the inherent value of the knowledge pursued, but in terms of the retail price of the skills we supply in wholesale quantities. The QAA is worth mentioning here, not for the sake of the cheap and cynical sneer which its bureaucratic intrusiveness has proved so ready and able to evince, but because theologians more than any other academics have reasons for exposing the distortions of intellectual values which it has sought to visit upon the conduct of our teaching. For they are distortions of a kind of post-modern reductivism for which substance is continually dissolved into process: the concrete, contingent, actuality of use-value to persons is converted into the abstract, vacuous neutrality of market exchange between 'consumers'. It would be bad enough if what this meant were only that our academic purposes are increasingly dictated by the market, as indeed they are. What the QAA, to infinitely greater insidious effect, collaborated in was an elaborate, socially and politically driven, complex of processes whereby intellect as such is reconceived as a market-place for the 'transferable skill' – a case, as it were, of the academy playing flirtatious footsie with the FTSE.

It is not, therefore, in such subject-neutral terms that our discipline needs a coherent account of itself, but rather in the subject-specific terms of what it contributes to the substantive agenda of the university, that without which there would be identifiable loss of intellectual integrity. And when one has said that one has already moved beyond the first reason why such an account is needed to a second, which is that our presence in the university and our contribution to its agenda is with excessive defensiveness promoted in the unchallenging terms of a given subject matter, the subject matter which consists in the phenomena of religions. If theology is something you do, then, like getting rich, that is something you are told you must do in your 'spin-off' company, outside the university; but religion is something you can study, so that, like economics, you can happily spend your time in duly underpaid and underfunded academic research into it. And it is true that there are good reasons why religions should be better studied and taught about than they are: but being an important topic of study does not by itself make for an important, or even a defensible, discipline, and for my part I have more theoretical and methodological doubts about the intellectual coherence of the academic project called 'Religious Studies' than I do of the academic credentials of theology. If, as of course it is, it is important to study religions in the university, it is not self-evident that what we call by the name 'Religious Studies' is the right way to do it. Why such doubts?

The first reason is simply the familiar problem of criteria and scope: as we all know, you cannot count the number of religions there are, until you know what is to count *as* a religion; and the obvious, over-rehearsed, problem with determining what counts as a religion is that you are either going to have to stipulate a definition, with the risks of arbitrary exclusion, or else go along with some entirely empirical and intuitive reckoning of what counts as religion, which risks a vacuous and criterionless inclusiveness. Either way, there is a much more serious problem: several of the central candidates for the category of 'religion' on the anthropologists' tally fiercely deny that they can be understood as belonging to some common category of 'religion' alongside other 'religions'. Muslims often do. And so do I, as a Christian.

You might say, it all depends on how you do it, on your criteria. You can, after all, generate a general 'concept' of religion without supposing it to be a genus of which religions are the species. Nor does a general concept of 'religion' have to rely on the identification of central cases – paradigms – on which others more or less proximately converge. Nor do you even have to define minimum conditions, as the Charity Commissioners do, in order to determine which charitable purposes qualify for tax-exempt status as 'religious'. You could see the word 'religion' as having 'analogical' uses, as one uses words like 'good', the point of the logic of 'good' being that of any kind of thing whatever, there is always what counts as a good one of that kind, and since anything at all can be a value of the variable in the expression 'a good x', you cannot give an account of the whole expression unless you know what x stands for. From none of which deconstruction of essentialism does it follow that the grammar of the word 'good' collapses into equivocity.

You might therefore think that a methodologically appropriate use of the word 'religion' is likewise analogical so that understanding what counts as a religion means determining some function which religion generally serves, hence any such thing will count as 'religious' within a given society which can be identified as having that function, not otherwise needing anything by way of common essence or description. Some functionalist anthropologists are among those who take this view of religion. 'Religions' do not so much possess common descriptive characteristics as explain a potentially unrestricted range of social or psychological phenomena by reference to a defining social purpose, or alternatively a psychological. One hears some opponents of the 'secularisation' thesis argue this way: it is not religion, they say, that has not been secularised away in post-modern Britain, just the traditional religion, which no longer serves the purpose as well as do supporting football teams, or millennium domes, or shrines in the street for dead princesses: I even heard a Cambridge colleague of ours on the radio once describe such phenomena as signs of the 're-Catholicisation' of British culture, because they are, he seemed to think, analogically what liturgies and pilgrimages and saints' cults were. Not descriptively the same, but for all that, solutions to the same (social, or, as the case may be, psychological) equation.

Attractive as such a proposition may be in solving some logical problems of taxonomy, it is still impaled on the horns of the familiar dilemma, in that whatever function itself is assigned to religion is either merely stipulated, yielding conceptually neat but empirically counter-intuitive results, or else is empirically satisfying, but conceptually too lax, to explain anything. After all, any 'function' which is served equally by the Islam of Iranian mullahs and by the Christianity of Irish Catholics in Salford is likely to be so vacuously defined as to serve just as well to explain the solidarities among the Salford criminal gangs – is likely, that is, to explain too much to explain anything at all. Contrariwise, any function which yields substantive explanation of any of these is unlikely to explain either of the others without procrustean distortion.

And though I know that there are all sorts of other ways sociologists and anthropologists have of defining 'religion' than by any form of functionalism, I shall not consider them here, partly because I do not have time, but mainly because I do not think that any project of defining 'religion' aprioristically is profitable, whether the *a priori* ground on which such a definition stands is mere stipulation, or whether it is the ground of social-scientific, anthropological or psychological methodological prescription. Nor do I foresee better hopes of profit in a definition inductively arrived at through the identification of descriptive common characteristics. But why rule them all out? Not I think because we do not need some sense for the word 'religion'; for I am sure that we do need some account of what it is that Christianity and Islam and Judaism all are, and some word will have to stand for whatever that is. The objection, you will guess, is to apriorism, to essentialist ways of getting at the notion.

Of course you might go the whole hog and say that no good purpose is served by *any* concept of 'religion', however arrived at. And one reason why one might think this, as I have said, is that most faith traditions are apt to think themselves trivialised and betrayed by being thought of as a religion, as if being thereby reduced to a mere instance of something more fundamental, more explanatory than what is distinctive, specific – including, of course, the distinctiveness of their own explanations of themselves. For self-reflective traditions, as the main faith traditions all are, the line between 'being explained at all' and 'being explained away' is always fine, and must seem to be crossed into a perverse reductivism for any faith tradition laying claim to ultimately fundamental truths. Besides, it is not even clear how far the description of a faith tradition as a 'religion' succeeds in explaining anything that matters. After all, which creative political, cultural or social movement in human history is best explained as having been inspired by a faith tradition in its character as a 'religion' precisely, as distinct from being inspired by what is specific to it as Islam, or Hinduism? What great architecture, or music, which literatures, what movement of social or moral reform, are explained better by their sources in 'religion' than by their sources in Judaism or Christianity? Which Christian or Muslim martyr gave up her life on account of religion? Which saint, in any tradition, understood his devotion in terms of a 'mystical core' common to all of them? How more fundamental and radical are the questions you raise out of a common religious motivation than are those which arise precisely out of the perception of difference and sometimes of opposition between specific faith traditions, understood precisely in terms of their differences and specificity?

There is, then, something to be said for the view that anything you could possibly value a religion for is liable to be lost in its characterisation as a 'religion' and that anything valuable lies in its specificness, and that it would be the first duty of ecumenical sensitivity to acknowledge that all major faith traditions seek to occupy the common territory of ultimacy, and therefore, at least at some point, are bound to contend over that territory. Therefore, faith traditions are either concerned with the discernment and proclamation of truths demonstrably ultimate, or else they deserve nothing better than to be 'explained', and if possible to be 'explained away' as human forms of idolatry. Which brings me back to the question of theology, and to its nature as argument, concerning which, all I can do here and now, for want of time in which to spell out a proper case, is asseverate: all theology arises out of the sort of disagreement which, though ultimate, is still of a kind which can, logically, be settled; or, if you like, will ultimately be settled; which is but to say that theology is inherently *argumentativa*, as Thomas Aquinas said.[1] Now, to say this much is to say something altogether foreign to our contemporary conceptions of argument and truth.

For it is a common contemporary prejudice of an informally logical kind, that the more ultimate your questions are, the less possible it is to determine the truth of competing answers, so that, the more fundamental your questions are, the less worthwhile it is to argue about them. A moment's reflection, however, suggests that this prejudice flies in the face of common sense. It seems to be a truth available to anyone whose mind is not captive to mere prejudice, that it is more obviously a matter of argument – and certainly that it is a question more worthwhile trying to settle – whether God exists or not, than which of us likes sausages most, for matters of taste are not in the same way *argumentativa*. And even if what would settle the question of God's existence is for the time being unavailable to us, that has nothing to do with the difference between the logical status of the proposition 'God exists' and that of 'I like sausages more than you do'. You can have an argument about whether God exists, because to the question, 'Does God exist?' there is a true and a false answer, even if you don't know which is which. And that is not the case in the matter of sausages, you

[1] *Summa theologiae* 1-1.1.8 *corp.*

cannot settle disputes about taste by argument – which is why, incidentally, when it comes to disagreements about sausages there is nothing much for it but to resort to blows; and it is also why blows are resorted to in the matter of God precisely when belief in God is placed logically on a par with a taste for sausages. Here, as elsewhere, a vacuum created by the rejection of reason will all too quickly be filled by unreasoning power.

At this point, therefore, we run up against the prevailing form of contemporary resistance to essentialism, widespread as a sort of academic ideology, the ideology of 'alterity'. For, of course, logically speaking, disagreement of the sort which makes argument profitable is possible only on the basis of agreement as to what one is arguing about: your saying that there is no cat on the mat is the negation of my saying there is one, only if we agree about what it would be for there to be a cat on the mat. As Aristotle says, *eadem est scientia oppositorum* – 'the knowledge of contraries is one and the same knowledge'.[2] But if you are of a mind which carelessly neglects to distinguish, within the many different ways in which things can be distinct, or 'other', between the non-exclusively and the exclusively distinct, that is to say between contraries and contradictories; or worse, within non-exclusive forms of distinction, between simple distinction and heterogeneity; and if within such laxity of thought you have cast all 'distinction' into the great logical stew-pot of 'radical alterity' or some such impressive nonsense about 'every other [being] completely other', as Derrida says; and if you allow thought to go that far abroad on holiday, as Wittgenstein put it, then you might be drawn to the conclusion, on merely *a priori* grounds, that such are the differences between faith traditions that genuine disagreement between them is theoretically impossible. At any rate, you may well conclude that those differences are such as to rule out any such disagreement as would make argument between them on matters of truth to be in any way profitable. Here, then, we meet with that contemporary fashion in anti-essentialism which results, as it were, in an absolutisation of relativism, an ideology of alterity.

Which is, in my view, as much to be resisted in the matter of understanding theology and religion as are the no more *a priori* doctrines of the methodological essentialists, and it will befit theologians of different faith traditions to be a little more subtle than current fashion calls upon us to be about how they are 'different'. Things differ in kind. But then too there are different kinds of difference. Aristotle thought that there were ten different respects in which things can differ from one another, as he

---

[2] *Peri Hermeneias* 17a, 31–3.

put it, 'univocally' – he called them 'categories'. Now suppose Aristotle is sufficiently right that we can, just by way of example, distinguish how things can differ quantitatively (one thing is six foot long, another five foot) from how they differ qualitatively (one thing is blue, another red); then we have thus far an at least plausible logic for distinguishing between those differences which can stand in relations of exclusion from one another and those between which no such relations can obtain. For a thing's being six foot long excludes its being five foot long, for they differ as lengths do; and a thing's being blue excludes its being red, for they differ as colours do. But its being five foot long cannot either entail or exclude its being red or blue, nor vice versa. Hence, if we are in possession of some such logical apparatus, then we are in command of some sort of distinction between profitable and settleable, and unprofitable and unsettleable, forms of disagreement – which, to simplify, will be the difference between difference and diversity.

It does not matter, for our purposes, how Aristotle got himself this apparatus for distinguishing difference from diversity. Nor does it matter whether he got it right. What matters to us is how we might get for ourselves a comparable apparatus which will equip us to distinguish between profitable and unprofitable theological disagreement, between difference and diversity as between religions, between beliefs in mutual exclusion of one another and simple heterogeneity of belief. And here again I think we must resist the temptations of the *a priori*.

I am inclined to think, in a vaguely Wittgensteinian fashion, of faith traditions as forming a sort of family. Historically, of course, some of them are like family members in having a common parentage, as the Abrahamic religions have, and as, loosely, Hinduism and Buddhism have. In other cases, as in many modern families, step-parentage will have to do, at best. But it was not that sort of genealogical analogy with families that I had in mind but that feature of families with which, being myself the seventh of nine exceptionally opinionated siblings, I am perhaps more than commonly conscious, which consists in their engagement in a certain kind of argument. You can tell any two or more members of my family from what we argue about and how we do it, and in what sort of language we embody our disagreements: as with others, so with Turners, *eadem est scientia oppositorum* – there is a Turner-like territory of disagreement. Of course the analogy is only partial. But for what it is worth, the analogy holds thus far that, as with families, so with faiths, pursuing disagreements is as productive a way as any of establishing both what common ground there is which makes our disagreements possible and profitable and where there is, on the contrary, but diversity, difference of a kind such that nothing is gained from trying to settle the matter, but can lead only to blows. If *eadem est scientia oppositorum*, then let us seek out that true *oppositio* on the ground of which will lie the *eadem scientia*. Thereby we will, I guess, discover the family of theologians: it is the kinship of those who occupy the common territory of *theological* disagreement, of those who know how to disagree about God.

So I say: if you want to do theology then argue. Argue where you know there is disagreement; argue where you are unsure there is disagreement, as being the best way of finding out where 'difference' is disagreement, or, on the other hand, pure alterity. Do you *know* whether your saying God is a trinity of persons and a Muslim's saying God is one is like saying God is red, not blue; or is it more like saying God is red, not six foot long? Is what the Muslim affirms by way of divine oneness that which is denied by the Christian's Trinity? Well, argue with the Muslim in order to find out, for you may find that you disagree as much (if not more) with some members of your own faith tradition than with Muslims or Jews. You may, of course, also have to argue about how properly to argue about such matters, for you may find you disagree also about the nature of our disagreements, as with a group of Birmingham theologians I discovered a year or so ago in debate with some Ayatollahs in Tehran. But that just adds to the fun of finding out just which your family is.

So here I come to one of two conclusions about the place of Theology within the university, this first one having to do with the curricular organisation of this subject. As you can gather, I am not at all happy with the nomenclature of 'Religious Studies', nor with the idea of it, if only because the widely established practice current in most UK universities in which the disciplines are taught and studied is intellectually and, as it seems to me, also morally, indefensible, whereby if it is Christian it can be taught as and called 'Theology', whereas if it is Muslim or Jewish or Buddhist, then it is taught as and must be called 'Religious Studies'. This is not a charmingly English, hence innocent, incoherence: it is an arrogant and patronising insult on the part of one, offered to all the other, major world faith traditions.

On the other hand, teach them all from the inside as Theology, at least in a broad sense as making contestable truth-claims, and so as *argumenta-tiva*, then you generate an agenda of questions which is not some artificial construct of theoretical questions you *could* ask if you happened to want to, but a set of questions you are constrained to ask, whether you want to or not. I really do believe that you ought to do only such theology as you cannot avoid doing without intellectual dishonesty; and I rather think that a great deal of what we do by way of theology isn't necessary at all: it is just stuff hanging around on the agenda long after anyone can remember how it found its way onto it in the first place, and we are no longer able to answer the question 'What problem does saying that solve?' But if Christians are forced to do theology in the light of Jewish or Muslim doubts, or apprehensions, fear, disgust or conceivably even admiration, and Jews and Muslims theirs in the light of like Christian reactions, the questions which arise as the tectonic plates crush up against one another are once again real, and will in the course of argument sharpen into a perception of where the common ground lies, the *eadem scientia*, on which to contest conflicting truth-claims. Such is how I envisage Theology being done within the university – as argument between traditions of truth-claim in contestation over the truths they make claim to.[3]

But if, as I have just said, the family of theologians is the family of those who know how to disagree about God, then, of course, atheists too are to that extent theological siblings. Unhappily today, however, atheists are in practice mostly runts, being intellectually under-weight and having little of interest to contribute to family life, not even decent levels of disagreement. There is in fact an important role for the university theologians in the re-education of atheists in what it would be worthwhile having them around to deny, because, even looking at it from their point of view, the superficiality of their negations gets them nowhere near a proper denial of God, but often little beyond the abandonment of an infantile fairy-tale: so that they are not even very good atheists. Likewise, there is far too little in common between what a Flew or a Dawkins tells us does not exist and what any theologians claim does exist for their denials to offer any real theological stimulus, so that there is a certain lopsidedness to the theological argument. The atheistical challenge being so generally lackadaisical, the consequence is that hardly anyone really argues about God any more, not even theologians much.

I think therefore that this lack equally of intellectual vigour and rigour on the side of the atheist does matter from the standpoint of the theologians too, for I suspect the theologians in turn often get away with far more than they should be allowed to and, for want of challenging atheists, I fear among theologians in particular a certain theistic complacency. Curiously, the one subject many theologians appear not to want to talk about much nowadays is 'God', and a certain kind of theologian, a case in point having been Colin

---

[3] I do not, by the way, think that that is all theology is. But I do think it is what 'university' Theology is for the most part.

Gunton, would really rather you did not, since proper theologians will talk about Christ, or the Trinity, and not, as Gunton thought, about pagan, 'monotheistic' notions, like 'God'. But when Thomas Aquinas asks himself what is the subject matter of theology, he rejects as insufficient the obvious answer that it is the truths of faith revealed through Jesus Christ – the incarnation, the Trinity, the sacraments, redemption and so forth; as he says, that is as mistaken as trying to define the sense of sight merely by listing the objects which you can see, because, of course, if you are colour-blind you can still see the same objects as the rest of us do. Rather, he says, the proper object of theology is all those truths of faith revealed to us and understood *sub ratione Dei* – precisely as showing forth God. And he has a point. You could very well detect a theological complacency in supposing that necessarily you are talking about God just because you employ a certain vocabulary of theological terms, or can work out some consistent way of talking about the Trinity of persons and the oneness of God, or because you know how to talk about the incarnation, or whatever; after all, Feuerbach showed just how you could do all that and more and not know yet how to determine the difference between a theologian's doing so genuinely *sub ratione Dei* and a Feuerbach's doing so *sub ratione hominis*, as just a roundabout way of talking about human beings. You aren't necessarily talking about God just because you talk theological terms – there are plenty of *Christian* forms of idolatry, and complacent Christians should take a lesson from the deluded aristocrat who when asked how he knew he was God replied that there was no difficulty in that since when he prayed he found he was talking to himself. I should have thought that working out some sort of account of how you would know that you are talking about God, never mind to him, was a basic epistemological task for theologians who wish to do more than chatter among themselves in a sort of tribal dialect; and perhaps the very best safeguard against such theological introversion is the challenge of a vigorous, and theologically demanding, atheism.

But if for that reason it matters to theologians, it is also from the point of view of the university that that argument needs to be had. For I believe that universities ought to be still what they were in their medieval origins, places of disputation, and that whatever else they do, it is their business to do it by means of argument. In which case, the quality of the work they do will consist, still today as then, in the quality of the questions they ask and in the general strategy of calling every answer back to the question it is an answer to, and so to the possibility of rival answers. And that precisely is the reason why any university should want to have in its midst the presence of theologians: for the 'Religious Studies' people ask only the same old sorts of questions that anthropologists, or psychologists, or historians, or sociologists ask, as it happens about religions, whatever we decide they are. Whereas theologians ask distinctive questions all of their own that no one else would have thought of asking, questions of such oddity that you are obliged, as a first sort of task, to demonstrate that they can be legitimately asked at all – like Leibniz's question, 'Why is there something rather than nothing?'

Now anyone can see how very odd that question is who can see how mangled is the syntax of the expression 'x rather than y' in this case, for, as relational expressions go, we would normally require a symmetry of values for the variables x and y: 'red rather than blue', being distinct as colours are, 'chalk rather than cheese', distinct as inorganic and organic substances are. Not so here: 'something' will have the value of some state of affairs, of course; but 'nothing' is not the name of some contrasting negative state of affairs, but the negation of there being any state of affairs at all. The position is, as Thomas Aquinas explains it, the same as that of the 'out of' in the expression: 'creation *out of* nothing'. The logic of the 'out of' here is not that what the world is made of is a sort of nothing in the way in which a Martin Heidegger might be described as 'talking about nothing' when *das Nicht* is the topic of his conversation; it is rather that the world is made but there is no 'out of' involved at all, in the way in which when anyone else but Heidegger is said to be 'talking about nothing', we take it rather more simply that he is not talking about anything. So, given its eccentric syntax, we might well ask whether there could be any legitimacy to the '. . . rather than . . .' in the question, 'Why is there something rather than nothing?', and so to the question itself. Well, yes there can, because it is the only way we have of construing the sheer contingency of the world: concerning any and all of it, we can say that it might not have been, and concerning anything else there could possibly have been, had it existed, it too might not have done so. So we have a *use* for the asymmetrical '. . . rather than . . .', we need it to be able to ask the question; and we need to ask the question for the reason that that there is anything at all is not to be taken for granted, it is *surprising* and *might not have been*; and there being nothing at all, would, of the two possibilities, have been by far the more likely outcome. But if we have a use for the eccentrically asymmetrical '. . . rather than . . .', nonetheless we have also, as it were, run out of *meanings* for it just at this point of ultimacy. And that, to me, sounds rather like the predicament which causes you to do theology: or perhaps it is better to say that to find yourself in that predicament *is* to find yourself to be doing theology: encountering a mystery, *quod omnes dicunt Deum*, as Thomas says.[4]

So you are doing theology whenever you are asking demonstrably ultimate questions about the world, questions you can make sense of because they lie in some continuity with questions we have regular and routine methods of handling in the different disciplines and sciences which form the received academic agenda; but the answers could not be ordinarily meaningful in the same way. For though the question lies, just, on the inside edge of language, and so just within the bounds of the sayable, the answer has to be on the other side of it. Our grip on the theological as a human discourse lies therefore in the questions we can ask; but what count as the answers must lie unsayably beyond those limits: theology is, as it were, our appropriation of this final loss of hold on language. Hence, insofar as questions of this sort press themselves upon us, insofar, that is to say, as they are demonstrably ultimate, they press upon us an unknowability about things, a sense of the world as mystery: as Wittgenstein says, it is not how the world is, but that it is which gives rise to astonishment. And if you were to ask me what I thought the place of Theology was within the university – I mean, what the reason is why it should be done there, the reason why it is needed – it would be for the same reason that we want to have universities themselves at all: there is reason enough for Theology, and for everything else that is done within the university, if they succeed in just this one thing within all the other things that they do, that in them all they give rise to an ultimate kind of astonishment concerning *how* the world is, which is science, and *that* the world is, which is theology.

---

[4] *Summa theologiae* 1-1.2.3 *corp.*

CHAPTER 3

Shaping the field: a transatlantic perspective

Sarah Coakley

INTRODUCTION AND OUTLINE

Let me start this short essay of salutation to Nicholas Lash with a quotation from his own writing with which many will be familiar. It is to be found in the opening section of his book *The Beginning and the End of 'Religion'* (1996), and runs thus:

> . . . the view that 'religion' is the name of one particular district which we may inhabit if we feel so inclined, a region of diminishing plausibility and significance, a territory quite distinct from those we know as 'poetry' and 'art', as 'science' and 'law', and 'economics'; *this* view of things, peculiar to modern Western culture, had a beginning in the seventeenth century, and (if 'post modern' means anything at all) is now coming to an end.[1]

In what follows I shall be taking much of these sentiments as read, however contentious they may remain in some quarters.[2] Yes, the falsely unifying, and inadvertently ghetto-ising, notion of 'religion' was indeed a distinctively Western, European product. It served particular political functions in an era of so-called 'toleration'; and it allowed 'other' 'religions' to be safely characterised as variations on a covertly assumed Christian norm. It also enabled such 'religions' to be theorised as intrinsically *interior* phenomena, and thus purportedly rendered them neatly distinguishable from the other more 'public' spheres and activities mentioned by Lash. It has been well said that this view of 'religion' was first shattered, symbolically, in British law on the day that a British immigrant Sikh refused to don a

---

[1] Nicholas Lash, *The Beginning and End of 'Religion'* (Cambridge: Cambridge University Press, 1996), p. ix.

[2] As we shall shortly mention, the American context of discussion, with its much-vaunted separation of Church and State, makes it considerably more difficult than in the UK to *dispose* of the concept of 'religion' as a category under which purportedly non-partisan academic study of faith traditions can cluster. However, for a trenchant critique from a post-modern perspective of this modern (and specifically American) notion of 'religion', see Talal Asad, 'The Construction of Religion as an Anthropological Category', in *Genealogies of Religion* (Baltimore and London: Johns Hopkins University Press, 1993), ch. 1.

motor-cycle helmet when riding his scooter (and was duly censured by the courts): his 'religion' manifestly failed to reduce to the appropriately interiorised Lockean accommodation.[3] Thus, like so many other 'achievements' of the European Enlightenment era (most notably, the idea of an autonomous, unitary self, which arguably goes along with it), this construct called 'religion' is now being demolished with glee by many scholars, especially in Europe.[4] And the *false* contrasts between this 'religion', on the one hand, and 'Christian theology' on the other, which were thereby set up (dispassion versus commitment, unbelief versus belief, 'scientific study' versus 'naïve religion' or 'enthusiasm'), have proved to be disjunctive binaries which no one represented in this volume, I presume, would wish any longer to defend.

My points of discussion with Nicholas Lash, therefore, will not lie in a *direct* challenge to his theory about the death of 'religion', even though I believe much more could be said than this simple account of mine would suggest. Especially is this true from the perspective of a comparison with North America, where the supposed separation of 'Church' and 'State' evokes different responses than in Northern Europe to the prospect of seeing off 'religion'.[5] But for the purposes of this short essay I shall don my British hat, and make just three suggestive arguments which draw attention to the paradoxical strategic realm we 'religious professionals' now inhabit in Great Britain. For here we find ourselves under constant strain, both *politically* (in our attempts to keep our subject funded, valued in the university, and attractive to the populace), and *intellectually* (in our efforts to keep our own integrity as scholars, and – in most cases – also as practitioners of specific religious traditions). We all know, both realistically and cynically speaking, that these two tasks can drag us in painfully different directions, especially

---

[3] See the relevant discussion in Paul Morris, 'Judaism and Pluralism: The Price of Religious Freedom', in Ian Hamnett, ed., *Pluralism and Unbelief* (London: Routledge, 1990), pp. 179–201.

[4] See for instance Denys Turner's contribution to this volume; but note that even he has to have recourse to the alternative epithet 'faith traditions' (instead of 'religions') at one point in his argument (p. 30). The idea of distinct historic strands of 'religious' practice and belief is hard to dissolve altogether.

[5] In North America there is an unrepentantly *secular* dimension to the 'study of religion' in some quarters, justified supposedly by the need to keep religious commitment out of the sphere of the university discourse: witness, for instance, the contentious current debate (in 2003–4) over whether to separate the Society of Biblical Literature from the American Academy of Religion, which is to a significant extent fuelled by this pugnacious secularism. (For a trenchant recent critique of this form of secularism, however, see Stephen Prothero, 'Belief Unbracketed: A Case for the Religion Scholar to Reveal More of Where He or She is Coming From', *Harvard Divinity Bulletin* 32 (Winter/Spring 2004), pp. 10–11.) My tentative hypothesis here is that the backcloth of established (though numerically failing) Anglicanism in England gives the discussion of 'religion' a different flavour: the inexorable mingling of religious commitment and politics is taken for granted, allowing (ironically) for a rhetorical *dismissal* of 'religion' in its distinctively modernistic sense.

given the *Realpolitik* of government funding-patterns; but I think we have to live with, and make creative use of, this ostensibly schizoid condition.

Let me then anticipate the conclusions of this essay before I argue them in detail. My three points are as follows, and in each of them I draw, dialectically, on a lesson I have learned from a continuing debate on 'religious education' that has been going on in recent years in North America. This multi-faceted debate deserves to be better known, I believe, if only as a contrapuntal 'cautionary tale', in British circles. In short, I write here from my *own* particular 'schizoid' perspective – as a British theologian domiciled in North America, but regularly visiting Great Britain, and made deeply aware, thereby, of certain characteristically 'American' mistakes that might be made at this crucial juncture in the supposed post-modern demise of 'religion' in Britain.

First, I shall argue that Nicholas Lash's account of the 'end' of 'religion' (along with David Ford's concomitant recent call in *The Christian Century*[6] to 'integrate' Religious Studies and Theology in the light of this shift of consciousness), are *dangerous* strategies if they thereby threaten to collapse completely the remainingly creative dimensions of the Enlightenment contrast between the 'study of religion' and 'Christian theology' which has proved so generative in the development of our subjects in the United Kingdom since the early 1960s. In other words, the apparently tired rhetorical contrast between 'religion' and 'theology' is one we Britishers have come to love to *hate*, for particular historical and contextualised reasons; and if we succeed in disposing altogether of what we love to hate, then there may actually be intellectual loss, not gain. (A cautionary aside here about what happens in North American 'liberal' circles when this distinction is effectively erased will perhaps provide an interesting object lesson.)

Second, I shall then illustrate the importance of keeping this dialectical *Nachlass* from the Enlightenment in play by indicating the far-reaching significance – as I see it – of feminist and gender studies for our respective fields. For these areas of critical reflection represent one of the most significant, if not *the* most significant, development of the last fifty years methodologically in 'Religious Studies' and 'Theology', in my view. And it is not a coincidence that the creativity of these approaches has emerged *within* the discussion of the dialectic between 'religion' and 'theology'; and not a

---

[6] See David F. Ford, 'Theological wisdom, British style', in *The Christian Century*, 5 April, 2000, pp. 388–91. Ford notes (approvingly) that 'In Britain . . . the trend has been to integrate theology and religious studies, to the extent of questioning the dichotomy', and that 'The historical reasons for developing a "neutral" religious studies program as opposed to dominant "confessional" theology . . . have largely disappeared in British theologies' (ibid., p. 388b).

coincidence either that when the dialectic is repressed – when 'Theology' withdraws, for instance, from interaction with 'Religious Studies' – that these methodologies also seem to be suppressed. Again, a brief contrapuntal aside about a false move, as I see it, in a particular North American association of 'feminism' with a socially conscious justice-seeking version of 'religious education', will be mentioned as an object lesson; for that ploy I believe destructively marginalises the very insights about 'feminism' it seeks to promote more widely.

Third, and finally, I shall make a playful – and not altogether tongue-in-cheek – aside about a potential new sub-faculty in any Marketing Department or Business School in Britain, which I shall call 'Spiritual Services'. I need hardly say that this would be a big money-spinner, and could lead to a lot of attractive consultancy work for our own departments. The idea for this came to me only recently, when I started a weekly training in a Roman Catholic hospital in Boston as part of a diaconal sabbatical year funded by the Lilly Foundation. As a sop, it seems, to the current ethos of pluralism and 'New Age' sensibilities, but also as a concession – perhaps unthinking – to the new American 'commodification' of 'religion', this Catholic hospital in Brighton, Massachusetts, has recently changed the name of its 'Clinical Pastoral Education' department. And so now, on Fridays, I proudly strut the hospital's corridors with my new gleaming badge: no longer am I a 'Protestant Chaplain', but rather a 'Spiritual Services Intern'. This unexpected turn of events has caused me to think afresh about a certain set of 'enterprise' opportunities that might await 'Religious Studies' and 'Theology' departments in Great Britain as they bemoan the governmental 'squeezing' of their budgets.[7] My institutional suggestion here for a lucrative extension of their expertise into the Business School is not merely cynical; my point is that the yearning for 'spirituality' (previously known as the yearning for 'mystical experience', so ably debunked by Denys Turner[8]), is a current cultural phenomenon too important and profound to be ignored by supercilious academics. Indeed, I suggest it can be turned to good account as an 'evangelistic' opportunity, one however that would ultimately *undo* the presumptions with which its 'customers' start; and one that probes more interestingly than did the long-running debate in North American seminary circles in the eighties over so-called

---

[7] For an astute set of essays on the 'enterprise culture' of the Thatcherite era, including some of its implications for 'religion', see Paul Morris and Paul Heelas, eds., *Values of the Enterprise Culture: Moral Debate* (London: Routledge, 1992). My suggestion here is scarcely a valorisation of that culture *per se*, but rather an idea for turning its impetus to a spiritually productive end.

[8] See Denys Turner, *The Darkness of God: Negativity in Christian Mysticism* (Cambridge: Cambridge University Press, 1995).

'religious *paideia*' to the way that 'practices' interact with 'beliefs'. (Here I will provide my last American contrapuntal aside, to the important work on 'Religious Education' by Edward Farley.[9]) In short, it is our commodified, globalising, corrupt Western culture – for all its frailties – that in its yearning for 'spirituality' is actually telling us here what it *knows* it needs to know: about how 'spiritual exercises' must undergird any philosophical and theological perceptions of integrity;[10] and how the 'beliefs' it ardently – if inchoately – seeks cannot even be entertained by 'untaught bodies'.[11] So, here, a cynical 'enterprise' opportunity meets an ingenious post-modern possibility for fashioning a spiritual and intellectual integrity amongst the secularised British business elites: if it is 'spirituality' that they want, let them consider their options under the best guidance that the university can offer them. This idea forces me finally to part company with the suggestion in my opening quotation from Nicholas Lash that 'religion' is a 'region of diminishing plausibility and significance'. *Au contraire*, I suggest. Although 'religion' (in the technical sense of a unifying construct of modern intellectual heritage) may by now be largely debunked by British academics, that does not mean that 'religious' yearnings and movements are any less vibrantly present, even in a 'secularised' country like Britain. There is still plenty of *religion* around, we might say;[12] it is, in contrast, the established churches in Northern Europe that are now in the direst trouble.[13]

So much by way of a brief introductory overview of my main themes. Now let me say a little more about each of these three theses in turn.

---

[9] See Edward Farley, *Theologia: The Fragmentation and Unity of Theological Education* (Philadelphia: Fortress Press, 1983), and Edward Farley, *The Fragility of Knowledge: Theological Education in the Church and the University* (Philadelphia: Fortress Press, 1988). The unfolding of the American debate about 'Religious Education' that was begun with Farley's work is ably discussed and assessed in David H. Kelsey, *Between Athens and Jerusalem: The Theological Education Debate* (Grand Rapids: Eerdmans, 1993).

[10] The reference here is to Pierre Hadot's essay, 'Spiritual Exercises', in *Philosophy as a Way of Life* (Oxford: Blackwell, 1995), which we shall discuss further at the end of this essay.

[11] This point is made in Talal Asad, 'Remarks on the Anthropology of the Body', in Sarah Coakley, ed., *Religion and the Body* (Cambridge: Cambridge University Press, 1997), pp. 42–52.

[12] That is, if we do not restrict 'religion' to *institutionalised* groups and churches; increasingly, sociological research in Britain reveals a vast preference for privatised affective 'spirituality' over institutional commitment: see Paul Heelas and Linda Woodhead, *Religion and the Rise of Spirituality* (forthcoming).

[13] On the phenomenon of North European state church decline, see the recent work of Grace Davie, e.g: *Religion in Britain since 1945: Believing without Belonging* (Oxford: Blackwell, 1994), and *Europe – the Exceptional Case: Parameters of Faith in the Modern World* (London: DLT, 2002). This work is interesting to compare with that of the prolific American sociologist of religion, Robert Wuthnow, e.g.: *The Restructuring of American Religion: Society and Faith since World War II* (Princeton: Princeton University Press, 1988), and *After Heaven: Spirituality in America since the 1950s* (Berkeley: University of California Press, 1998).

KEEPING THE DIALECTIC BETWEEN 'THEOLOGY'
AND 'RELIGIOUS STUDIES'

Let us take a step back, once more, to the reflections in our introduction. It might seem a reasonable ploy, having historicised and criticised the
notion of 'religion' in the way that Lash does (or that Michael Buckley has
again done in his contribution to this volume), to see off the notion of the
study of 'religion' altogether. As Jonathan Z. Smith puts it, famously: there
seem to be '*no data*'[14] for the study of 'religion', in this falsely hypostasised
sense. And certainly it might seem even more legitimate, from a Christian
theological perspective, to un-yoke the enterprise of Christian 'systematics'
from this spuriously concocted subject matter of 'religion'. For there are, of
course, famous Barthian reasons for such a disjunction between 'dogmatics'
and 'religion', even in a *modernist* milieu;[15] and, in a *post-modern* milieu,
the pressures to divide the disciplines, or to dissolve the 'study of religion'
altogether, seemingly only become greater. Consider John Milbank's entic-
ing call to a 'meta-narrative of peace', one in no way dependent, it appears,
on the close study of the messy realities of contemporary lived 'religion'.
Indeed, since modern 'sociology of religion' has apparently been given its
marching orders by Milbank, it is unclear how the study of such realities
could now even credibly proceed.[16]

But my suggestion here is that such a reasserted institutional *disjunction* between 'Theology' and 'Religious Studies' would be a false move of
great seriousness; and even worse would be the simple swallowing-up of
'Religious Studies' under the aegis of 'Theology'. For even if we cannot
any longer give a fully convincing or consistent account of the meaning of
'religion'; even if we become fully aware of its European Enlightenment
genealogy and of certain embarrassing concomitant associations that we
would now rather eschew; and even if the supposed disjunction between
dispassionate description and normative evaluation now seems entirely

---

[14] Jonathan Z. Smith, *Imagining Religion: From Babylon to Jonestown* (Chicago: University of Chicago
Press, 1982), xi: '. . . while there is a staggering amount of data, of phenomena, of human experiences
and expressions that might be characterized in one culture or another, by one critierion or another,
as religious, *there is no data for religion*. Religion is solely the creation of the scholar's study.'

[15] Like Bruce McCormack and others, I read Barth's 'dialectical' revelationism as equally informed by
Kant's modernistic epistemology as it is by political dissent from late nineteenth-century German
theological 'liberalism': see Bruce L. McCormack, *Karl Barth's Critically Realistic Dialectical Theology:
Its Genesis and Development 1909–1936* (Oxford: Clarendon Press, 1995).

[16] See John Milbank, *Theology and Social Theory: Beyond Secular Reason* (Oxford: Blackwell, 1990),
which conjoins a blistering critique of classical sociology of religion with an exhilarating call to
'recover the possibility of theology as a metadiscourse'. I question Milbank's apparent disassociation
from humdrum contemporary religious realities in ch. 1 of my *God, Sexuality and the Self: An Essay
'On the Trinity'* (Cambridge: Cambridge University Press, forthcoming).

spurious; nonetheless, the teaching of 'traditions' other than Christianity,[17] and the acute observation of a variety of religious traditions *as lived*, may still provide the most creative dialectical context for the forging of systematic Christian positions (and indeed, the forging of contemporary Jewish, Hindu or Buddhist positions). Without this dialectical *frisson* between Christianity and its 'competitors', Christian theology would be in danger of a more arid intellectualism, a more smug authoritarianism, or – at the other end of the spectrum – a more pallid descriptivism. By this last tag I have in mind the lazy tendency in circumstances which do not call for a clearly normative, or contestable, stance simply to describe what other theologians have said about some matter in the past. Much of what is called the teaching of 'theology' in our universities tends, on closer inspection, to veer towards this unengaged regurgitation of 'facts'. But then the undertaking becomes what the Dutch Jesuit Frans Jozef van Beeck has called 'theologology' (talking about talking about God), not *theology* in the strict sense;[18] and it is much easier and more tempting, I suggest, to rest with lazy 'theologology' when one's inter-religious interlocutors are safely off the scene. Similarly, and ironically, it is easier to shout very loud, in an authoritarian Christian voice, when one's inter-religious interlocutors are likewise out of earshot.

So, if I am right, we now find ourselves in an odd and paradoxical position. We have come to a point in 'post-modernity' when the well-established institutional distinction between the 'study of religion' and 'theology' no longer pleases us (if it ever did). But if we dispose of it altogether, the last case may be worse than the first. Even John Milbank's immensely creative theological project in *Theology and Social Theory*, note, was originally sponsored in, and arguably most fittingly resides in, the 'oppositional' context of a department of 'Religious Studies' (in Lancaster, UK). But when it now gets taken up enthusiastically by ultramontane Roman Catholics operating from entrenched theological bunkers in America, even Milbank becomes distinctly, and visibly, nervous.[19] The point is that, when divorced from

---

[17] As I mentioned before, it is notable that even Denys Turner (in his companion essay in this book, which also takes issue with the category of 'religion'), cannot forbear at one point to use the alternative term 'faith tradition'.

[18] For his use of the term 'theologology', see Frans Jozef van Beeck, S. J., 'Trinitiarian Theology as Participation', in Stephen T. Davis, Daniel Kendall, S. J., and Gerald O'Collins, S. J., eds., *The Trinity* (Oxford: Oxford University Press, 1999), pp. 295–325, at pp. 315–18; and Frans Jozef van Beeck, S. J., *God Encountered: A Contemporary Catholic Systematic Theology*. Volume 2/4: *The Revelation of the Glory* (Collegeville, MN: The Liturgical Press, 1999), pp. 47–9.

[19] Milbank's commitment to a form of Christian 'socialism' fits uneasily into the American milieu, with its long-standing near-identification of socialism and communism. For his most recent exposition of his 'socialist' vision, see John Milbank, *Being Reconciled* (London: Routledge, 2003), ch. 9: 'Politics: Socialism by Grace'.

the creative interplay of 'religious studies' and 'theology' as understood in the British context, Milbank's project is capable of a sort of 'Babylonian captivity' by the American theological 'right' that eviscerates it of its distinctive socialist impetus. In short, Milbank's undertaking, I aver, not only *assumes* the 'study of religion' that it ostensibly despises, but also takes for granted the Church/State collusion of Anglicanism that it seeks to revitalise. When removed from either, or both, of these conditions, the effect of Milbank's message is disarmingly different from its original intent.[20]

What, then, has our first argument established so far? It does not seek, note, to return to the artificial notion of 'religion' as *separable sphere* that Lash has so ably criticised; and still less does it propose that the 'study of religion' is somehow more appropriate for the university setting than 'theology' because the latter, given its 'commitment', will necessarily evidence less intellectual rigour than the former.[21] Rather, what it urges is that an over-hasty rush to declare 'religion' defunct, and thus to announce the 're-integration' of the two realms of study, could have the unintended effect of subsuming one into the other, and thus of erasing the hard task of the recognition and negotiation of contentious religious 'otherness' which lies at the heart of today's most challenging political crises.

Before passing on from here to my second main thesis, then, a brief aside about the effective collapse of the 'religious studies'/'theology' distinction in 'liberal' theological circles in North America may be instructive for the British context. It is not that the British theological world is ever likely to embrace this distinctively American mixture of intellectual and political commitments ('liberalism' in the United States having in my view a greater historic tendency to covert 'illberalism'); but more that the American example acts as kind of symbolic warning-system against the erasure of the 'theology'/'religion' distinction altogether. In the United States, we find in the remaining contexts where theological 'liberalism' is still regnant, an intense suspicion of metaphysical claims, *tout court*, brought about, first, by a particular reading of Kant's religious epistemology,[22] and, secondly,

---

[20] This difficulty was manifest in a recent Dulles Seminar in New York devoted to John Milbank's work.

[21] This latter view is however still actively in play in some American exponents of the study of 'religion': see again Stephen Prothero's recent article in the *Harvard Divinity Bulletin*, 'Belief Unbracketed', which takes issue with precisely this line of approach in the work of the American religionist Robert Orsi.

[22] The early work of my predecessor at Harvard Divinity School, Gordon D. Kaufman, is particularly exercised with the neo-Kantian difficulty of God's *noumenal* status, and with our supposed restriction therefore to 'constructive' theology about the 'available God' of our cultural imaginations: see *God the Problem* (Cambridge, MA: Harvard University Press, 1972). Kaufman's later work veered away from this strict neo-Kantian position to a much more subtle enunciation of a form of modified

by the 'post-modern' chastening of the 'grand narrative'.[23] With that goes a pervasive assumption that pluralistic 'toleration' should rightly involve the whittling away of any absolutist claims, lest one's convictions be seen as inappropriate 'hegemonic' bids for power. A more 'humble' approach, allowing space for a diversity of theological voices from the margins, can only, it is urged, be supported by some form of uncontentious philosophical pragmatism; religious beliefs and doctrines come to be seen as merely *hermeneutical* perspectives, no longer axes on the 'truth' in a metaphysical sense.[24]

But the task of then delineating the difference between the constructive and critical hermeneutical claims of a *theologian* (representing a particular faith tradition), and the equally creative and critical hermeneutical reflections of the student of 'religion', becomes very difficult indeed. As my Harvard colleague Francis Schüssler Fiorenza has attempted (in several important articles) to defend that distinction, it ostensibly lies in the fact that only the 'theologian' has the task of owning and taking on the tradition – of reconstructing it hermeneutically with an eye to its *practice*. But this is a slim distinction from the (equally hermeneutical) task of the religionist, perhaps even a distinction without a real difference.[25] Not insignificantly, Margaret Miles (another notable exponent of this American 'liberal' tradition of theology) opened her 1999 presidential address to the American Academy of Religion with the frank assertion: 'it is time . . . finally to lay to rest the debate of fundamental differences between "theological

Hegelianism (see *In Face of Mystery: A Constructive Theology* (Cambridge, MA: Harvard University Press, 1993)); but arguably Kaufman's more simplistic earlier position had much greater influence on 'liberal' American theology of the eighties and nineties than his later stance, as witnessed for instance in the feminist work of Sallie McFague.

[23] See Jean François Lyotard, *The Postmodern Condition: A Report on Knowledge* (ET: Minneapolis: University of Minnesota Press, 1984), a work that had extraordinary influence in the United States in deflecting theological thinking away from attempts at metaphysical or epistemological realism.

[24] The 'hermeneutical turn' in continental philosophy (witnessed in such writers as Hans-Georg Gadamer and Paul Ricoeur) thus gains a particular flavour in the work of American 'liberal' theologians such as David Tracy and Francis Schüssler Fiorenza.

[25] For Fiorenza's views on 'religious' and 'theological' studies see his 'Theological and Religious Studies: The Contest of the Faculties', in Barbara G. Wheeler and Edward Farley, eds., *Shifting Boundaries: Contextual Approaches to the Structure of Theological Education* (Louisville: Westminster/John Knox Press, 1991), pp. 119–49; and his, 'Theology in the University', *The Council of Societies for the Study of Religion Bulletin* 22 (April, 1993), pp. 34–9, and 23 (February 1994), pp. 6–10 (the latter section responding to a critique from Don Wiebe). The gist of Fiorenza's position is the insistence that neither 'religious' nor 'theological' studies can avoid a *double* hermeneutical move of both retrieval and reconstruction. This of course leaves the difference between the two very slim; but only the latter, according to Fiorenza, reconstructs the identity of a particular tradition with reference to its *practical* outcomes. To be fair, Fiorenza does strenuously resist, rhetorically, the collapse of one discipline into the other, as do I; but one is left wondering if the particular 'distinction' he draws makes any serious 'difference', since students of 'religion' are often also interested in practical outcomes to their work.

studies" and the "study of religion" . . . [I]n 1999, their distinctions are without a difference.'[26] And, further, the important recent attempts by Ronald Thiemann at Harvard[27] and Clark Gilpin at Chicago[28] to redefine the job of the theologian in the university Divinity School, as a 'public intellectual' commenting on the place of 'religion' in the 'public sphere', also, and similarly, comes close to an erasure of the distinction between theology and religious studies. For such a 'public intellectual' walks a fine line short of any robust theological claims; there is an intense coyness about doctrinal or credal tradition, lest – it seems – the wider university look unfavourably on such commitment as offensive proselytism. In Gilpin's book, *A Preface to Theology*, talk about the churches becomes minimal, connections with Christian devotional practices unmentioned, and God-talk is replaced with elusive references to 'symbols' and (occasionally) to 'the sacred'.[29]

In short, and not to belabour the point further, if we want to keep questions of 'God', 'truth' and metaphysical ultimacy robustly in play in our theological discourses, we also need to defend *in some form* the traditional distinction between 'religious studies' and 'theology', like it or not. To be sure, the American 'liberal' danger of passing off as 'theology' what has virtually ceased to be anything more than the old (dispassionate) 'religion' is unlikely to be the particular danger that British theologians – for historic reasons – find the greater temptation. Retrenchment into a smug,

---

[26] Margaret R. Miles, '1999 Presidential Address: Becoming Answerable for What We See', *Journal of the American Academy of Religion* 68 (2000), pp. 471–85, at 471–2.

[27] See Ronald F. Thiemann, *Toward an American Public Theology: The Church in a Pluralistic Culture* (Louisville, KY: Westminster/John Knox Press, 1991); Ronald F. Thiemann, *Religion in Public Life: A Dilemma for Democracy* (Washington, DC, Georgetown University Press, 1996); and for his explicit views on 'religion' and 'ministry', see his *Toward the Integrated Study of Religion in the University* (Pittsburgh, PA: The Association of Theological Schools, no date). In this last short (13 pp.), but revealing, document, Thiemann strenuously defends the specific mandate of the theologian to exercise 'normative' judgement, in contrast to the spuriously 'neutral' position of some 'religion' departments' ideology, and speaks of his hope for a 'mutually fruitful dialogue' between divinity schools and religious studies departments (ibid., p. 11). However, the language of 'religious leaders' and 'public service' largely replaces that of 'pastors' and 'church' in this document – presumably out of a desire to placate those who fear the dominance of robust statements of 'faith' in a divinity school, and who see them as inappropriate in a research university setting. Unlike Fiorenza, Thiemann makes no attempt to locate the *differentia* of 'theology' in 'praxis' as such; but he suggests, somewhat blandly, that what 'ministry' as 'a peculiar profession' can offer to the university is a particular sense of *'public responsibility'* (ibid., p. 12). The document ends, significantly, thus: 'Universities need vigorous, self-confident divinity schools, institutions devoted to preparing intellectually acute *leaders* for lives of *service* in *public affairs*' (ibid., p. 13, my italics). I myself find it difficult to see how that statement could not equally be made of the vocation of a politically aware professor of 'religion', social worker, doctor, diplomat or CEO.

[28] See W. Clark Gilpin, *A Preface to Theology* (Chicago: University of Chicago Press, 1996).

[29] See ibid., esp. ch. 5, for Gilpin's recommendation for the contemporary theologian's vocation as 'public intellectual'. References to 'symbols' and 'the sacred' feature significantly in the closing pages of the book: pp. 181–3.

uncontested Anglicanism or Scottish Presbyterianism is arguably a more insidious possibility in the United Kingdom than the adoption of a British form of illiberal religious 'liberalism'. But even so, *pace* David Ford, the simple 'integration' of 'theology' and 'religious studies' is perhaps not quite what we want, if, that is, it suggests any danger of fusion of the two poles, or the collapse of creative tension between them.

GENDER STUDIES AND THE STUDY OF 'RELIGION'

My second point, then, is related, but perhaps not so obvious, *prima facie*. And that is that without this creative dialectical *frisson* between 'religious studies' and 'theology', the immensely important insights of feminist and gender studies which have so fructified and regenerated theological and religious studies in the last generation are likely to get repressed, or else to lose their practical contemporary application. For what feminist theology, at its best, persistently and importantly reminds us of is the multi-textured way in which – covertly or overtly – gender themes are entangled with doctrinal pronouncements; and how, in *application*, doctrines which may appear purely abstract and anodyne disconcertingly display gender bias;[30] or how, again, some renditions of doctrine are intrinsically connected with practices and habits which condone the subordination or abuse of women.[31] What I have elsewhere called the 'messy entanglement' of doctrine with questions of sexuality and gender requires, of course, eyes to see it; and these eyes need to be trained precisely in the methodologies of what Geertz calls the 'thick description' of religion.[32] So 'theology' without 'religious studies' 'taking a look' (as Nicholas Adams memorably put it at our conference in honour of Nicholas Lash) is likely to be theology without awareness of its own gender bias and texture, and so, concomitantly, theology without self-reflective consciousness of its own rich set of entanglements with practice and application at every level. And that, in my view, is deeply *impoverished* – as well as self-deceptive – theology.

The problem is, that even – or when – this point is well taken, other dangers immediately confront us which threaten to re-inscribe a false disjunction of the disciplines which we seek to keep in productive 'play'. And here a second, cautionary, point of comparison with American theological

---

[30] I demonstrate this with regard to some crucial features of the history of the doctrine of the Trinity in *God, Sexuality and the Self*.

[31] See the chilling examples (both Protestant and Catholic) of the appeals to Christian 'orthodoxy' to justify incestuous abuse in Annie Imbens and Ineke Jonkers, *Christianity and Incest* (ET: Minneapolis: Fortress Press, 1992).

[32] See Clifford Geertz, *The Interpretation of Cultures* (New York: Basic Books, 1973).

circles may prove instructive as a brief object lesson for our reflection on the importance of a continuing dialectic of 'religious studies' and 'theology'.

Ironically, it is in the realm of an institutionally 'successful' *feminism* of one variety that our lesson here resides. For I think here of feminist or 'womanist' theology of a particular, pragmatic sort in North America, powerful especially in denominational seminaries and (some) university Divinity Schools, which has tended to focus exclusively on a curiously a-historical notion of 'justice' as the central goal of its view of 'Religious Education'. This type of 'theology' has eschewed 'the study of religion' for *different* (and at points explicitly anti-intellectual) reasons from that of extrication from Enlightenment views of 'religion'. And unfortunately it has done this in a way that abstracts from, and virtually ignores, the sophisticated 'gender studies' so illuminatingly being developed, almost simultaneously, in 'Religious Studies' departments by historians and 'religionists' working on particular moments of the Christian tradition.[33] This feminist/womanist movement in 'Religious Education' has, in contrast to the concomitant developments in 'gender studies' in 'religion', tended to favour the 'practical/political', and to deride the aridly 'intellectual'; it has also shown a marked resistance to 'spiritual practices' other than those with obvious and immediate political impact.

The now-classic feminist/womanist text on Religious Education by the so-called 'Mud-Flower Collective', entitled *God's Fierce Whimsy*,[34] is perhaps the most striking instantiation of this type of 'theological' method. Its authors combine a method of autobiographical narrativity with an insistence that 'the primary theological and educational task of the church [is] the work of *justice* . . .'[35] The book does not attempt a contextualised definition of what that 'justice' might consist in,[36] but adds a curiously sneering rejection of spiritual practices as a-political, narcissistic, and propelled merely by a desire to 'feel good about myself'.[37] (To this last point I shall return shortly, in the third 'thesis' of this essay.) But there is a notable

---

[33] For a historically astute and revealing account of the waves of fashion since the 1970s in 'women's studies', 'feminist studies' and 'gender studies' in the realm of Christian history, see Elizabeth A. Clark, 'Women, Gender, and the Study of Christian History', *The American Society of Church History* 70 (2001), pp. 395–426. Clark, being involved in 'religious' rather than 'theological' or 'ministerial' concerns, is ostensibly unaware of the debate on 'Religious Education' and does not cover material relating to it.

[34] The Mud Flower Collective, *God's Fierce Whimsy: Christian Feminism and Theological Education* (Cleveland, OH: Pilgrim Press, 1985).

[35] Ibid., p. 33 (my italics).

[36] A comparison with the nuanced contribution of Maleiha Malik to this volume (on the issue of 'justice' considered trans-religiously), will prove instructive.

[37] *God's Fierce Whimsy*, p. 162.

lack of integration of *scholarly* feminist or 'gender' studies of the Christian tradition in this approach; and there is an accompanying assumption that 'practices' which are not overtly political must be insidiously a-political. In short, what we see in action here is a particular style of (somewhat anti-intellectual) 'theology' that consciously majors in political activism, and so sets itself at a distance from the supposedly dispassionate and intellectual 'study of religion'. But it equally distances itself from personal *spiritual* practice on the grounds that such endeavours are time-wasting and narcissistic. Both 'high' intellectual research, then, and also 'spirituality', are seen as suspicious elitisms which divert attention from the needs, 'experience' and voices of the dispossessed. Whilst these aversions are surely understandable, especially in the North American context of what can only be called institutionalised racism, the more worrying question is whether this policy ultimately marginalises and disempowers the very feminist/womanist projects that it seeks to promote.

Even Rebecca Chopp's infinitely more rigorous work on feminist theological education, *Saving Work*,[38] shares with the Mud Flower Collective the same de-historicised appeal to justice ('theological education is not just *about* justice, it is in a sense justice itself'[39]), and a persistent avoidance of a head-on discussion of 'God' and metaphysical claims about God-self, as well as a classic 'liberal' avoidance of interest in habituated spiritual practices of relation to such a God. There is a connection here, I suggest, between 'liberal' American theology's lack of confidence about the very possibility of truth-claims about the divine, and this particular sort of feminist theology's tendency to hypostasise and de-historicise 'justice' whilst becoming disassociated from the complexities and riches of historical and spiritual tradition (and scholarly gender studies thereon). Again, a disjunction between 'theology' and 'religion' leads, I believe, to unfortunate intellectual – and indeed spiritual – consequences.

'SPIRITUALITY' IN THE POST-MODERN UNIVERSITY

And that brings me, finally, to my playful third point, which focuses explicitly on the question of spiritual practices in relation to theology. I have been arguing so far for maintaining institutionally what is *good* about the dialectical tension in British universities between 'Theology' and 'Religious Studies', despite all our new-found scruples about the meaning

[38] Rebecca S. Chopp, *Saving Work: Feminist Practices of Theological Education* (Louisville, KY: Westminster/John Knox Press, 1995).
[39] Ibid., p. 106.

and evocations of the term 'religion', and despite our suspicions about any false disjunction between dispassion and commitment. But now I propose an extension of our operations – a cunning, but not cynical, application of our expertise to a blatant *Anknüpfungspunkt* in our commodified post-modern culture. And so I ask: why not literally *sell* 'spiritual services', if that is what is a perceived cultural need? If the burnt-out executive seeks 'spiritu-ality' for himself and his workforce, why should we leave the teaching of such important matters to relatively untrained amateurs? Why not take on the task and 'cure' the exhausted CEO's 'soul', not only of its spiritual lassitude, but of the very ambition to add 'spirituality' to an already-extended list of 'leisure pursuits'? In short, why not lead him/her, through the development of sustained 'practice', to a point at which commodified 'spirituality' may ultimately give place to a transformative metaphysical commitment? And why, exactly, does this prospect embarrass us? Can we not grasp this oppor-tunity and turn it to good account, economically, as well as theologically and spiritually?

The reason for our embarrassment, I suggest, lies in another long-established split connected with the Enlightenment project: between theo-retical exposition, on the one hand, and ascetic practice, on the other. And it is this which makes the sort of undertaking I propose seem more than faintly inappropriate in the contemporary university setting. But again, I propose that we need to get beyond this modernistic coyness. Whereas the Mud Flower Collective, as we have seen, derides 'spirituality' for other reasons (as a narcissistic and a-political undertaking), other teachers of 'Theology' or 'Religious Studies' who *are* also practitioners remain curi-ously inhibited or secretive about their personal commitment. But does not this fear of 'commitment' belong precisely to the disengaged or dispas-sionate notion of the study of 'religion' that post-modernity has effectively criticised? We lag behind here, it seems. Pierre Hadot had already in the late 1980s drawn attention, in his famous essay 'Spiritual Exercises', to the accompanying practices of ancient philosophy deemed to be indispens-able for 'a transformation of [one's] vision of the world', and thus for the philosophical task *per se*.[40] Practice and theory inexorably belong together for Hadot, as indeed they did for most pre-modern philosophies and theologies.

Whilst this appeal of Hadot's to re-integrate philosophical argument and practice has been enthusiastically promulgated of late by no less eminent a

[40] Hadot, 'Spiritual Exercises', 82.

philosopher than Hilary Putnam at Harvard,[41] theologians and religionists in the same university – even at the Divinity School where scholars are engaged in the professional training of ministers! – often treat such matters as virtually unmentionable.[42] Moreover, the productive and long-running debate over Edward Farley's book *Theologia* (1983),[43] which drew attention precisely to the lack of *paideia* (educative formation) as an integrating factor in 'Theological Education' in American seminaries, ran into the sands, it seemed, when it hit the big university Divinity Schools, where such imitative training in ascetic practice seemed to the then-dominant academic elites curiously out of place. Why was this so? Apparently the 'public intellectual' theologians of the Thiemann or Gilpin school would not think it appropriate for their students (let alone for their faculty) to be caught *praying* publicly in the university. Why so (or why not)? It would seem that the newly minted 'public intellectual' approach of the university Divinity School deans was still caught in the *modernist* need to evacuate intellectual leadership in 'theology' from any taint of 'commitment'. Yet at the very same moment, respected leaders in the philosophical faculties were leading a charge back to a pre-modern integration of committed practice and intellectual argument. The ironic result is that Divinity School students in these leading institutions may now find themselves more encouraged in the cultivation of a disciplined practice of prayer and asceticism by the *philosophy* professors in the university than by their own Divinity School leaders. Is this a rational or defensible state of affairs? That is an interesting question for debate, on which there is so far an almost deafening silence.[44]

In sum, leaders in 'Theology' and 'Religious Studies' in British universities should surely take note of these lessons from the North American university milieu. If the embarrassed disjunction between reason and commitment is no longer one that can be credibly sustained in a post-modern intellectual climate, then there is no intrinsic reason why highly trained

[41] This shift in interest in Putnam's philosophy (which accords with the re-embracing of his Jewish faith and practice) is already evident in his Gifford Lectures, *Renewing Philosophy* (Cambridge, MA: Harvard University Press, 1992), esp. chs. 7–8 on Wittgenstein's views on religion.

[42] See again my discussion of Thiemann's and Fiorenza's views of 'ministry' and 'theology', above; and Prothero's call in 'Belief Unbracketed' to resist Robert Orsi's insistence that '[religious studies] exists in the suspension of the ethical' (p. 10b).

[43] Farley, *Theologia*.

[44] Honesty would also call us to admit that the political and historic valences of a *Jewish* call to integrated 'practice' are subtly different from that of a parallel Christian call in contemporary America. Not only is Judaism associated in the culture at large (rightly or wrongly) as more concerned with 'practice' than 'doctrine', I suspect that the fear of a charge of anti-semitism significantly – and fortuitously – protects certain university discussions about 'religion' which might otherwise be constrained or cut off if overtly undergirded by Christian faith commitments.

practitioners of a variety of religious backgrounds (from the department of 'Theology' and 'Religious Studies') should not 'sell' their wares in the wider university. Indeed, we have come to a strange pass when the Business School prefers a collection of self-educated New Age proponents of quick-fix 'spirituality' in its programmes of self-help and relaxation over highly trained representatives of faith traditions available in a nearby university department. To the cynical riposte that the Business School only *desires* quick-fix 'spirituality', and that it necessarily reduces 'religion' to 'relaxation', I must declare that I have myself found intelligent MBAs-in-the-making more religiously discerning, and less gullible, than they are often characterised. And to the suspicious riposte that the religiously practising members of the 'Theology' and 'Religious Studies' departments would use such an opportunity for inappropriate *proselytism*, I would declare the same: if their (different) wares are presented with intellectual and spiritual integrity, the members of the Business School will be quite able to make their own rational choices in the matter.[45] If I am right, the current difficulty and resistance here lies more in the 'scruples' of the theological and religious scholars of the university, than in the intelligence, spiritual yearning, and potential commitment of the inhabitants of the contemporary Business School.

CONCLUSIONS

Let me now sum up the results of this short essay. In this tribute to Nicholas Lash's work on the 'end' of 'religion', I have attempted to bring some (admittedly refracted) light to bear from America on our current British *aporiai* about the future of 'theology' and 'religious studies'. In three different ways, I have tried to show that what I have called the remaining 'dialectical *frisson*' between 'theology' and 'religious studies' should not be dissolved without extreme caution and always with the acknowledged danger of reductive loss. I have freely acknowledged in the process of this argument that (1) a falsely hypostatised, unified, and interiorised notion of 'religion', (2) a misleading disjunction between dispassion and commitment, and (3) an equally insidious divide between theory and ascetic practice, are all products of the 'modern' period that we are now attempting

---

[45] Here, interestingly, my argument finally converges with that of Denys Turner, from whose position – in significant other respects – I have diverged in this essay. The confidence we have in the possibility of 'rational' discussion, 'rational' *arguments*, over 'religious' and 'theological' issues in the university, will clearly affect our attitude to their relation. It has been one of the burdens of this essay to suggest that the integration of spiritual 'practice' and theological enquiry will make that 'rationality' *more* telling and nuanced, not less.

to correct or allay. Of the first two of these dangers we are seemingly more aware in Great Britain than we are of the last; and hence my playful – and surely contentious! – call to test our commitment to the new intellectual ethos of post-modernity by responding creatively to the perceived cultural longing for 'spiritual' authenticity in the university setting.

I end this essay, however, with the reiteration of a double irony about the American theological scene that has emerged in the course of my argument, and which seems to demand a measured reflection and response beyond the limited confines of this current essay. Feminist theology at its most theologically productive, I have suggested, should have certain ends in view that *cohere* with the current interest in Pierre Hadot's work. Both approaches seek to explore how 'practices' are entangled with beliefs, *all the way down* – for good or for ill. Yet a form of feminist theology dominant in 'liberal' circles in America tends to eschew interest in 'spiritual practice' altogether; and the American university departments (whether Divinity Schools or departments of Religion) most adequately placed to explicate the relation of spiritual practice to belief in such a way that a false quest for high-point 'experience' is chastened, also tend to avoid the teaching of 'practice'. Whether we in Great Britain can adjust our post-modern methodological lenses to meet these strange bifurcations and challenges, and to avoid some of the misleading choices evident in the North American 'liberal' scene, seems to me a good test of how to continue, in this new century, the productive interaction of 'theology' and 'religious studies' (however re-defined) that has served us here so well since the 1960s.

CHAPTER 4

The study of religion as corrective reading

Gavin Flood

At the end of the sixteenth century John Donne writes:

> . . . On a huge hill,
>   Cragged and steep, Truth stands, and hee that will
> Reach her, about must, and about must goe;
> And what the hill's suddennes resists, winne so;
> Yet strive so, that before age, deaths twilight,
> Thy Soul rest, for non can worke in that night.[1]

This is a striking image that identifies truth with religion, but one that today does not resonate with us. Donne stands near the beginning of a path that will lead, some hundred and fifty years later, to an Enlightenment that would retain his image of Truth standing on the 'huge hill, cragged and steep', but which would break the link between truth and religion. With the Enlightenment truth becomes identified with reason (*logos*) and religion becomes identified with story (*mythos*) and, as de Certeau reminds us, from an Enlightenment perspective the history of religion becomes the history of error.[2] Truth becomes the truth of reason rather than of faith. The story continues, as we know, with reason itself being held up to scrutiny, particularly by those masters of suspicion Nietzsche and Freud, and this suspicion continues into the late modernity of our present age. Reason comes to be seen by some, not as the means of accessing truth, but rather as part of story, part of *mythos*.

A second, contrasting, image is offered by Walter Benjamin's angel of history. Inspired by Klee's painting *Angelus Novus*, which he owned, Benjamin presents us with an image of the angel of history whose face is turned towards the past. The angel does not see a sequence of events but only 'a single catastrophe that keeps piling wreckage upon wreckage and hurls

---

[1] John Donne, 'Satyre: On Religion', in Helen Gardner, ed., *The Metaphysical Poets* (Harmondsworth: Penguin, 1966), p. 50. Thanks to Martin Davies in English Studies, Stirling University.
[2] Michel de Certeau, *The Writing of History*, trans. Tom Conley (New York: Columbia University Press, 1988), p. 23.

it in front of his feet'.[3] The angel wishes to move back into the past to repair the things that have been broken, but a storm is blowing from paradise, blowing the angel inexorably backwards, into the future. He wrote this between his release from the internment camp and his death at the Spanish border. In an earlier essay on the idiosyncratic thinker Karl Krauss, Benjamin again evokes Klee's painting as a representation of the angels who are created in countless throngs each moment to sing God's praise and then immediately pass into nothingness before his glory.[4] But Klee's angel is captured and cannot fulfil its purpose of glorifying God, nor can it return to heal the past. This is a tragic angel, prevented from fulfilling its purpose by the winds of modernity. The image offers a pessimistic vision and a tragic view of history which, in spite of Benjamin's theological leanings, implicitly rejects Donne's vision of religion as inviolable, timeless truth. Benjamin's angel is impotent, driven by no other force than history.

But there is a position between the totalising claim implicit in Donne's verse and the tragic angel of history, although it is a position that cannot be evoked in a single image, or perhaps in no image other than that of the meticulous scholar at work with her text. This position concerns the 'corrective reading' of tradition by tradition; the constant re-reading and reinterpretation of the past that is also an attempt to heal the past and thereby to constitute the future. All communities have some mechanism for understanding their pasts, but some traditions have deep conceptions of the past and sophisticated mechanisms of interpretation and remembrance, particularly the Jewish and Hindu traditions, closely linked with future hope. The criticism of religion, in its rationalist forms claiming a value-neutrality, has itself developed within an intellectual tradition that has both broken with the past while undoubtedly having continuities with it. This is the tradition of rational critique of which we are all a product, which Peter Ochs calls the Cartesian-Kantian epistemology, but which itself has offered totalising claims that are set against the claims of religion (Marx might be an example).

Against this background, I wish here to describe the recovery of traditions of interpretation or corrective reading as performed by Peter Ochs. Secondly, I wish to claim that the study of religion needs to take note of this discourse and to look at the possibility of Religious Studies as corrective

---

[3] Walter Benjamin, *Illuminations* (London: Pimlico, 1999), p. 249.
[4] Walter Benjamin, *Reflections: Essays, Aphorisms, Autobiographical Writings*, ed. Peter Demetz, trans. Edmund Jephcott (New York: Harcourt Brace, 1978), p. 273. Reference from Handelman, *Fragments of Redemption: Jewish Thought and Literary Theory in Benjamin, Scholem, and Levinas* (Indiana University Press, 1991), p. 168.

reading, through reflexive critique of its own tradition and through reading across cultures. In this way, I would hope to posit the development of a post-critical study of religions which we might call a dialogical Religious Studies. This is not so much the application of a method developed by Ochs, but an orientation towards text and tradition necessitated by Ochs's post-critical position. Thirdly, I would wish to claim that such a programme of post-critical corrective reading allows the recovery of subjectivity and explores the relationship between subjectivity and macro-cultural analyses of history or the place of subjectivity within wider temporal forces.

THE IDEA OF CORRECTIVE READING

In his work on Peirce, Ochs develops the idea of 'corrective' or 'pragmatic' reading, although this work is of importance beyond Peirce scholarship. Let me quote Ochs himself. The basis and aims of his project are to find

reasonably precise ways of talking about imprecise things without losing the meaning of the impression itself; a belief that phenomena of everyday language, including the everyday practices of religion, are among those things; a love of critical reasoning but a distrust of criticism that has lost sense of having a purpose; disillusionment with 'modern' or Enlightenment attempts to make a metaphysics – and also a religion – out of rational critique of inherited traditions of knowledge and practice; a conviction that post-Enlightenment anti-rationalism – including romanticisms, emotivisms and a variety of totalizing ideologies of power, history, experience and so on – may prove logically to be the other side of the rationalist coin . . .[5]

The thesis that Ochs presents is simply a claim to pragmatic reading as the performance of correcting definitions of imprecise things. Such a reading, he argues, cannot be done in general but only for someone or for some community of readers, as new contexts disclose new meanings for different purposes.[6] The field of his inquiry is within the Cartesian-Kantian tradition, examining problems in the philosophy of Peirce and offering ways forward for the community of readers concerned with those problems, such as the theory of Pragmatism and Peirce's critique of Cartesianism. Ochs develops various levels of reading that involve the initial collecting of explicit texts, and the analysis of those texts with categories that foster the development of hypotheses which in turn allow the identification of

[5] Peter Ochs, *Peirce, Pragmatism and the Logic of Scripture* (Cambridge: Cambridge University Press, 1998), p. 4.
[6] Ibid., p. 5.

leading tendencies in the texts, themes, problems and methods. Ochs develops strategies for distinguishing between the explicit text and the implicit text of which it is a sign and develops a sophisticated schema of levels of interpretation.[7]

I do not intend to describe these problems or Ochs's ways forward, but simply to draw attention to the method of pragmatic reading based on a distinction found in medieval Jewish scholarship between the 'plain sense' (*peshat*) of a text and the 'interpreted sense' (*derash*). Pragmatic or corrective reading is the interpreted sense. New contexts will bring out new meanings for different communities of readers. We might see such corrective reading as a recovery of tradition and an attempt to heal the things that have been broken; making the past, through tradition, relevant for particular communities at particular times as both an exercise in healing and an exercise against forgetfulness. All traditions offer corrective readings in this way, although some more overtly than others, namely the Jewish and Hindu traditions which developed systems and methods of interpretation.

In a modern context, Ochs outlines a 'corrective' or 'pragmatic' method of reading that reveals both the horizon of the text and the way the text meets the world. He takes the text to be two kinds of sign, a sign as an explicit statement about a possible world envisioned by the text's author and an implicit index of events in the actual world from which the statement emerges.[8] We might say that on the one hand we enter into the world imagined by the text or its author(s) – into the text's religious *imaginaire*[9] – while on the other we see how the text expresses events and power in the 'real' socio-political world. The text is an index both of wider history and of its author(s). Each text evokes its own *imaginaire*, its possible world or horizon which the reader, receiver, or community of receivers learns to inhabit. Learning to inhabit the world of the text, and thereby entering the tradition of practice of which the text is an icon, is the first step in the act of reading. This initial reading is getting to know what Ochs calls the 'plain sense' of the text in contrast to the 'interpreted sense'. It is this level that I penetrate through reading, and repeated reading, and, unless it is a text of a tradition that I am inside, I can never wholly enter into it.

---

[7] Ibid., pp. 24–41.   [8] Ibid., p. 24.

[9] My use and understanding of the term is based on C. Castoriadis, *The World in Fragments: Writings on Politics, Society, Psychoanalysis, and the Imagination*, trans. D. A. Curtis (Stanford: Stanford University Press, 1997), pp. 5–18. For a discussion of this term and a constructive use of it see S. Collins, *Nirvana and Other Buddhist Felicities* (Cambridge: Cambridge University Press, 1998), esp. pp. 72–89.

Pragmatic reading is tradition- and community-specific; there can be no general pragmatic reading that has universal application or validity.

PRAGMATIC READING AND THE STUDY OF RELIGIONS

In Ochs's account all texts that share a theme or leading tendency and 'which belong to a demonstrable 'chain of transmission' are considered icons of a tradition of practice'. By 'chain of transmission' he means a 'historically identifiable series of interpretations according to which one practice serves as interpretant to another practice and so on'.[10] Corrective reading, on this view, is tradition-specific and discourse-internal, integral to the tradition's historical trajectory and the practices that contextualise it in any contemporary world.

Religious Studies, I would argue, has to pay attention to this idea of tradition-internal, pragmatic reading as a model of an intellectual tradition's reflexivity. First, because traditions external to the discourse of Religious Studies are its proclaimed objects. Secondly, because it raises the very question of the possibility of Religious Studies as an externalist programme giving an account of tradition in terms of other discourses (sociology, psychology, or phenomenology). The problem is whether pragmatic reading is possible in a discipline that claims a plurality of its objects, namely 'religions' or even 'religiosities'; that stands outside of those objects in an aspired-to scientific objectivity; and that is both implicitly and explicitly comparative in nature. Put even more simply, the question is: what is the relation of Religious Studies to its objects or the primary traditions that comprise its fields of inquiry?

This is not to question the legitimacy of 'outsider' claims, which is surely not in question. The human sciences – anthropology, sociology, the cognitive sciences, and even biology – have a claim in explicating all areas of human experience, including the religious. But there is clearly a difference between claiming to speak for a religion and claiming to speak about it. There are deep problems that cannot be developed here about the place of 'insider' voices representing religions in the publicly funded academy. Religions are polymorphous so there is the question of *which* voice is represented and there are pedagogical problems about only one religious voice representing a tradition to an increasingly pluralist student body. I suspect that the more important issue is one of pedagogy rather than position – surely somebody cannot be barred from teaching Karl

---

[10] Ochs, *Peirce*, p. 34.

Barth because she is Catholic or from teaching Islam because she is an atheist. Expertise is more important than confession at this level. To my mind, regardless of position, what is important is that all participants in conversation share a common method of rational inquiry.[11]

But given these problems, if Religious Studies is to move beyond a surface description of phenomenology, which might be identified with the 'plain sense' reading of a text, to modes of analysis and understanding that are equal in sophistication to tradition-internal modes of pragmatic reading performed, say, in Jewish or Hindu traditions, then it needs to learn from them and be humble before them. How can the comparative endeavour of Religious Studies relate to tradition-specific pragmatic reading? It is this important question and tradition-specific, internal discourse as a model for the study of religions that we have to address and that Religious Studies needs to respond to.

I would wish to argue that Religious Studies can be understood in terms of corrective reading and that such corrective reading has two referents: a reflexive, corrective reading of its own tradition, especially Phenomenology, and corrective reading of primary traditions or the objects of its inquiry, which is implicitly or explicitly a reading *across* traditions. Let us examine each of these in turn.

Reflexive corrective reading

Religious Studies can clearly be regarded as a discipline distinct from Theology in so far as it now has a certain historical density, a strong institutional base in Western universities, and an intellectual tradition and reflexive critique. This is not to deny that Theology is the parent, or grandparent, of Religious Studies or that both are engaged in the secular university in the same practice of conveying rational method, but it is to claim that they have different narrative bases. The discourse of Religious Studies is wide, embracing within it philological scholarship on traditions' scriptures, particular historical descriptions, phenomenologies of contemporary practices, along with Marxist, feminist, and post-colonial critique. But central to Religious Studies – especially, but not only, in the UK – has been the Phenomenology of Religion with a history stretching back into the nineteenth century.[12] This discourse has been and continues to be of central importance in departments of Religious Studies and in schools and colleges

---

[11] I have discussed this elsewhere in *Beyond Phenomenology: Rethinking the Study of Religion* (London and New York: Cassell, 1999), ch. 1.

[12] E. Sharpe, *Comparative Religion* (London: Duckworth, 1975), pp. 220–50.

where the teaching of 'world religions' largely develops from the phenomenological enterprise.[13]

Pragmatic reading in Religious Studies as a reflexive discourse is an internal, corrective reading of its tradition that needs to proceed dialogically through the mapping of the discourse and then moving on to corrective readings of it. Of key importance here is Phenomenology. For Peirce, Phenomenology is perceptual judgement. It diagrams collections of perceptual judgements which are then abstracted to degrees of abstraction that become mathematical.[14] The Phenomenology of Religion does not derive its method from Peirce, but rather from Husserl, whose Phenomenology nonetheless compares with the Peircian programme. For Husserl, Phenomenology is the mapping of perceptions or appearances to consciousness that entails the bracketing of their objective referents. Through simply mapping appearances to consciousness and bracketing ontological questions, he thought he could avoid the problems of idealism and materialism that had plagued the history of philosophy. Bracketing (*epoché*), or the first phenomenological reduction, is followed by a second reduction – paralleling Peirce's 'precisive abstractions' – which is the intuition of the essence (*eidos*) of phenomena through as complete a picture gathered in the first reduction as possible. This process is inevitably always incomplete. In terms of the Phenomenology of Religion this has been interpreted as the organising of religious phenomena, gathered through description, into types. Empathy (*Einfühlung*) is central in the process as the penetration of the object by the external observer. It is empathy and typology that have characterised the Phenomenology of Religion as practised by Ninian Smart, for example, who has defined Phenomenology as 'informed empathy' and 'a morphology or classification of types of religious phenomena'.[15]

While this discourse has had a deep effect on the representation and study of religion, taking the Ochsian idea of corrective reading, Religious Studies needs to continue to bring out the theoretical problems of this discourse and to offer corrective readings internal to its tradition.[16] One example, but an important one, will suffice to illustrate this. Husserl's *epoché* has

---

[13] For a clear assessment of phenomenology in the classroom and its critique see R. Jackson, *Religious Education. An Interpretive Approach* (London: Hodder and Stoughton, 1996), pp. 7–29.

[14] Ochs, *Peirce*, pp. 119–21. E.g., 'The car is red' becomes '– is red, white', becomes '– has a given color – has a quality', becomes 'whiteness; quality; Firstness (monadicity),' and so on.

[15] Ninian Smart, *Dimensions of the Sacred: An Anatomy of World's Beliefs* (London: HarperCollins, 1996), p. xxiii.

[16] For a critique of the Phenomenology of Religion see T. Fitzgerald, *The Ideology of Religious Studies* (Oxford: Oxford University Press, 1999), ch. 2, p. 237; for a critique of Eliade, R. McCutcheon, *Manufacturing Religion: The Discourse on Sui Generis Religion and the Politics of Nostalgia* (Oxford: Oxford University Press, 1997), pp. 74–100; Flood, *Beyond Phenomenology*, pp. 91–116 and *passim*.

been of central importance in the phenomenological study of religion in its attempt at value-free description and understanding the 'other' through empathy. Husserl's idea seems to have entered the study of religion through Max Scheler in 1921 but was taken up by van der Leeuw in his *Religion in Essence and Manifestation* (1938) where his understanding is in consonance with Husserl, that the *epoché* is the suspension of questions about the reality behind appearances; about the being of the meanings presented to consciousness.[17] However, within Religious Studies discourse the *epoché* has often been taken to mean the suspension of *subjectivity* rather than the objective status of appearances. Gaston Berger, writing before van der Leeuw, speaks of the need to put into parentheses our own beliefs and personal feelings, while admitting to the difficulty or impossibility of suppressing subjectivity.[18] And Phenomenology in a classroom setting is often presented as the suspension of subjectivity.

There is a deep contradiction here. On the one hand Phenomenology is concerned with consciousness as intentional – indeed the intentionality of consciousness might be taken to be its central idea – yet on the other it is represented as proclaiming the suspension of subjectivity. We might state the contradiction more formally: that consciousness has the defining property of being intentional (the *cogito* always has an object, a *cogitatum*) and consciousness has the property of being able to suspend subjectivity. If subjectivity is defined as the subject of first-person predicates, the response to the question 'who',[19] then because consciousness is intentional it can deny its intentionality and we are left with the contradiction, if it is intentional it can be non-intentional.

It is in instances such as this, where the plain sense of the texts of Phenomenology renders contradictions, that corrective reading needs to take place. We can fruitfully examine this in terms of Peirce's A- and B-reasonings. Ochs describes these as follows: 'B-reasonings appear, alone, to offer significant information about the world, but they are often faulty. A-reasonings appear to offer little information, but serve as reliable criteria against which to judge errors in the B-reasonings.'[20] Let us say that for some Religious Studies scholars, bracketing is the suspension of subjectivity rather than the suspension of the 'natural attitude' that for Husserl

[17] See Flood, *Beyond Phenomenology*, pp. 97–8; G. van der Leeuw, *Religion in Essence and Manifestation* (London: Harper Torchbooks, 1973 (1938)), p. 674.

[18] Gaston Berger, 'On Phenomenological Research in the Field of Religion', *Encyclopédie Française*, translated in J. Waardenburg, ed., *Classical Approaches to the Study of Religion*, vol. I (The Hague, Paris: Mouton, 1973), p. 665.

[19] Paul Ricoeur, *Oneself as Another* (Chicago: University of Chicago Press, 1992), pp. 57–61.

[20] Ochs, *Peirce*, p. 77.

means the suspension of the objective status of appearances. We might take bracketing as a B-reasoning which claims that this method can offer significant information about the world, in this case the revelation of a truth about religions for one who stands outside of them. But there is a contradiction here that needs to be addressed, between the idea of intentionality, and the suspension of subjectivity. In this particular case, corrective reading can be made by a return to Husserl; a contradictory B-reasoning about the *epoché* can be addressed by another, corrective, B-reasoning which then functions as an A-reasoning when put to this use. We can use Husserl's coherent account to offer corrective readings of the incoherence of suspending subjectivity, especially as Phenomenology is so centrally concerned with consciousness as intentionality. Husserl writes in the *Cartesian Meditations:*

This universal depriving of acceptance, this 'inhibiting' or 'putting out of play' of all positions taken toward the already given Objective world and, in the first place, all existential positions (those concerning being, illusion, possible being, being likely, probable, etc.), – or, as it is also called, this 'phenomenological epoché' and 'parenthesizing' of the Objective world – therefore does not leave us confronting nothing.[21]

Husserl's account functions to correct the imprecision of the religionist who takes the *epoché* to be the suspension of subjectivity. Rather than subjectivity, it is objectivity or the question of the being of appearances that is suspended, and the plain-sense reading that renders contradictions can be initially rectified through a corrective reading using Husserl; he in turn can, however, become subject to corrective reading, as when Derrida highlights the problem of distinguishing the first *epoché* that distinguishes a realm of the purely psychic (i.e., the stream of the *cogitationes*) from the transcendental *epoché* that reveals the transcendental subject.[22]

While Husserl himself has been subject to corrective reading from the perspective of *différance* which denies the distinction between meaning and being intended here, the application of the *epoché* in Religious Studies, when used responsibly, has nevertheless intended to liberate the study of religion from distortion and to bring out the web of values and beliefs implicated in any particular practice. Smart writes that Phenomenology allows for accurate description and so does not misrepresent other traditions. When Bishop Heber writes that 'The heathen in his blindness/Bows down to wood

---

[21] E. Husserl, *Cartesian Meditations*, trans. Dorian Cairns (Dordrecht, Boston, London: Kluwer, 1993), p. 20.

[22] Jacques Derrida, *Speech and Phenomena and Other Essays on Husserl's Theory of Signs*, trans. David B. Allison (Evanston: Northwestern University Press, 1973), p. 11.

and stone' he is guilty of phenomenological mis-description, being 'more interested in conversion than in being scientific'.[23] Although this concept of science as offering a value-free account is problematic thirty years on, the Phenomenology of Religion did intend that other voices should be heard and that Christianity should not be privileged above other religions: all religions are equal before the gaze of the scientific phenomenologist, as it were.

Corrective reading that draws on the sources internal to the tradition can therefore function to highlight and correct contradictions at the level of plain-sense reading or B-reasonings. Interpretation needs to be brought to bear when contradictions appear in the plain-sense of the text. But we must not forget that corrective readings are always for a particular community, perhaps a later generation within a particular tradition. These interpretations are integral to an intellectual tradition's self-modification and, in the case of the study of religions, to the very existence of the discipline as a coherent discourse. Because of the diversity of the field, for Religious Studies to be operative as a coherent discipline there needs to be a meta-discourse – which we might take to be the series of A-reasonings – that reflects common concerns and allows communication between different fields within it.[24] It is as a kind of meta-discourse that Religious Studies can operate in comparative mode and it is here that we see the possibility of Religious Studies as corrective or pragmatic reading operating beyond the narrow confines of its own internal dialogue. A Religious Studies pragmatic reading must also be able to operate across traditions if it is to be relevant to a wider community.

Corrective reading across traditions

While the Phenomenology of Religions has claimed to be descriptive, there is another sense of Religious Studies as social science that makes claims about the explanation of religion from the perspective of sociology, psychology, or even genetics, where 'explanation' means the location of a cause. These are classically naturalist or reductionist explanations,[25] legitimate

---

[23] Ninian Smart, *The Science of Religion and the Sociology of Knowledge* (Princeton: Princeton University Press, 1973), pp. 20–1.

[24] Flood, *Beyond Phenomenology*, pp. 3–8.

[25] I do not like to restrict reductionist to naturalist explanations, as all representations of knowledge are reductionist in some sense. On kinds of reductionism in religion see I. Strenski, *Religion in Relation: Method, Application and Moral Location* (Columbia: University of South Carolina Press, 1993), section 2; for a sustained critique of socio-biological reductionism see J. Bowker, *Is God a Virus?* (London: SPCK, 1995).

discourses that have claims on religion in giving accounts of it. Religious Studies as an *explanatory* discourse attempts to interpret why communities and individuals perform religiously. The question arises as to what the relation is between Religious Studies as explanation and the traditions it seeks to 'explain'; what is the relation between the texts of Religious Studies and the primary texts of their object traditions? While Religious Studies is explanatory – even phenomenological description is explanatory in one sense – it can nevertheless intersect with the corrective praxis of tradition. It can itself function as a corrective form of reading in relation to a tradition's primary texts and in offering corrective understandings of imprecise things.

But what is it to read texts outside of their cultures and traditions and in what sense could Religious Studies offer corrective readings relevant to traditions? The scholar engaging in primary and interpretative readings is participating in the fate of all texts, to be 'entextualised' and 'contextualised', to use Silverstein and Urban's phrase; taken out of one context (entextualisation) which is a simultaneous placing in a new context (contextualisation).[26] Benjamin speaks of translation as 'a relation between two objects which is intimate but not mimetic which always involves the displacement of the original into some other realm'.[27] With religious texts, my reading will not be the religious reading of their reception in the traditions of their origin. My 'consumerist' reading, in Griffiths' terms,[28] is in order to describe these texts in their historical tradition and to bring them into juxtaposition in the sphere of an academic enterprise. For the purposes of scholarship, such as Philology, the world of the text is entered by a reader or community of readers for purposes other than those envisaged by its composer(s) and earliest receivers. Within the field of Religious Studies, for example, religious texts of Europe and South Asia are studied by those standing outside of the traditions with varying degrees of distance from the texts' *imaginaires.* As Ochs says, there will be different communities of readers for whom different readings will be resonant.[29] Different communities of readers will therefore engage with a text at different levels and for different purposes,[30] and we might add that the same reader might engage

---

[26] M. Silverstein and G. Urban, eds., 'Introduction', *Natural Histories of Discourse* (Chicago: University of Chicago Press, 1996), p. 1.

[27] Benjamin, *Illuminations*, p. 30.

[28] P. Griffiths, *Religious Reading: The Place of Reading in the Practice of Religion* (Oxford: Oxford University Press, 1999), pp. 42–5.

[29] Ochs, *Peirce*, pp. 246–7. In ch. 8 Ochs takes leave of the 'general reader' and offers readings to particular communities of readers.

[30] Griffiths, *Religious Reading*, pp. 40–54, 60–76.

with the same text in different ways: the Religious Studies scholar might also belong to the tradition whose text she is studying and so read the text in different ways on different occasions.

To enter into the world of the text is to inhabit, to an extent, the subjectivity or subjectivities it articulates. If the first task in Religious Studies reading is to understand the text in its own horizon (Ochs's primary sense), then the second task is to understand the text as an implicit index (Ochs's indexical symbol) of the text's context. How does the text relate to wider culture and history? Of which power group or pressure group is it an expression? It is at this level of reading that we see how the subjectivities expressed in a text articulate with macro-cultural history and how the text functions within a specific time-frame and narrative base. Beyond description, corrective readings are offered at the level of the edition through Philology, that is, in establishing the parameters of the text itself, and also at higher levels of social and cultural critique. For example, Sanderson's historical mapping of the Hindu tantric traditions, based wholly on manuscript sources, is a very significant contribution to the history of religion in South Asia, primarily written for the scholarly community of Indologists, South Asian historians, and religionists.[31] But that this work could have relevance for the remnants of those traditions themselves is clearly possible. A more obvious example of work that has an agenda to affect tradition is feminist reading of religious texts from outside of the religious tradition (although this is less clear in the case of Christianity where it could be argued that feminist readings are tradition-internal). In this case a feminist scholar will offer critical readings at variance with the readings of tradition.[32] Yet such readings make legitimate claims on tradition and need to be taken seriously by the tradition itself, if it is to thrive in the contemporary world in a way that fosters the non-closure of possibility. Again, readings of tradition through the lens of power, as exemplified in the writings of Foucault, are vitally important for traditions.[33] Religions can only avoid 'secularist' critique if they turn inwards in a retrogressive way that attempts to ignore the changed historical, global conditions in which contemporary religions function. Put simply, Foucault throws down a gauntlet that needs to be taken up.

---

[31] A. Sanderson, 'Saiva and the Tantric Traditions', in S. Sutherland et al., eds., *The World's Religions* (London: Routledge, 1988), pp. 660–704.

[32] E.g., Elisabeth Schüssler Fiorenza, *In Memory of Her: A Feminist Reconstruction of Christian Origins* (London: SCM, 1983); G. Jantzen, *Becoming Divine: Towards a Feminist Philosophy of Religion* (Manchester: Manchester University Press, 1998).

[33] J. Carrette, *Foucault and Religion: Spiritual Corporality and Political Spirituality* (London: Routledge, 2000), e.g. pp. 142–52.

Corrective or pragmatic reading from outside the tradition is possible and, I would argue, desirable. We might also call such pragmatic reading 'dialogical' which – unlike the phenomenological *epoché* – assumes a socially and historically situated position outside the text and tradition, and which in many cases will be an implicit critique of text and tradition. Indeed, we might replace empathy with corrective reading as allowing the ability to understand and through understanding (the 'plain sense') to offer help, to correct. Ochs speaks of two functions of corrective reading, hearing and healing.[34] Religious Studies is ideally suited to this enterprise and *can* have this moral function for those who wish: a tradition can adopt a Foucaultian reading of its past and in so doing attempt to understand and to heal that past. Ochs uses the image of a healer. He writes in a passage worth quoting at length:

Let us define 'suffering' as the condition of someone who cannot fix some everyday problem and, therefore, cannot identify the problem with precision. A 'healer' will be someone who, after engaging the sufferer in dialogue, can eventually *hear* in the sufferer's report symptoms of an identifiable problem. To 'hear' successfully, a healer must possess a relationship of trust with the sufferer, the ability to read explicit reports as symptoms of inexplicit conditions, the knowledge to recognize these symptoms, and the imagination to envision how the sufferer might live and not have these problems. Healing and hearing are therefore not only complementary but also interdependent activities, since, with respect to a given purpose, each one presupposes and makes use of the other.[35]

A Religious Studies discourse can hear successfully and so possess an element of trust with the host tradition. The academic discourse is receptive to the hospitality of the tradition and the tradition in turn, through the academic discourse, can learn to make sharper definitions of imprecise things. Here pragmatic reading offers what Benjamin's angel cannot do, a retrieval of the past and a healing of the things that have been broken.

Does Religious Studies really have a healing function? Yes and no. The primary effect of Religious Studies is the representation of traditions to a scholarly community, a community comprising people who may or may not be inside the object tradition. This representation might be an analysis of history, text and community that offers explanations of behaviour, that offers descriptive mappings of history based on primary sources, or that offers readings of texts that are implicitly or explicitly comparative. In representing an account of a historical trajectory, the primary purpose is just that and it is not necessarily healing, but it *may* be so as a consequence. An analysis of the conditions that gave rise to the discourse of

---

[34] Ochs, *Peirce*, pp. 253–4.   [35] Ochs, *Peirce*, p. 254.

Orientalism or Indology might be a healing process in so far as corrective reading has an ethical dimension in revealing conditions within which a mis-representation occurs or a misreading of history due to certain presuppositions about the nature of the other community, or whatever.[36] But the healing function is only such if adopted by a community or tradition, as has happened with feminist critique, Christian, Jewish, Buddhist, and Hindu.

Given that Religious Studies can offer corrective readings of texts of specific traditions, it furthermore supports the claim that Religious Studies is inherently comparative. Comparison is essential to understanding in both the human and the natural sciences. New knowledge depends upon comparison with the old and with other, parallel, forms of knowledge. But within the study of religion, comparison has often been done to show the superiority of Christianity to other religions, to show that diverse religions are pointing to a common truth, or to show that Indian traditions are equal to, if not better than, Western ones.[37] This is not the place to develop a history of comparative religion and philosophy,[38] but given the critique of European approaches to other cultures in recent years, especially of Indology and Orientalism from the perspective of post-colonial critique, it is important to address the issue of how a comparative religion is still

[36] R. King, *Orientalism and Religion: Postcolonial Theory, India and the Mystic East* (London: Routledge, 1999), e.g. ch. 4.

[37] Within theology, one of the first and little remembered theologians to compare Christianity with another religion, in this case Hinduism, was Rowland Williams who, while being sympathetic to Hindu thought, sought to establish Christianity's superiority (Williams, *Parameswara-jnyana-goshti: Dialogue of the Knowledge of the Supreme Lord in which are compared the claims of Christianity and Hinduism* (Cambridge: Deighton Bell, 1856)). Other theologians such as Karl Barth claimed that Christianity in essence is not a religion (but rather revelation of the Word) and so is beyond comparison with others (H. Hartwell, *The Theology of Karl Barth: An Introduction* (London: Duckworth, 1964), pp. 87–91), while liberal theologians on the other hand, such as John Hick, have claimed that all religions are in some sense equal responses to 'the Real', their transcendent reference (Hick, *An Interpretation of Religion: Human Responses to the Transcendent* (London: Macmillan, 1989), pp. 10–11, 236–40). In the nineteenth century secular comparative religion, whose assumptions are implicitly critical of religion, was most famously advocated by Max Müller in his idea of a 'comparative science of religion' (*Chips from a German Workshop* vol. I, *Essays on the Science of Religion* (London: Longman, Green and Co., 1867), pp. 18–19). Müller, in consonance with his age, sought an objective, truly scientific understanding of religions. P. Masson-Oursel popularised the idea of comparative philosophy, although, as Halbfass observes in his interesting essay on 'India and the Comparative Method', it was a Bengali scholar, N. N. Seal, who may have first coined the phrase 'comparative philosophy' in his *Comparative Studies in Vaishnavism and Christianity* in 1899 (W. Halbfass, *India and Europe* (Albany: SUNY Press, 1988), p. 422).

[38] See Sharpe, *Comparative Religion*; Halbfass, *India and Europe*. For a critique of the enterprise see McCutcheon, *Manufacturing Religion* e.g. pp. 101–4; Fitzgerald, *The Ideology of Religious Studies*, pp. 33–53. On a discussion of comparative philosophy with reference to Halbfass's work see Eli Franco and Karin Preisendanz, eds., *Beyond Orientalism: On the Work of Wilhelm Halbfass and its Impact on Indian and Cross-Cultural Studies* (Amsterdam, Atlanta: Rodopi, 1997).

possible and what can be gained by it.[39] How can a comparative religion be done that avoids essentialism or that does not inevitably bring with it the remnants of a colonial discourse?

I think that pragmatic reading offers a way forward, which, for Religious Studies, must be implicitly comparative. Different texts address different communities of speakers and for different reasons, and a text that addresses one community but is used by another will be reconfigured in fresh ways. A comparative religion is yet possible, but a kind that is dialogical, and language and communication centred. Indeed, as I have argued elsewhere, a dialogical research programme open to the otherness of its 'object' while retaining its 'outsideness' is the only way we can now responsibly offer a comparative religion.[40] By 'dialogical' I mean that knowledge within human communities assumes language and that language not only presupposes the existence of the language system (grammar) but also the chain of utterances through time (and therefore the community of language users).[41] Language is dialogical in its very nature – every utterance is preceded by another to which it in some sense responds, and is succeeded by a further response. Utterance looks back in responding to other utterances and looks forward in anticipating response; it has the quality of addressivity.[42] The comparison lies in the pragmatic reading, an approach that entails the close reading of texts, their mutual interrogation and the relation of these readings to macro-historical concerns. The dialogism inherent in the chain of utterance entails the notion of time and that utterances form part of a historical sequence. The historical sequence of utterance also entails the idea of historically located text and of subjectivity expressed through text. It is to these two concepts – text and subjectivity – that we must briefly and finally turn.

TEXT AND SUBJECTIVITY

Religious Studies as corrective reading places text at the centre of scholarly praxis. The two primary justifications are that text is an index of

---

[39] Among the most important, of course, is Edward Said, *Orientalism* (New York: Pantheon, 1978). For a critique of colonial constructions of India and Indian religions see R. Inden, *Imagining India* (Oxford and Cambridge, MA: Blackwell, 1990) and the work of the subaltern studies group, e.g. R. Guha and G. Spivak, eds., *Selected Subaltern Studies* (Oxford: Oxford University Press, 1988). For important discussions of the issues see F. Dallmayr, *Beyond Orientalism: Essays in Cross-Cultural Encounter* (Albany: SUNY Press, 1996); King, *Orientalism and Religion*. On the critique of the category 'Hinduism' see G. D. Sontheimer and H. Kulke, *Hinduism Reconsidered* (Delhi: Manohar, 2nd edn 1997) and Gavin Flood, ed., *The Companion to Hinduism* (Oxford: Blackwell, 2003).

[40] Flood, *Beyond Phenomenology*, p. 214.

[41] M. Bakhtin, 'The Problem of Speech Genres', in *Speech Genres and Other Late Essays*, trans. Vern W. McGee (Austin: University of Texas Press, 1986), p. 69.

[42] Ibid., pp. 68–9. See Flood, *Beyond Phenomenology*, p. 155.

tradition and society and text expresses subjectivity. The focus on text in the history of religions and thereby on the literate, power-wielding and ideology-creating echelons of a society has often been at the cost of understanding folk cultures, the mass of the population, cultures of resistance, and material culture, including the plastic arts and music. In the study of South Asian traditions, this occlusion is being addressed in recent work that focuses on oral traditions[43] along with a turn to the image. In Hinduism, Eck and Davis have focused on the importance of the image,[44] Schopen has argued that through a neglect of the image and archaeology, a distortion has occurred in our understanding of early and Theravada Buddhism,[45] Faure has emphasised the role of mediation in Chan Buddhism,[46] and Trainor has focused on the material culture of Theravada, showing the centrality of relics.[47] Harpham has written intelligently and at length on Grünewald's Isenheim Altarpiece, relating readings of it to narrative theory and to wider medieval culture.[48] But it is nevertheless still the case that our historical knowledge of religious traditions and the contents of those traditions is based primarily on texts. Text is the foundation of culture and while texts can be art objects, not all art objects are texts (because they lack language).[49] Even Grünewald's painting needs narrative to be brought to it, as the painting itself disrupts a unified narrative sequence.[50] Any understanding of religion needs to focus on the texts and narratives embodied in them, while of course taking into account material culture. But text and language remain our primary resource, especially in understanding the subjectivities that produced them.

The subjectivities expressed through text are moulded by the *longue durée* of their history; a text is clearly a product of its age. Yet texts express

[43] See for example S. Blackburn, *Singing of Birth and Death: Texts in Performance* (Philadelphia: University of Pennsylvania Press, 1988); A. Hiltebeitel *The Cult of Draupadi* vols. I and II (Chicago: University of Chicago Press, 1988, 1991); P. Lutgendorf, *The Life of a Text: Performing the Ramacaritmanas of Tulsidas* (Berkeley: University of California Press, 1991); John Smith, *The Epic of Pabuji* (Cambridge: Cambridge University Press, 1985).

[44] D. Eck, *Darshan: Seeing the Divine Image in India* (Chambersburg: Anima, 1985); R. Davis, *Lives of Indian Images* (Princeton: Princeton University Press, 1997).

[45] G. Schopen and D. Lopez, *Bones, Stones and Buddhist Monks: Collected Papers on Archaeology, Epigraphy, and Texts of Monastic Buddhism in India* (Honolulu: University of Hawaii Press, 1997).

[46] B. Faure, *The Rhetoric of Immediacy: A Cultural Critique of Chan/Zen* (Princeton: Princeton University Press, 1991), pp. 7, 65–6.

[47] K. Trainor, *Relics, Rituals, and Representation in Buddhism: Re-materialising the Sri Lanka Theravada Tradition* (Cambridge: Cambridge University Press, 1997).

[48] G. Harpham, *The Ascetic Imperative in Culture and Criticism* (Chicago: University of Chicago Press, 1987), pp. 137–96.

[49] J. J. E. Gracia, *Texts: Ontological Status, Identity, Author, Audience* (Albany: SUNY Press, 1996), pp. 6–7.

[50] Harpham, *The Ascetic Imperative*, p. 175.

the subjectivities of their authors (even though meaning exceeds author's intention), especially religious texts that are clearly a product of tradition and are integral to the individual life-path, to his or her intentions and goals. The *longue durée* of history articulates with the subjective time-frame of the subject in the text. Pragmatic reading in a Religious Studies context, we might even say, has an existential dimension that allows the close engagement of the scholar with the 'object' tradition and with the subjects of that tradition to which and to whom the text points. Through text we see, on the one hand, the force of religion as symbolic order that has exerted power over individual lives, determining social relationships, and constructing particular forms of subjectivity, and on the other as expressing subjective concerns about meaning, human relationships, interiority, and death. Text lies at the heart of culture and text points to subjectivity.

By way of conclusion, let us return to Ochs's healing dimension to corrective reading. I have argued here that Religious Studies needs to pay close attention to the model of tradition-specific pragmatic reading and that a pragmatic reading from outside of tradition, across cultures, is possible and desirable. We can no longer believe Donne's image but we do not have to go down the route of scepticism. Pragmatic reading is partly an attempt to mend the things that have been broken in a way that Benjamin's angel cannot, and Religious Studies is partly a discourse that has traditionally had this concern. Religious Studies can interact with the praxis of the host tradition not only as explanation but also as corrective reading. This healing or ethical dimension to corrective reading is in consonance with Ninian Smart's endeavour to represent world religions, which was undoubtedly driven by a strong humanitarian ethic that maintained an equality of representation and, arguably, a belief in a unified human nature. Some months ago, standing by Ninian Smart's grave in Lancaster, I noticed two Sanskrit words in devanāgarī inscribed on the white, marble stone: *kalyāna mitra*, 'true friend'. These simple words, so apt in that context with their resonance of 'spiritual friend' and 'good teacher', perhaps summarise the healing aspiration behind much of the Phenomenology of Religion: a discourse friendly towards tradition – but a tradition of which we must offer corrective readings and move on.

PART II

Meetings on Mutual Ground

Section 1: Understanding Faith

CHAPTER 5

God

Rowan Williams

Religious Studies as a discipline would not, of course, exist if people had not used and reflected on the word 'God'; but where do we start in specifying the issues that might arise in defining the word, especially when its users have habitually shrunk from offering what would usually count as a full-scale definition? What I have aimed at in the pages that follow is an investigation somewhere on the borderlands of theology strictly so-called and the phenomenology of religious discourse, in order to clarify a little of the 'grammar' of God in the Abrahamic traditions of faith – those whose material origins lie, broadly, in the eastern Mediterranean regions and which ascribe something like personal agency to the divine, creative causality in respect of the entire contingent universe and providential love towards it. I am not claiming that this is the best place from which to begin constructing a theology. But perhaps it corresponds to what one tradition would have considered as the treatise *de deo uno*: i.e., considerations of the kind of issue that needs clarification if we are to be sure it is *God* we're talking about.

A wholly understandable reaction against a theology apparently beginning from considerations of God as a solitary transcendent individual, capable of being considered independently of the history of divine engagement with human experience and history, has led to some impatience with such grammatical exploration. In the Christian world, this can mean a reaffirmation of a robust trinitarian discourse, systematically critical of abstract theism and tending to identify any *de deo uno* reflections with such abstraction: thinking of the unity of the divine nature can be seen as giving a kind of priority to some reality lying behind the concrete relationality of God to God as Trinity, let alone the relations of God with the world's history. This is occasionally linked with a more radical alienation from the tradition of grammatical investigation that, in the name of giving priority either to revelation or to experience, declines to affirm (and even regards as actively damaging) the common conventions of philosophical exposition of God's transcendence – conventions common to Judaism, Christianity and Islam.[1] And this revisionism may or may not be linked with a trinitarian agenda in Christian theology.

Thus a fair amount of new writing on the question of God pleads for one or another kind of modification of what might have been regarded as the classical norm for such talk. Influential feminist essays have posed questions about a language of divine transcendence that might be understood as simply transcribing a rhetoric of the superiority of mental to physical, and have argued in various ways for a more obviously immanentist account; and other, equally influential, voices have been raised in criticism of the language of immutability and impassibility, demanding a God who is not so much 'beyond' suffering and change but what we might (awkwardly) call an endlessly resourceful manager of suffering and change. These two sorts of challenge are, of course, less compatible with each other than they might appear, though they are often merged with one another by writers whose main issue is the supposed inadequacy of the classical model. A suffering and mutable God (such as is said to be found in the Bible) must be, in a very strong sense, a psychological subject comparable to ourselves; an immanent God is not obviously a subject in anything like this sense. The virtues of the mutable God are sometimes argued in terms of the need to say what must be said about God's compassion; but this is difficult to state intelligibly if God's subjectivity is not, at the level that matters, different from the totality of the experience of contingent subjects.

My purpose in these brief reflections, though, is not to mount a detailed critique of contemporary challenges so much as to ask a few questions as to how the 'classical' Jewish, Christian and Muslim model ever evolved, with particular emphasis upon my own Christian discourse, against its Jewish background . I shall be arguing that it represents a complex fusion between that narrative specification of the identity of God about which Hans Frei wrote so seminally[2] and the familiar considerations in the philosophical world about the grammar of transcendence, the kind of 'being' that could be ascribed to what was not an item in the world. Nothing specially new about that; but I hope to suggest that the fusion was something other than a confusion, and that the narrative identification of the God of Israel and of Jesus raises precisely the kind of questions that can't be answered without reference to those grammatical issues sketched in the philosophical tradition of antiquity. In other words, I shall argue that the patristic and medieval

[1] For an important discussion of this, see David Burrell, *Knowing the Unknowable God: Ibn-Sina, Maimonides, Aquinas* (Notre Dame: University of Notre Dame Press, 1986).
[2] Hans Frei, *The Identity of Jesus Christ* (Philadelphia: Fortress Press, 1975).

reading of Exodus 3:14 in connection with a metaphysical preoccupation with what existence actually meant – the reading already canonised by the Septuagintal rendering of 'I am who I am' as 'I am the one who is' – is neither muddled nor opportunistic. It may become clearer how, in David Burrell's words, '[t]he unity of God can hardly be comprehended as a purely philosophical assertion'.[3]

The God of Hebrew scripture in its canonical shape is a god whose identity is consistently clarified in terms of what he has done and whom he has known, called or spoken to; in the Exodus 3 passage, he is the god of the 'fathers' even before he is the 'I am' of the great self-declaration. The Exodus and covenant themes then add to this the specification that God is defined or self-defined as Israel's covenant partner and thus also as the source of Israel's law. Israel's God is recognisable as the one who initiates the law-governed life of Israel, the one who gives regular, coherent, continuous unity to the distinctive life of this community. Everything that makes Israel the community it is has to be referred to the commands of God, given to Israel in the wake of the act of liberation by which this rather inchoate and ill-assorted group of people become independent. Here is the governing theme of (in particular) the Deuteronomic literature; and Deuteronomy itself (see especially chapters 4 to 6) stresses the oddity of what God has done in this respect. It is, says Deuteronomy 4:34, not a general characteristic of gods that they set out to create a new nation by a process of prolonged upheaval and suffering; this, it is implied, is what is signified by the uniqueness of the experience (4:33) of hearing God 'in the midst of the fire'. And the whole of this process, divine decision and human testing, establishes (4:35) that this God is the only true God.

Much is regularly (and rightly) made of the connection between God's freedom to set people free and God's difference or transcendence; but there is another question to be thought through in this complex of theological narrative. God constitutes a people not simply by the creation of a discernible community but by the giving of law to that community. God is known and served by the keeping of the law, in every detail. But this establishes that God's claims upon the human community are not the claims of a divine monarch to worship only, but are identical with the claims of justice between human agents and towards strangers (the latter a point well made in John Milbank's essay on God in Jean-Yves Lacoste's *Dictionnaire de théologie*). God is not an object competing for attention: to know God is to be involved in the entire range of actions specified by law; or, indeed, more

---

[3] Burrell, *Knowing the Unknowable God*, p. 111.

particularly, a writer like Hosea can put 'the knowledge of God' more than once as a parallelism for 'fidelity' and *hesed*, compassionate commitment (4:1, 6:6). The famous 'What does the Lord require?' passage of Micah 6:6–8 reinforces the same point: in no sense is the knowledge of God or the idea of action pleasing to God something that occupies a place of its own alongside other duties. There *are* cultic duties, their priority variously assessed and understood by different writers; but the canonical conclusion is that these are unintelligible outside a whole system of injunction about the form of the common life.

God's relation to the chosen community is thus not *an* element in the community's life, it is the constitutive fact for there being a community at all. To be a conscious participant in this community is to be able to recognise who God is, and to be outside that participation is to lack that skill – not because sharing in the community provides an initiate's knowledge of the divine in the normal cultic sense, but because the whole of the law-governed life is acquaintance with God. And if the identifying of God cannot be confined to what cultic activity prescribes, there is already a blurring of the idea that God's claim on the community's life is one among others – and so of the implicit idea that *God* is one among others. You cannot discharge God's claim by performing a determinate set of actions; you cannot therefore work on the assumption that responding to God's claim is something that can be enumerated along with the doing of other things. In this sense, cultic and social action alike both are and are not 'adequate' responses to God, since no one act or kind of act alone tells you what the nature is of the God to whom you are responding; that depends upon the entire pattern of 'lawful' existence that is enjoined upon the people of the covenant. God's priority in the life of the covenant community is not a matter of ascribing to God a greater significance than is possessed by anything else; God is that to which every action in some sense refers, that which every action manifests or fails to manifest; and, as such, an agent who cannot be compared with other agents.

Very cautiously and confusedly, this is, I believe, moving towards the fundamental recognition in classical Christian (and Jewish and Muslim) theology, that divine life can't be discussed in the terms in which we speak of finite activity, as a contingent and interdependent reality. It is this sort of consideration that makes possible and desirable the appeal by Jewish and Christian thinkers of late antiquity to the Platonic language of God as 'beyond being', God's nature as capable of being characterised primarily by the stripping away of the attributes of contingent agency. Action, for the agent within the universe, is always bound up with response, passivity as well as initiative. But what determines the meaning of any human (any finite?) action, what determines what it communicates or 'carries', cannot itself be wholly determined by other actions within a system. The traditional ascription of impassibility to God, so very unpopular today, is not so much a radical departure from a scriptural God possessed of a psychology like ours as it is a somewhat abstract rendering of what is awkwardly understood in the definition of God as the source of law and covenant, that is, the source – for the community that embodies his 'name', his 'public identity' in the world's history – of the meanings that are to be ascribed to, or perceived in, every action and relation.[4]

Specifically for the Christian, this is reinforced by what is implied in incarnational faith. Already in the New Testament, the involvement of divine action in the life of Jesus is something that is not restricted to specific areas of his biography or understood as episodic inspiration. Paul can describe Jesus as simply the power and wisdom of God (1 Cor. 1:24) – that is, he can write as though Jesus were as a whole to be characterised as God's action, admittedly a very strange way of speaking. John's formulation of the Logos made flesh (John 1:14) works in much the same way: at the foundation of everything in the world is an active relation to God, a relation designated as Logos, 'word', 'structure', 'expression', a relation so intimate that the Logos is concretely the way God acts both to establish the universe and to direct the universe towards himself; this relation is embodied without reserve or qualification in the human life that is about to be narrated, the life of Jesus. But the implication is, as in Paul, that this is not a life episodically inspired by God, let alone interrupted by God at moments of crucial importance. God is not 'in' Jesus as an element in his biography, but as what the entire biography expresses, transcribes or communicates. The divine life which is eternally realised in the Logos is not an overwhelmingly important dimension of Jesus's life, but the deepest source of that life's meaning in all the actuality of its historical and narrative detail. Thus both the action and the passion of this life are held together as one coherent phenomenon by, ultimately, the act of God; and the presence of that act in the history of Jesus of Nazareth is not an element or moment alongside the contingencies of the history. It is the point that is laboriously clarified in the Christological debates of the early Christian centuries and remains a focal theme in the Christology of high scholasticism. The pervasive and determinative work of divine action in Christ takes nothing from his specific

---

[4] A fine and exhaustive treatment can be found in Thomas Weinandy, *Does God Suffer?* (Edinburgh: T&T Clark (Continuum), 2000).

human identity, replaces no aspect of the outer or inner integrity of a finite agent.

One of the boldest and most extraordinary contributions to theology made by Michel de Certeau was to note that in modern intellectual discourse the 'religious' no longer marks off a clear and discrete area of study. 'Comprendre, en sciences humaines, c'est avoir, par méthode, à surmonter la régionalisation des faits religieux'.[5] Speaking about religious phenomena is always describing social and psychological facts and processes; to use terms like 'God' and 'grace' is to conceal (in his words) the conditions of the production of these phenomena. Religious language does not describe a set of independent things, but offers an 'equivocal' account of their significance[6] – or, more accurately, of their *reality*. Theology's temptation is to introduce such reality into the systems of the world's processes, to bring the secret substances 'behind' the world's process into the light of day. But this would be only to reduce what theology talks about to the level of all other subjects of human discourse. Theology has to learn to work differently, or at least to understand its own difference. Instead of being the language that brings hidden things to light, it is more, for de Certeau, a language that points to and holds on to what is 'un-said' in the various regions of 'scientific' language, the various analyses of the world's processes – not least by pondering out loud about the very nature of scientific process as always facing what is *not yet* thinkable in the terms already fashioned. Thinking constantly confronts otherness – a truth that is, de Certeau argues, more than ever visible in the human sciences of modernity (ethnology, psychoanalysis, sociology, new historical methods), though it is true of all the sciences in their fashion.[7] If there is always a tension between the thinkable and the unthinkable, the same and the other, thinking Christianity will have the same character. And, although we have to advance cautiously here, de Certeau seems to be suggesting that Christianity does offer a kind of methodological clue to how we think, if only because its fundamental narrative is so conspicuously one of absence: it rests on an absent body, not a graspable set of teachings and institutional rules laid down by a 'normal' historical founder.[8]

De Certeau can be read – quite inadequately, I believe – as another exponent of the triumph of 'neutral' modern epistemology, of the all-sufficiency of secular reason and explanation. This is to miss both the post-modern and the biblical edge of his thinking – as well as the powerful Hegelian echoes.

---

[5] Michel de Certeau, *La faiblesse de croire* (Paris: Seuil, 1987), p. 192.
[6] Ibid., p. 194.   [7] Ibid., pp. 208–9.   [8] Ibid., pp. 211ff.

To say that religion has lost its territorial integrity is not to reduce religious discourse to an optional gloss on a world that is already accurately described by secular reason (we could turn for illumination here to Nicholas Lash on *The Beginning and the End of 'Religion'*[9]). It is certainly not that a grid of universal explanation has been imposed on the world: quite the contrary. The various practices of interpreting and structuring, tracing processes in the world, intertwine and sometimes prompt each other, sometimes simply confront each other in non-communicating plurality. No discourse can offer a systematic way of relating the regions of thought to each other. Thus, the 'real' is, says de Certeau, always receding, always 'lacking'.[10] It is precisely not something capable of exhaustive secular description; but equally the lack which is marked in scientific discourse is not a gap capable of being filled, because the 'un-said', the not-yet-thought, is something quite other than a specific problem within the system. As for Hegel, so for de Certeau, thinking has to become newly conscious of itself in acknowledging its own movement through contradiction, a confrontation with an otherness that is always being assimilated and always escaping and repositioning itself.

Equally, for de Certeau, if one can speak of revelation at all, it is in terms of what brings to speech that absence which makes possible the shifting space of prayer and witness that is Christian life. God's act is never identified with a segment of history that will stand still under scrutiny (de Certeau's convergence with Barth would be valuable to explore here). The founder has disappeared, surrendered himself to the absent Father, become part of the divine absence itself, so that, in the Church, there is never a single all-sufficient source of authority in which and in which alone the founding reality is decisively embodied.[11] At every point in the Christian narrative, meaning recedes from anything that might be read off the immediate and contingent and appears only in the ways in which the whole of a story consistently evokes the absence that makes space for us. It should be possible to see how this converges with what has already been said about God's act in relation to the scriptural narrative of the formation of a corporate practice referred in its entirety to God as agent in a sense that cannot be accommodated in terms of the world's interactions.

I am proposing that this kind of understanding is the most effective possible transcription into contemporary intellectual terms of the belief that God is 'pure act'. The superficial paradox that we are invited to speak

[9] Cambridge: Cambridge University Press, 1996, esp. chs. 5, 10 and 12.
[10] De Certeau, *La faiblesse de croire*, p. 198.   [11] Ibid., pp. 215–18.

at one and the same time of divine absence and the fullness of divine activity should not alarm us if we have read our Bibles with attention. Divine action can be 'pure' only if it is in no sense in 'negotiation' with specific agencies. And so far from this leaving us with a God uninvolved in creation's life – as the polemic of revisionist theologies so often suggests – this allows some grasp of what is being claimed in saying that God is 'pure' *giver* (and therefore that any talk of God's favour or grace or goodwill must be a way of honouring the primacy of God's action rather than a drama of seeking and winning a desired reaction). The removal of the religious from the status of a category among others, like the denial in Hebrew scripture of a single privileged area for acting so as to gain or retain divine favour, is not a way of privatising or marginalising what faith speaks of (though it may require, as de Certeau bleakly and frequently suggests, a certain honesty about the actual *social* marginality of the voices of faith at the present time): it allows what religious discourse purports to be about to retain its place at the source of communicative action while proscribing any battles to secure a place among other places for 'the religious'. The encounter with God, paradigmatically seen in the life and language of the 'mystic', always moves us towards a non-place: the mystic's actual worldly identity becomes an inscription of otherness – in the dissolution or paradox of the mystic's language and in the sense of mystical awareness as the growth towards a joy generated by nothing but the life of the other in the self.[12] By being an individual in this world whose pattern of life and language insistently subverts and fractures itself in reference to this alien joy, the mystic occupies a place that is not determined or defended (or defensible) and so gives the only sort of content that can, in contemporary intellectual terms, be given to the language of God as *actus purus*.

There are a lot of questions raised by this – not least the issue discussed by F. C. Bauerschmidt in his 1996 article on de Certeau,[13] whether de Certeau is adequately clear on how the non-place of the mystic is also a space of corporate practice (even if that space cannot be identified with the territory of what is unambiguously religious in the world). I suspect that a fuller untangling of what de Certeau says about the practice of confronting and accepting otherness would in fact lay bare a more specific theology of the Church and its characteristic moral practice than might initially appear if we concentrate primarily on the anonymous or contested

---

[12] Michel de Certeau, *The Mystic Fable. Volume 1: the Sixteenth and Seventeenth Centuries* (Chicago: University of Chicago Press, 1992), pp. 176–7, 197–200.
[13] 'The Abrahamic Voyage: Michel de Certeau and Theology', *Modern Theology* 12.1 (January 1996), pp. 1–26.

or simply inarticulate nature of believing life as sketched by de Certeau. The point of discussing him in the context of a reflection on the grammar of God in contemporary theology is that he, more than any other recent analyst of religious language, offers both a way of making fresh sense of some aspects of classical Christian discourse about God and a set of implicit questions about what might be entailed in abandoning that discourse in favour of one more immediately sympathetic to some aspects of the late modern mindset.

What might such questions look like? Say we allow ourselves to speak of God as changeable and capable of suffering – not just as a rhetorical moment, a conscious deployment of myth, but as a systematic principle. If we really mean what we say, the implication is that there are agents or agencies that are strictly external to the agency of God; even if we grant that God is in some way the ultimate source of their existence, creation – as it were – bestows on them a life on the other side of an ontological frontier such that they may modify not only each other but their source. But this is bound to have at least two significant effects. If the source is in this way modifiable, is it still possible to say that it is unequivocally the source of the meanings constructed or enacted in the world? And if it is not to be thought of as source, it has to be thought of as standing with, negotiating with or even contesting other possible meanings. Does this lead us back into the trap so eloquently characterised by theologians like John Milbank and James Alison as a capitulation to 'foundational violence'? That may be putting it rather extremely; but in the sense that an *irreducibly* plural understanding of how human meanings are ultimately created and sustained leaves us with an inevitable element of contest, the concerns are real. And to claim that the divine action can be trusted to prevail (following some varieties of process thought which privilege the resourcefulness of love while allowing a kind of passibility to God) is only to claim that, in the long run, God has more resource than other agents. The story remains one of contest and victory rather than the complex convergence imagined by classical theology and spirituality between growth in integrity and actualisation as a creature and conformity with the 'will' or 'purpose' of God. And thus conversion, sanctification and so on become precisely the kind of issues they are regularly represented as being in modern, emancipatory theological rhetoric: they are about power, who has it and who doesn't, who has more of it, what counts as power and so on.

This in turn has implications for the understanding of the contemplative practice and experience that de Certeau discusses. In his brief but revolutionary account of what Teresa of Avila is doing in the writing of her *Interior*

Castle,[14] he demonstrates how Teresa's models of the soul as castle, crystal and diamond cannot be reduced to a single momentary representation: there is no way of depicting the soul as Teresa speaks of it. The image 'already has a narrative structure'; the soul *is* the action or motion of the text that unfolds its reality, and God's presence in and to the soul is capable of being spoken of only in this movement, this structure. To show how God is there in the soul, how the soul is the place of this divine other, you have to relate a history and lay out a sequence of metaphors, to 'shape' yourself in speech, as opposed to providing a description at a distance of what the soul and God are like. In so doing, you show a self becoming 'other than itself', a self that is the site of what was earlier called alien joy. The ordering of a life story exhibits 'what cannot be there . . . , unless it be in metaphors and passages. In this way, [Teresa] can equally affirm that the castle is the book or the soul, that she is the author or that God is . . . , and that she is speaking of the writing, the soul, or prayer.'[15] What prompts or directs the ordering is all that makes the soul a stranger to itself – anguish, ecstasy, the interweaving of the two that is characteristic of Teresa and others – and refuses a graspable and lasting identity. It is another aspect of what de Certeau writes about in the pages on *rupture instauratrice* in *La faiblesse de croire*: no aspect of the Christian system of speech and practice represents alone or in itself the absent 'transcendent' origin, the events that make Christian life possible; only together do they evoke this absent ultimate resource, 'not without each other'. Once again, God is spoken of truthfully only in the entire complex of talk, narrative, action.

But if God comes to be characterised as an agent among agents, all of this becomes enormously problematic. It is not clear how contemplation can be conceived in such a context as an embodiment of the other in the self, since two agencies are bound to be confronting each other within a contested 'territory'. When one triumphs, that constitutes a clear representation or inscription of God within the world. Once again, there is an underlying issue about power, about the risks of identifying some area of the world's discourse unambiguously with God. Or, if there is no guaranteed 'triumph' for God, if contest is perpetual and unresolved, we are stuck with a meta-physic (the fact that it is commonly presented as a kind of alternative to metaphysics is irrelevant) in which what is unambiguously good has no necessary relation to how things fundamentally are, or are thinkable. Good becomes a function of the will, separated from 'nature', as in the familiar forms of debased Kantianism, and from intellect. If the former problem

[14] *The Mystic Fable*, ch. 6, esp. pp. 192–200.   [15] Ibid., p. 200.

(God as an agency confronting others) tends to a reduction of God to an item in the world, the latter allies the reality of God to the workings of an 'inner' life, detaching God from the processes of learning that take place in a material and historical environment. In plainer terms, while the former interprets God's existence as being on the same footing as that of contingent realities, the latter moves towards evacuating talk of God's existence of all content.

The classical conventions of speaking about God are precisely devised to steer between these two positions. To say that God is pure act, or that God is being itself, that God is *esse*, or *non aliud*, with all that these imply about the inappropriateness to God of language about change or suffering, is to register the difficulty of ascribing *existence* to God, if our talk of God is indeed grounded in the kind of history that Jews and Christians relate. Two factors have made a difference to the present possibility of reclaiming these conventions (which is why a perspective like that of de Certeau is so suggestive as a way of recovering these concerns in a quite other idiom). The first is summed up by Joseph O'Leary.[16] The language of absolute being, *ipsum esse subsistens*, and so on has become problematic in the wake of the dissolution of those elements in earlier metaphysical discourse that worked against a univocity in speaking of being. When 'being' has become a more unproblematic and territorialised concept than it is in Platonic and early medieval (including Thomist) thought, the risk is of seeing God as possessor of an unlimited quantity of it – or as a synonym for the totality of what there is. God is either a supreme individual or an all-pervasive quality or force in what exists. We forget in such a context the inseparability in Aquinas of the language of pure act and the language of God's 'excess' in respect of being. What was, to use O'Leary's expression, a 'strategy' for indicating God's freedom from circumscription may become in a changed intellectual environment a narrowing theoretical construct which has lost sight of how the classical language intends to evoke a unique difference (the true sense of Cusanus's *non aliud*, of course). In short, the language of 'being' has become muddied; O'Leary speaks of its having lost its 'radiance'. Readers of Jean-Luc Marion will recognise some convergence of themes here: for Marion, the separation between being and God is what permits the reading of being as gift and 'icon', a reality that does not *represent* what is other to it but is a space for God's self-donation in the events in which God deals with us. But O'Leary is in fact rather cautious about Marion's project, arguing that Marion is at best cavalier about the *extended* social and historical processes

[16] *Religious Pluralism and Christian Truth* (Edinburgh: Edinburgh University Press, 1996), ch. 6, esp. pp. 188–90, 197.

whereby the name of God appears, concentrating instead on the luminous, timeless act of God in the eucharist; so that his focus upon love and gift as the words needed to speak of a God beyond, prior to, or other than being threatens to become abstract.[17] John Milbank further questions whether Marion is not himself caught in the early modern misapprehension that assumes a univocal sense for being, thus missing the nuance typical of the entire Platonic tradition by accepting too uncritically the Heideggerian insistence on the ideologically malign character of ontology.[18]

Nonetheless, the point remains: the language of being has come to be charged with these ambiguities, for good or bad reasons, and this is bound to affect any attempt to articulate persuasively the concerns of classical theology in classical terms. But the second modern and post-modern development that makes a difference here is, I suspect, one that works obliquely in favour of the classical emphases, and that is what we might call the new sense of the politics of discourse. Revisionist models of divine life in terms of possibility and so on have commonly been innocent or simplistic about this. The typical protest on behalf of emancipatory concerns has been that the traditional view sets in philosophical concrete a hierarchically ordered model of reality in which mind is privileged over feeling, spirit over body, male over female and so on; God's transcendence (including, for some writers, the doctrine of creation *ex nihilo*) as expressed in the classical 'attributes' places God in irreconcilable opposition to a world of chance and vulnerability. God becomes a metaphysical transcription of unexamined power structures in the world.

In this framework, the obvious but naïve resolution is to salvage divine credibility by refusing the classical grammar of transcendence, so as to relocate God with and in the world's vulnerability. It is a strategy given much persuasive power by the undoubted fact that the rhetoric of Christian proclamation from the very beginning apparently does just this, insisting (as in 1 Corinthians) on God's adoption of the weak as vessels of grace and of course, above all, on the mortality of Jesus as the supreme vehicle of God's transforming work. But there is a misunderstanding here: Paul's language is professedly a way of asking where we might expect to discern God in the world's experience, and displaying how God's actual presence upsets those expectations. To read it as endorsing a projection onto God of the vulnerability of subjects in the world is, ironically, to remove the upset by removing the paradox. If God as such is vulnerable in the sense that we

---

[17] Ibid., pp. 186–91.
[18] John Milbank, *The Word Made Strange: Theology, Language, Culture* (Oxford: Blackwell, 1997), pp. 46–9.

are, God becomes a case of contingent passibility and discerning God in the cross of Jesus or in the action of grace in the poor, the voiceless, the failed and the spiritually incompetent is no longer surprising. What has been changed by the emancipatory move in theology is the locus of power and of suffering, not the nature of power relations themselves. To put it a little mischievously, it is like the demand made by sections of the British public in the wake of the death of Princess Diana that the Queen should show public signs of grief. What consoles is that the powerful should become vulnerable ('interesting and weak like us' in W. H. Auden's telling phrase). And what is left unchallenged is how power is conceived. The difference of transcendence as specified in the Christian narrative is eroded.

And, as I have been consistently arguing, such a theology in fact leaves us with a more, not less, politically problematic model, in which God occupies the same conceptual space as we do, so that our relation with God is never wholly free of contest. If that is the model we are using, we shall have difficulties coherently explaining why the gospel creates substantive and distinctive community: on the traditional model, the non-rivalrous relation with God (pure act, *non aliud*), by shaping the self as a 'place of the other', in de Certeau's words, challenges a territorial account of the self, in such a way that the *created* other finds place in my self, and my 'interest' is shifted from an individual focus to one that prescribes reciprocity and involvement. Leave God as an agent among others, and the fundamental miracle of the self's fruition in the unequivocally other, that which is so different as to be *non aliud*, different from all differences, never happens. Contest, violence, rivalry, is allowed to remain ontologically basic, without a 'difference from difference' that permits the formation of a revelatory community.

My argument began with the biblical theme of the formation of a community as constitutive of the naming of God in the world – a community which, by tracing its entire law-governed character to God and refusing a merely religious revelation, began to raise the conceptual question of how to imagine a 'non-territorial' God. The evolution of belief in Jesus Christ as bearer of simultaneous divine and human identity represents an intelligible outgrowth of the same understanding and raises the same issues. Thus, I have proposed, when Jewish and Christian (and, I must suppose, Muslim) thinkers undertake the meta-narrative job of clarifying the grammar of their discourse, they reach for the radical language of transcendence available in the Platonic world – both the Middle Platonist disciplines of *aphesis*, the 'taking away' of predicates of contingency, and the venerable but constantly puzzling idiom of God's transcendence of 'being'. That they do so is not, I believe, a betrayal of revealed or scripturally founded faith but an attempt to render more adequately the radical implications of that faith. To return to the insights of David Burrell, referred to at the beginning of this discussion, we have to recognise that clarification of the grammar of 'God' is in fact not easily separable from the study of how religious languages are formed and learned; which in turn should remind us that there are theological questions that need examining *by way of* history and phenomenology; that theological clarification may be had – without questioning the autonomy of theology – from 'religious studies'.

So we shall not straightforwardly recover 'classical' insights simply by repeating the familiar tropes of classical theology, however lucidly rendered (though it does no harm to remind an intellectually careless theological public of what the tradition actually does and doesn't say). Since we have become sensitive to the politics of our language, it may well be that an analysis of the implications of our theology in respect of power will prove the most fruitful way towards recovery. I have discussed de Certeau at some length; the presence of Girard in the background will have been, I am sure, equally obvious. Their significant contribution to contemporary theology is surely to have begun this task: de Certeau in his seminal notion of the contemplative self as a 'non-place', a non-territory, in virtue of its relation to God, and his account of foundational absence in the origins of faith; Girard in his analysis of the Christian and Jewish narrative as a dissolution of human assumptions about foundational violence. Questions remain for both, which this essay has had no space to examine in detail; but the methodological importance of this approach is what matters if theology – in the strictest sense of discourse about God – is to avoid a degeneration into sentimental mythology, unexamined narratives of a supernatural individual.

To conclude with a more immediate Christian theological and ecclesial point: the implication of all this is also, of course, that the recovery of what I have been arguing is the pivotal concern of classical theology is impossible unless the believing community takes seriously its own character and acts accordingly. In a church that is in many ways deeply wedded to 'territorial' preoccupations, it is unlikely that the gift and promise of the non-territorial God will be clearly discernible. In other words, a church that is concerned about its internal politics will not transform the political in the way that is in fact made possible by Jesus. The desire to secure purity and control in the Church (which can be a preoccupation as much of 'progressives' as of 'traditionalists') looks to a territory in which believers may see in one another a reassuring sameness; and when believers are looking at one another to test that assurance, they are less likely to be attending to the foundational absence on which the life of the community rests. And if the contemplative life is central in some way to the integrity of the Church at large, it is because of this: not to point to 'values' above and beyond the concerns of the world, not to pass judgement on the unspiritual conflicts of the Church or society, but to witness to the way in which a life may be constructed in which all acts are referrable to God and in which the consequent 'deregionalising' of the life of the spirit, life before God, impacts increasingly upon the understanding of prayer. It is to do with the poverty and wealth of the everyday; with the fullness and emptiness of faith.

CHAPTER 6

Love

Julius Lipner

There is a hoary view – the legacy of generations of works of Christian theology, and endlessly resurfacing in the syllabuses of Theology departments in the Christian world – that theology proper is the preserve of Christian self-reflection, or at most, of the 'Abrahamic' traditions. All other faiths do not have theology in this sense; as such they belong to the 'religions' of the world, and must be studied under some rubric called Religious Studies or the Study of Religion.

No one quite knows what goes into the dumping-ground of Religious Studies or the Study of Religion. But it is not 'theology'. For, in this view, it is only in the 'great monotheism(s)' of Christianity or the Abrahamic faiths that the cosmic drama of the production of the world and the healing and redemption of the human condition can properly be considered. It is only in this domain that there exist the ingredients continually to recover – historically, ontologically, epistemologically – the basis for the appropriate conception and grammar of what it means to be truly human in terms of the human community's ultimate source and end, 'God'. And by some process of mission-creep in much modern intellectual discourse, theology has been appropriated to Christianity, and the teachings of non-Christian religions, or more precisely, the non-Abrahamic faiths, have been relegated to the Study of Religion.

What, then, happens in the Study of Religion? On a grand scale, here the faiths are studied as 'religions' – as congeries of competing doctrines, rituals, institutions, myths, symbols, narratives, testimonies. They are a human-based and human-inspired endeavour to bestow meaning and purpose to life. By an act of academic egalitarianism it is sometimes allowed that even Christianity and its Abrahamic colleagues, Judaism and Islam, may be studied in this way. But whilst such study may be interesting and even important – after all, it is useful to teach in a 'pluralist' society that Hindus and Buddhists, for example, behave and believe religiously in many ways similarly to Christians, Jews and Muslims – it doesn't get to the heart of the matter. The critical distance it inculcates so usefully, phenomenologically, puts it at a disadvantage when it comes to dealing with what really count: issues of ultimate truth and value. Those belongs to the Christian enterprise (and/or the Muslim or Jewish).

I have never been satisfied with this hoary or glory view, this view of unreconstructed orthodoxy. It is so riddled with dubious totems of the past in the disciplines of both Christian theology and the comparative study of religion as to be untenable. In what follows, I shall examine some of these totems with reference to the hermeneutics of love as a heuristic device. This may yield some corrective insight into the future of theology and the study of religion in the academy.

This is where love first steps in: not for arbitrary reasons, but because 'love' is regarded in Christian self-reflection, not least in the unreconstructed view we are critiquing, as occupying centre-stage for articulating the Christian enterprise. The Christian theologian Anders Nygren's well-known *Agape and Eros*[1] provides a useful starting place, not only hermeneutically but also because it is a good example of what we may call the strong version of the unreconstructed view.[2]

Nygren distinguishes two kinds of love: *agape* and *eros*. As representing two 'fundamental [leit-] motifs' of human existence, *agape* and *eros* are qualitatively different; they have nothing in common. 'It is . . . of the utmost importance that we should accustom ourselves . . . to the idea that we cannot count on any *direct* correspondence and commensurability between Eros and Agape' (*AE*, p. 31). *Agape*-love is declared to be distinctively Christian:

We have . . . every right to say that *agape*[3] is the centre of Christianity, the Christian fundamental motif *par excellence* . . . Agape comes to us as a quite new creation of Christianity. It sets its mark on everything in Christianity. Without it nothing that is Christian would be Christian. Agape is Christianity's own original basic conception. (*AE*, p. 48)

Eros-love is the mark of other religions and cultures, past and present, of an unregenerate, ungraced humanity.

---

[1] This work was originally published in Swedish in two Parts, the first Part being a study of the Christian idea of love (first published in 1930), and the second Part being a study of the history of this idea till the Reformation (first published in 1936). It was published in an English translation (the 'Authorised Translation') by P. S. Watson in one volume in 1953. All references are taken from this translation (London: SPCK, 1953, abbreviated in this essay as *AE*).

[2] 'Strong' in the sense of regarding the Chrisian dispensation as absolutely unique (see further). As for love's hermeneutic role in the Christian project: 'To describe the changes that the Christian idea of love has undergone through the centuries would be ultimately the same as to write the entire inner history of Christianity'; *AE*, p. 29.

[3] Written in Greek letters in the original.

What then are the distinguishing characteristics of *agape* and *eros*? *Agape* is a self-giving, disinterested love: it loves the other for the other's sake, not for its own ends, however noble these may be (for example, to acquire some good, even the highest good, or for friendship or companionship, or to bring about an increase in virtue, etc.). It is sovereign and spontaneous: it has no ulterior motive, it is not based on need. It is value-free, that is, it does not seek value from the other but bestows an equal value on the other *qua* human. Humanly speaking, it is an egalitarian love. Finally, it is 'theocentric'. This means that it is initiated by God, and, through one's response in (Christian) faith, it extends in fellowship to the other as one's 'neighbour', and seeks its end in God for God's sake (not as one's 'highest good', for that would once more be to love for one's own ends).

Eros is the opposite of all this. It is a gainful, acquisitive love, even though the gain envisaged may be exalted (friendship, virtue, peace, the highest good, 'fulfilment'). Some of its forms may be less exalted than this, degenerating into sensuality and greed, but all forms of *eros* have this in common, that they are fundamentally egocentric. The other is loved, not for his or her own sake, but for what can be got out of them. *Eros* is based on need, and originates 'from below', in the human condition (see *AE*, p. 210). Other than Christianity, there is no religion or form of life which can be characterised originally as agapeic. 'Paul knows nothing of Eros, and Plato nothing of Agape [p. 33] . . . the difference between them is not one of degree but of kind. There is no way, not even that of sublimation, which leads over from Eros to Agape [p. 52]'. '[T]he legal piety of Judaism and . . . the Eros-piety of Hellenism' – typological forms of non-Christian piety – are wholly opposed to Christian *agape*, the *agape* of the Cross (p. 143). Thus, the unregenerate love of non-Christian faiths and cultures can be neither a path for authentic human life in the world nor a resource for accomplishing the ultimate purpose of that life.

It follows from this that the discourse on God based on this understanding of the human project is theology proper (a weaker version of this view might hold that discourse on God arising out of Jewish and Islamic self-reflection might also be theology in the proper sense, but to a lesser or more erroneous degree).[4] All other forms of 'theology' are theology by

---

[4] But note, the concept of the 'great monotheisms', as applying homogeneously to Judaism, Christianity and Islam, is itself contentious, and this for two reasons: (i) historically, the Christian doctrine of the Trinity, of three 'Persons' in one Godhead, has been granted only concessive status as a monotheism in mainline Jewish and Muslim theology: the 'monotheism' of Christianity seems to be the odd one out, and (ii) as contemporary study shows, the prejudices of the past can no longer stand against affirming as robust monotheisms the theologies of other world faiths such as Sikhism and major strands of Hindu devotionalism.

courtesy, that is, phenomenologically. They purport to do theology; they go through the motions, they might even make similar moves and draw similar conclusions, but they are unfounded. They do not have the proper theological legitimation to yield critical insights about those truths and values that guide us to our final goal and help us grow fully as human beings; they are misguided *ab origine*.

It should be clear that this position is not only fundamentally *a priori*, but also logically circular (for after saying that only Christian theology is theology proper, it then goes on to say that soteriological insights into the nature and goal of human existence can be granted only to and by Christians). It encapsulates a declaration of faith, rather than a demonstration of argument. It is not remarkable that there is not a single argument in Nygren's extensive work to *show* that the doctrine of altruistic love originates in the Christian tradition alone. The premise is simply assumed, and the conclusions follow. But as such, the premise and its implications for the teaching of theology have no academic merit whatsoever, and should not form the basis of education on religion in a secular institution funded by public money and purporting to teach, and to foster research, on 'scientific' grounds, that is, on grounds that are not epistemologically privileged in any way, but whose premises and conclusions are transparently subject to rational (rather than supra-rational or extra-rational) processes of legitimation. The 'theological' stance might be at home, perhaps, in seminaries and confessional educational institutions of one faith or another, but since such institutions often seek academic accreditation themselves, they too must pursue their inquiries with more than half an eye on the epistemological implications of their basic assumptions. We shall return to this point in due course.

I realise, of course, that an increasing number of Christian theologians accept neither Nygren's basic premise nor its implications for doing theology. This bodes well, in my view, both for doing Christian theology and for teaching it in the university. The point is, however, that the unreconstructed view continues to insinuate itself, as a dangerous relic of the past, in all sorts of ways in the academy, and there bedevils our understanding of the relationship between theology and the study of religion.

Is there, then, no scope for describing what we do in some university departments as 'Theology *and* Religious Studies/the Study of Religion'? There may be, but only in a restrained sense. That is, 'theology' may be studied in the secular context only as an aspect of the study of religion, not as a project evaluatively privileged on the basis of commitment to a particular faith. Indeed, the study of Christian theology in many of our universities seems often to be accorded such privilege: funded by public money, it is given more resources, more posts, and more curricular importance than the study of other theologies. This is an alarming prospect in multi-faith democracies modelled on a secular, liberal agenda in which the principle of equal rights and standing before the law is constitutionally embedded.[5]

But the egalitarian study of theology, as a special focus of the study of religion, would not accord a privileged evaluative status to the theology of any particular faith. It would be a phenomenological inquiry into quidditative aspects of a particular religious tradition from the point of view of that tradition's understanding and expression of the nature of ultimate reality and its relationship to the world, not a legitimation or endorsement of one tradition over others. In this sense, one could even have a theology of Buddhism (which famously seeks to eliminate appropriative discourse about a personal supreme being or God), if by 'theology' is meant a phenomenological inquiry into the nature of ultimate ends and their means.[6] Admittedly, this would be to strain the use of 'theology' somewhat, but it drives home the point I am making. For though the term 'theology' is derived from the Latin *theologia*, of course, which came into its own in early medieval Christianity as the *scientia Dei*, viz., that knowledge of the Christian deity derived from the proper use of reason reflecting upon (what was believed to be) the divine self-disclosure in history, the vicissitudes of time have conspired to enable the term to supersede its etymology (rather like the term 'religion' itself, which has metamorphosed so substantially over the centuries from its original (Roman) form of *religio*).[7]

Here, let me raise a further matter. There can be no objection, I think, to the forging of close relationships of study and teaching between departments of religion and institutions in which confessional theologies are taught. But these relationships cannot be one-sided, in the form of straightforward endorsement or ratification. The secular contribution could be to

---

[5] The only way, it seems to me, that a case can be made for privileging the study of one major religious faith over another in this context is on grounds extrinsic to any judgement about the rightness or wrongess of the theologies of these faiths, viz. the availability of appropriate teaching expertise, counterbalancing tendentious emphases of the past, being attentive to demographic and cultural needs, and so on.

[6] I am using 'phenomenological' in both senses identified by Gavin Flood in his contribution to this volume, viz. in the 'objective' sense, that is, as the intentional object, and in the 'subjective' sense of suspension of the inquiring agent's commitment and belief.

[7] See Michael J. Buckley's essay in this volume for an account of the medieval concept of *religio* and its development. He locates a radical change in the meaning of *religio* – to refer not only to piety or virtue, but also to such external things as ritual, teachings and beliefs – among theologians of the sixteenth and seventeenth centuries, especially in the influential textbooks of Francis Suarez.

maintain a watching brief on historical-critical standards of study that must inevitably form a crucial component of any responsible confessional theology. The study of other faiths (including rival strands of one's own faith), for example, in the context of one's performative theological overview must abide by these standards in the interests not only of acquiring as accurate an understanding of these faiths as possible, but also of pursuing the values of truth, justice and human affirmation that such an overview should seek. Indeed, even the study of the history of one's own faith, subject to the narrative of doctrinal and other conflict as it inevitably must be, must conform to these norms. For its part, confessional theology can inject a certain verve into the academic study of theology; it can show the ongoing relevance of religious faith in the lives of ordinary people in what Nicholas Lash has called a world that 'has now become, to an extent that was unimaginable even a few decades ago, one single complex fact, one seamless web of cause and consequence'.[8] Equally importantly, it continues to provide an important dimension of the raw material of the critical study of theology: the making of theology must precede its academic study.

To summarise the argument so far: the reader will have noticed that I have signalled the use of 'theology' in two senses: (i) performatively, if you will, and (ii) descriptively or phenomenologically (the 'egalitarian' sense). In the performative sense, the theological premises are *accepted as* true, and conclusions are then drawn. In the egalitarian sense, premises are assumed to be true *for argument's sake*, and various conclusions are drawn and/or scrutinised. Theologising in the performative sense is a function of the commitment of religious faith – in this sense, it is *a priori* – whereas theology in the egalitarian or descriptive sense invokes the stance of the critical observer. Nevertheless, as I have noted, there can be a symbiotic relationship between the two; indeed, this seems to be a desirable state of affairs.[9]

I have argued that performative theology does not really belong in departments of (Theology and) Religion in the secular university where, in fact, it is descriptive or egalitarian theology that is truly at home. However, because of the theological (in the performative sense) assumptions of the past and the inertia of history, this distinction is often blurred in our secular

[8] *The Beginning and the End of 'Religion'* (Cambridge: Cambridge University Press, 1996), p. 3.
[9] From this one can see that I fully endorse Sarah Coakley's recommendation (see her contribution to this volume) that we should maintain a real methodological distinction between Theology and the Study of Religion or 'Religious Studies' (but not, of course, in the way Nygren implies, where only Christian theology is 'theology' in the proper sense because it is supposedly based on the true revelation of God). Coakley's distinction (if I understand it aright) and mine are based on the epistemological difference of justification on the one hand, and description on the other.

institutions of learning, and a great deal of confusion and prejudice of one sort or other is perpetuated thereby.

To clarify the point, let us inquire into the kind of exercise an egalitarian theology of love in the study of religion might be. This would be a fascinating task, not only because love is so central to human purpose and meaning, but also because of the term's polyvalent and somewhat elusive semantics.

In the first place, it is in this context that Nygren's basic distinction between *agape*-love and *eros*-love could be considered. As a distinction *per se* between two kinds of love, it is a useful one. After all, there is a fundamental and consequential difference between love that is essentially other-seeking and love that is essentially self-seeking, between altruistic and acquisitive love. We do speak of love in both these senses. But one cannot engage with this distinction in more than the most superficial and misleading of ways without delving into its conceptual and behavioural roots in a particular linguistic-cultural tradition. For it is here that the *notae* or marks of the forms of love, whether in terms of Nygren's distinction or not, could be teased out, their ramifications for an ethics of love followed through, their interaction for an understanding of the relationship between love and other virtues and passions discerned.

Indeed, the full-blooded context of Nygren's distinction could only be a Christian one. A critical inquiry would need to ask on what grounds Nygren could maintain at all that *agape* is 'the Christian idea of love in its original sense' (*AE*, p. 56), that it is 'the qualitatively new and distinctive element in Christianity' (p. 62), that it is the 'specific achievement of Christianity' alone (p. 61). A contextual exegesis of the Christian scriptures and a survey of the history of Christian teaching seem essential ingredients of our inquiry's initial phases. But a comparative element also enters forthwith, beginning with those traditions most deeply involved with the articulation and early development of the Christian faith. Nygren singles out two in particular: 'the legal piety of Judaism' and the 'Eros-piety of Hellenism'. Framing it thus would seem to prejudge the question. But beyond pointing this out, our study would have to inquire further whether the radical disjunction Nygren is so keen to posit between the piety of the ancient Jews in particular and Christian piety in a matter so centrally definitive of the latter does not fatally undermine a fundamental teaching of Christian theology down the ages, viz. that the Christian message of love is not sprung on us as a bolt from the blue, *but is rooted in the cumulative religious history of ancient Israel,* which has been nurtured, guided and sustained by God himself. Radical disjunctions of the order of Nygren's linguistic hiatus sit ill at ease in such historicist theological perceptions of religio-cultural development. If this is the case, then as a Christian theologian in the first sense, is not Nygren at odds with himself? Surely a decisive element of the *agape* of which Nygren speaks must be discernible in the piety of the ancient Jews, not to mention in the Hellenistic piety that increasingly influenced the formulation of both Jewish and Christian faith?

Here the logic of descriptive theology is doing no more than holding the logic of performative theology strictly to account, a task it is constrained to perform. But descriptive theology can go further: it can also bring the contemporary insights of the social scientific study of language to bear on the way meaning is changed and transmitted across religio-cultural boundaries. Where such basic human sensibilities as love and their expression are concerned, the transmitted meaning is not a meaning *ex novo* – created out of nothing (as if human beings were ignorant of authentic other-regarding love before the Christian message came on the scene) – but a sense *ex ovo*, so that radical *continuities* between the terms of semantic change may be discerned. This argument too would seem to undermine Nygren's claim for the absolute uniqueness of Christian *agape*.

It is important to note that we are engaged in the analytical processes of a phenomenological inquiry, that is, in an *a posteriori* seeking out, prompted by the particular starting point of our study: the putative uniqueness of the *agape* of Christian discourse. Thus, having included Jewish and Hellenistic piety within the compass of our inquiry, we cannot stop there. To assess how unique Christian *agape* in its basic sense might be, we are prompted to inquire whether other contemporary world faiths, such as Hinduism and Buddhism, draw distinctions parallel to that of *agape* and *eros*. Here, as we leave the constitutive religio-cultural matrix of Christian tradition, we are confronted, more urgently than hitherto perhaps, by a fresh problematic: that of cultural translation. According to what methodology can we proceed? Is there a nexus of terms and ideas in the Indian traditions (perhaps clustering around the words *bhakti* in Hinduism and *karuṇa* in Buddhism) – a horizon of discourse – properly analogous to the *agape* and *eros* of Nygren's distinction? What is the role of the imagination, of tropes such as metaphor, of symbols and myth and images, in comparative methodology?[10] It is not the purpose of this essay to pursue this further. Here I am inquiring into differences of method in the study of theology

---

[10] In an increasingly globalised world, such comparative work is becoming more and more sophisticated. On the topic of love as a comparative study, see my own contribution, 'The God of Love and the Love of God in Christian and Hindu Traditions', in J. Runzo & N. M. Martin, eds., *Love, Sex and Gender in the World Religions* (Oxford, Boston: Oneworld Publications, 2000).

and religion, and the issues raised as we consider the systematic application
of these methodological differences.

But perhaps this is not quite Nygren's point? He may concede that, from
the viewpoint of the external observer, there appear to be close analogies
in other religions to his fundamental distinction vis-à-vis the Christian
faith. But he may argue that the point is that the Christian faith is oper-
ational soteriologically while other religions are not: this is precisely the
difference underlying phenomenological and theological (in the performative sense) understanding. In fact, Nygren does seem to say that even
phenomenologically *agape*-love is absent as a regulative category in other
religious traditions. This is one of the implications of his characterising the
piety of ancient Israel and of Greece as 'legal' and '*eros*' respectively. But
it is not the task of egalitarian theology to pronounce in the performative
sense on Nygren's theological stance. Rather, its task is, on the one hand, to
lay bare the latter's theological presuppositions and their implications for
doing theology, and to explore from a critical distance the theological alter-
natives available, and, on the other, to examine, equally critically, whether
his distinction has counterparts in other faith traditions.

In our discussion so far, the reader will not have failed to notice the range
of disciplines that have come into play in our survey of the methodological
and other issues raised by a descriptive theology of love in the study of religion. These disciplines would include anthropological and ethnographic
inquiry, the philosophy of religion with special emphasis on ethics, philosophical theology, the historical-critical exegesis of scripture, the study of
the history of ideas, comparative methodology, and social scientific theory of language and behaviour. Quite an array. No doubt scholars would
specialise in certain areas of the inquiry, but increasingly today, scholarly
expertise needs to be cross- and inter-disciplinary. By this I do not mean
that Religious Studies or the academic study of religion must make some
attempt to colonise other discourses; rather, part of its purpose is to function as a 'go-between' discipline. As Gavin Flood says in his essay: 'Because
of the diversity of the field, for Religious Studies to be operative as a coherent discipline there needs to be a meta-discourse . . . that reflects common
concerns and allows communication between different fields within it.'[11]

(In my argument I am not advocating, of course, some methodological stance of Olympian impartiality, some unattainable vantage-point of
Enlightenment neutrality. It is well understood today that such a stance
was based on a simplistic misunderstanding of what we still like to call

[11] Above, p. 65.

on occasion the objective method. Today's objective method retains more than a *soupçon* of ingrained perspectivalism. But this does not mean that our approach cannot strive to be non-partisan, or that we cannot achieve appreciable success in the attempt. If we could not, the disciplines mentioned above would lose all academic and functional respectability, and could in no wise be perceived as yielding some harvest of truth. In that case, the critical apparatus undergirding our legal, political, social and entrepreneurial systems (which depend crucially though not exclusively on the truths derived from social scientific and analogous inquiry) would have no credibility whatsoever. We shall take up this matter again. Here I am simply affirming the critical approach consensually underlying these areas of study in their context as feeder-disciplines of the study of religion too.)

But to return to our theme: Nygren's distinction, *qua* distinction, is an important guiding starting point in our understanding of the meaning and purpose of love. It points to two incommensurable kinds of love: other-regarding, selfless, love, and self-regarding, gainful, love. In Nygren's hands, this distinction is taken further, of course. He claims that it is Christian love alone that is the former kind of love, and that all other faiths teach the latter. We have seen how it is one of the tasks of an egalitarian theology of love to lay bare the (confessional) theological presuppositions of this claim. But there is an additional evaluative component to Nygren's distinction: not only is it the case, he contends, that erotic love so called is morally inferior to agapeic love, but it is also intrinsically morally corrosive; it is a tainted and tainting love. It is inherently (morally) 'egocentric'. It originates in the human condition, and is the only kind of love human beings are capable of by themselves (theologically, it is an ungraced love). As such, it can play no direct role in accomplishing the proper end of human existence, which in this life is agapeic love for one's fellow human beings founded on (the Christian) God's agapeic love for us, and in the next life is communion in such love with this God and those who have been saved. In short, the only kind of love we are capable of as human, in this view, is in fact essentially degrading.

Of course, this is a theological standpoint, and one of the tasks of descriptive theology would be to point to alternative Christian stances, not to mention patterns of discourse in Christian foundational texts, such as the Gospels, which appear to run counter to Nygren's position. For example, in the latter context, does not Christ himself, the exemplar for Christians of God's love for us and our love for God, seem to endorse *eros*-love, viz., gainful love, love for the sake of some reward or other (see, e.g., Matt. 5 and 6, John 2 (the wedding at Cana), Luke 10:7, and *passim*)? Perhaps not surprisingly, during centuries of discussion and teaching, Christian thinkers have regularly affirmed *eros*-love as both humanising and good in circumstance after circumstance.

Descriptive theology could seek to explore this position from *within the premises* of Christian discourse. This is different from affirming, as performative theology does, that Christian discourse is based on foundations that are true; rather, it is accepting a starting place as if it were true, and then testing the coherences and implications of its form of life both internally and in interaction with other forms of life. This entails a process of *internal* evaluation in contrast to the externally evaluative presuppositions (external to other faiths, that is) on which the starting place of performative theology is predicated. Such a scrutiny will show that Nygren's uncompromising devaluation of *eros*-love is contested within the universe of Christian discourse itself.

In an important article in which he considers an analogous problematic, viz. the ambivalence of desire – 'an ambivalence as to whether the peace at which our hearts are set *fulfils desire or springs from its suppression*' – Nicholas Lash, as a Christian thinker,[12] suggests a solution to our problem of the ambivalence of erotic love:

Perhaps we might say that the Christian project of discipleship, conceived as lifelong schooling in the purification of desire, is a matter of discovering that, whatever we desire, our desiring of it is only the desire of God in the measure that it is conformed to and transformed by God's previous desire of us. Our yearning, purified, shares in that yearning by which the world is made. (p. 6)

Thus self-referencing love, the fundamental dynamic of *eros*, is acceptable only in so far as it is subject to the demands in our lives of agapeic love, whose selfless nature stems from the Source of agapeic love itself. Put theistically, it is the expression of God's love in our lives – the prevenient love of self-giving – that enables *eros* to become a humanising love. All forms of erotic love – the desire for food, shelter and clothing, the mutuality of companionship, the love of virtue, knowledge and learning, even the striving after our highest good – are justified only in so far as their seeking does not transgress *agape*'s altruistic constraints. Thus, though as types of love *eros* and *agape* may be incommensurable, *eros* as *eros* can be validated and transformed into a humanising love when it is guided and informed by the selflessness of *agape*, when it becomes submissive, that is, to *agape*'s decentring dynamic. This is the alternative and deeper Christian understanding

[12] See his 'The Purification of Desire' (abbreviated in this essay as *PD*), in J. Lipner, ed., *The Fruits of our Desiring: An Enquiry into the Ethics of the Bhagavadgītā* (Calgary: Bayeux Arts Inc., 1997).

to which Nicholas Lash points, and not only the Christian, for 'these fundamental facts about the world have been familiar, from the beginning, to all the great traditions' (*PD*, p. 4).[13]

But is understanding, profound though it may be, sufficient for the academic study of religion? Can there be no search for, no grasp of *truth*? Well, understanding itself can be true, or false. And it is generally agreed that the study of religion seeks an understanding that is true, or at least that becomes truer and truer as it delves deeper into and ranges ever more broadly over its subject. This is an arduous and ongoing task, requiring a skilled discipline in the science of hermeneutics and the art of empathy.[14] But if it did not promise a yield of even limited success, some progress in the grasp of truth, we could lay no claim to acquiring any real knowledge at all from the scholarly expertise of the historian, the scriptural exegete, the philosopher of religion, the social scientist, the comparative religionist.

It is by its search for right understanding of a central human endeavour, by its own accrual of *a deposit of truth*, that the study of religion validates the religious enterprise and helps establish it as an important focus in the public forum. It is the academic study of religion that gives us the tools for intelligent, open debate about humankind's religious quest. It is the academic study of religion that helps rescue religion from its own worst excesses.

Nicholas Lash has written that 'it is the role of religion as a medium of truth that has been privatised. Religion, in societies that imagine themselves secular, is, like art and music, allowed to be about the Beautiful. Sometimes,

---

[13] In *PD* Lash considers the *Bhagavadgītā*, which teaches through the mouth of Krishna, the *Gītā*'s supreme deity: 'Your concern is with action, never with its fruit. Neither let your motive be the fruit of action, nor be attached to inaction' (2.47). This is the teaching of *niṣkāma karma* or unselfish action. It is noteworthy that in a well-known Sanskrit text on *bhakti* or 'devotion' to the deity, the *Nārada Bhakti Sūtras* (c. tenth-twelfth centuries CE), *bhakti* is paraphrased as an *āsakti* or 'attachment/adhering to' of various kinds (see Sūtra 82). Attachment/adhering to implies a centrifugal, other-regarding impetus rather than a centripetal, self-referencing one.

[14] See my 'Seeking Others in their Otherness', *New Blackfriars* 74 (March 1993), pp. 152–65. I note with interest Clifford Geertz's sarcastic dismissal of the 'myth of the chameleon fieldworker, perfectly self-attuned to his exotic surroundings, a walking miracle of empathy, tact, patience, and cosmopolitanism', in his contribution to R. T. McCutcheon, (ed.), *The Insider/Outsider Problem in the Study of Religion* (London & New York: Cassell, 1999) p. 50. However, Geertz then proceeds to undermine his own disavowal by delineating the sensitivity of his own anthropological approach, culminating in the statement that 'Understanding the form and pressure of . . . natives' inner lives is more like grasping a proverb, catching an allusion, seeing a joke – or, as I have suggested, reading a poem – than it is like achieving communion' (see his '"From the Native's Point of View": On the Nature of Anthropological Understanding', p. 63 in the same volume). For my part, I do not dismiss the exemplar of the myth or indeed 'communion' as the ideal to strive for, but these are, after all, ideals. And considerable empathy is required if one is systematically and cumulatively to grasp a proverb, catch an allusion, see a joke, or understand a poem, of another culture or way of life. This may well be close to a form of 'communion'.

it is allowed to be about the Good. What is excluded, by the dominant
ideologies, is any suggestion that the business of religion is, no less than that
of science, with public truth.'[15] But we have looked at one way in which
religion may have to do with public truth, may help make our societies
and cultures, by common consent, more fully human. Its egalitarian study
draws to our attention a great deal of the cumulative wisdom that the
human race has considered desirable and necessary for living the good
life, notwithstanding the active rivalries, falterings, incompleteness and
incoherences of this history. But such study cannot decide for us which
paths to choose. It can yield only descriptive, not prescriptive, truths; it can
help us arrive at more informed and discerning choices.[16]

After the cataclysmic events of September 2001, our secular societies are
re-learning, haltingly, it is true, to speak the word 'God' (or its equivalents)
again. Since the world has now changed, people will experience a greater
need for the exigencies of theological discourse, in both senses of 'theology'.
And responsible talk of love will be central to this discourse, for it is only
appreciation of something like the sovereign self-giving of love in its agapeic
mode, where nothing is sought in return, where love is freely given and freely
received, that will be able not only to initiate and complete processes of
genuine reconciliation where hostility now prevails, but also to penetrate
the hard carapace of our consumerist mentalities. We are growing used
to setting a price on everything: everything is becoming a commodity, a
'good' to be bartered or sold in the market-place of human interaction.
Theology/the study of religion has a chance to break this mould. It can do
so in two ways: (i) by providing descriptive truths about such things as love,
hope, and sharing, laboriously derived with the care of scholarship from the
legacy of the world's wisdom, and (ii) by enabling those whose task it is to
dare to counsel, challenge, guide, that is, the utterers of prescriptive truth,
among whom we may number religious leaders and theologians (in the
performative sense), to do so with a transparent sense of responsibility. But
this will not be possible unless they are willing to incorporate the knowledge
offered by the descriptive truths of which we speak, and to be sensitive
in their utterances to the *methodological restraint*, viz. to the epistemic
provisionality, that the science of religion inculcates. Those who continue

---

[15] *The Beginning and the End of 'Religion'*, p. 16.
[16] I do not wish to suggest that we can draw an absolute distinction between 'descriptive' and 'prescriptive' here, for the 'descriptive' of the scholar is not free from a form of perspectival transformation
of the content of the object described. Nevertheless, there is a real, qualitative distinction methodologically between the description of the scholar and the prescription of the religious adherent or
performative theologian: a distinction that legitimates the academic enterprise and the truths it
consensually yields. It is this distinction that I am endorsing here.

to isolate themselves from the fruit of scholarship will show themselves to be power-mongers serving vested and divisive interests, and will run the risk of their words falling on dismissive ears. And it is here, I suggest, in the discipline of attentive scholarship, that the future of theology in both its modes and of the study of religion lies, in a world becoming ever more nearly 'one single complex fact, one seamless web of cause and consequence'.

CHAPTER 7

Scripture

Peter Ochs

INTRODUCTION

Here is a scriptural text: from the biblical book of Nehemiah (8), part of the narrative of the return of Israel after the First Destruction, under the guidance of Ezra the Scribe:

Ezra came up from Babylon, a scribe expert in the Teaching of Moses . . . (Ezra 7:6)

On the first day of the seventh month, Ezra the priest brought the Teaching before the congregation . . . He read from it . . . to the men and women and those who could understand . . . Jeshua, Bani, . . . and the Levites explained the Teaching to the people . . . They read from the scroll of the Teaching of God, translating it and giving the sense; so they understood the reading. (Neh. 8:2–7)

And here is a Talmudic commentary on this biblical text, drawn from the first generations of rabbis who renewed the religion of Israel after the Second Destruction:

It has been taught: R. Yose said, Had Moses not preceded him, Ezra would have been worthy of receiving the Torah for Israel. Of Moses, it is written, 'And Moses went up to God' (Ex.19:3), and of Ezra it is written, 'He, Ezra, went up from Babylon' (Ez 7:6). (*Bab. Talmud, Tractate Sanhedrin*)

We may recall from the Exodus narrative that, enraged by the Israelites' sin of the golden calf, Moses broke the first tablets he brought down from Mount Sinai (Exod. 32:19). From then on, the Israelites were guided only by words brought down a second time. This is to be a prototype for Jewish teaching ever since: where each teaching (from the root *l'shanot*) is a second-ing . . . or 'repetition' (*mishneh*), inscribed after some experience of terrible loss, on stones carved *by human hands* (see Exod. 34:1). This time, it is the shattered tablets. Another time, it is the Destruction of the First Temple, followed by Ezra's re-teaching the Torah. Later, it is the Destruction of the Second Temple, followed by the Mishnah itself, the re-teaching that initiates the literature of Talmudic Judaism. But what Jewish hermeneutic will emerge today, after the Shoah?

The question before us in this essay is what the reading of texts in scriptural traditions may show us about the future of the study of theology and religions. For the past century and a half, even before the Shoah, it has been difficult for Jewish scholars to consider the *future* of their field, or even the present. Their preoccupation has been on the past: not the past of their field, but of Judaism itself. Since the birth of modern Jewish Studies as the *Wissenschaft des Judentums* and until quite recently, Jewish scholarship has been strictly a history of Jewish writing. Scholarship has focused largely on the reception history of Jewish sacred writings, from the Tanakh, or Jewish Bible, through the classics of rabbinic Judaism – Mishnah, Talmud and the midrash collections – to the codes, commentaries, philosophies, esoteric writings and, finally, literatures, of the Jewish Diaspora in Europe and North Africa and now also America and Israel.

MODERN ACADEMIC VS. CLASSICAL RABBINIC MODELS OF SCRIPTURAL STUDY

On one level, the classic texts in this tradition also appear to be about the past: the story of ancient Israel retold by a later, sadder Israel, and the laws of a Temple cult redescribed by the rabbinic sages who survived the loss of Temple. On another level, however, these classic texts are written about the future: stories of Israel in the desert that warn a later, Israelite monarchy about the wages of sin on a national scale; and laws of the priesthood that prepare Jewish householders of the Diaspora to conduct their family meals as if they were priestly cults. This is what we might call 'typological history': history narrated as a source of types or models for conduct in the future. To seek such models is, however, to narrate one's history for the purpose of responding to the crises of the present. In this sense, many of the classic texts of Jewish tradition belong to a literature of crisis.

There is therefore a significant discontinuity between the form of modern Jewish historiography and the form of the classic texts it studies. This is, I trust, not because Jewish historians have been unmoved by the crises of modern Jewish life, but because they fear that 'typological history' would be too subjective truly to meet the needs of the day. What we need instead, they suppose, is dispassionate documentation of the decision-making processes of the past, so that anyone concerned to respond to any crisis will be armed with as much evidence as possible about the cause-and-effect relations between certain classes of action and certain results. Towards the end of this essay, I will ask which of these two models of study better serves contemporary theological and religious studies – the modern historian's induction or the classic authors' typological history. For most of the essay, however, I will attend to a form of recent scholarship that may represent a third model.

A THIRD MODEL FOR SCRIPTURAL STUDY
THEN AND NOW

For our purposes, this third model will be illustrated by the hermeneutical writings of David Weiss Halivni, survivor of Auschwitz and widely regarded as the twentieth century's most innovative Talmudist. Lucius Littauer Professor of classical Jewish civilization at Columbia University, and rector of the Institute of Traditional Judaism, Halivni is widely known for his historical-critical commentaries and re-readings of the Talmud: *Mekorot Umesorot* (*Sources and Traditions*).[1] In the past decade, he has added English language studies of the method he uses to reinterpret the Talmud and of the theological implications of his work for Jewish life after the Shoah. In brief, his method is to practise *both* inductive *and* typological history, or what we will call 'depth historiography'.[2] In the way he practises *both* of these, he places his *academic* work within a hermeneutical tradition that links him to the practices of the Mishnaic sages, or *tannaim*, and links them to the practice of Ezra the Scribe. This to receive and *repair* the written traditions of Torah (*l'kabel ul'drosh et hatorah*) for the sake of renewing Judaism after yet another Destruction. The historian's *Wissenschaft* is as central to this work as were the rabbinic sages' new philological and interpretive technologies.

Halivni argues that, for a significant stream of Talmudic thinking, Ezra acquires a status near, or in some ways equal to, that of Moses.[3] There is a tradition, for example, that the Torah texts transmitted by the priestly scribes to Ezra were imperfect ('maculate', in Halivni's words), that Ezra

---

[1] David Weiss Halivni, *Sources and Traditions: A Source Critical Commentary on the Talmud* [Heb.] (Tel Aviv, 1968; Jerusalem: Jewish Theological Seminary, 1975, 1982 and cont.).

[2] For Halivni, 'inductive' or 'plain-sense' history examines 'factual events as best as these may be established from the evidence [of ancient texts]'(David Weiss Halivni, *Peshat and Derash, Plain and Applied Meaning in Rabbinic Exegesis* (New York: Oxford University Press, 1991), p. xvi. His original term for typological history was 'transcendent history', but he has accepted my re-labelling this 'depth historiography'. See David Weiss Halivni, *Revelation Restored, Divine Writ and Critical Responses* (Boulder: Westview Press, 1997), p. 10; and 'Foreword by Peter Ochs', p. xvi.

[3] *Peshat and Derash*, passim; and *Revelation Restored*, passim.

instituted a process of restoring those texts, and that the dots that appear over ten verses in the Torah (the *eser nekudot*) mark places where Ezra had not yet carried out the revision:

Some give another reason why the dots are inserted. Ezra reasoned thus: If Elijah comes and asks, 'Why have you written these words' [why have you included these suspect passages?], I shall answer, 'That is why I dotted these passages.' And if he says to me, 'You have done well in having written them,' I shall erase the dots over them. (*Bamidbar Rabbah* III.13).

The text implies that the Torah that was received by the scribal priests, by the Pharisees, and by the proto-rabbis in Second Temple days was not a self-sufficient record of God's spoken word; it displayed its meaning only through the mediation of an interpretive tradition that the rabbis named the Oral Torah (*torah she b'al peh*). According to the Mishnah, the rabbis received this Oral Torah from Moses by way of Ezra: 'for Ezra had dedicated himself to seek [/interpret, *l'drosh*] the Torah of the Lord so as to observe it, and to teach laws and rules to Israel' (Ezra 7:10). In Halivni's words, *Ezra was thus a principal architect of the oral law.* We will later ask what kind of scholarship enables Halivni to make a statement like that. For now, let us simply unpack the layers of text reading that are folded into it.

1. Moses and Sinaitic textuality

The first layer is the narrative of Exodus 19 and 20: 'Moses brought the people out of the camp to meet God. Moses went down to the people . . . Then God spoke all these words: I am the Lord your God . . .' This, we are accustomed to saying, is the foundational text of Sinaitic revelation, the Torah *per se*. But the canonical Torah of the Jews is irreducible to any one of its sub-texts or verses. As Halivni argues, for the early rabbinic sages who canonised the Torah, the *peshat*, or 'plain sense', of a biblical text is the meaning of the text in its literary context within the canon. *Peshat* here displays its etymological meaning as 'what is spread out' – the text within its literary spread. The plain meaning of Exodus 20 cannot, therefore, be detached from its relation to the narrative of Exodus 32–4:

Then Moses turned and went down from the mountain, carrying the two tablets of the covenant in his hands . . . The tablets were the work of God, and the writing was God's writing . . . But as soon as he came near the camp and saw the calf and the dancing, Moses' anger burned hot and he threw the tablets from his hands and broke them at the foot of the mountain. (32:15–16, 19)

YHVH said to Moses: Carve two tablets of stone like the first ones, and I will write on the tablets the words that were on the first tablets, which you broke... YHVH said to Moses: Write these words... And [Moses] wrote on the tablets the words of the covenant. (34:1, 27–8)

According to these words, the Torah that God gave to Moses is a broken Torah. The Torah that Moses gives to the people Israel is a second giving – in this sense already a *mishneh torah*. It is written by God's hand, but on stone that Moses carves *because the first stones were broken*. The Torah that Israel receives from Moses is therefore already thick with its own internal history, and the history is already broken by human sin, as much as *adam*, the human creature who makes it out of the garden, is already broken by his/her sin. And that is not all.

2. Deuteronomy and reading the relations between the verses

In the final, Deuteronomic, narrative Moses offers of Israel's wanderings, the text of Torah already appears different from the text recorded in Exodus 20. In the earlier text, the Israelites are to observe the Sabbath day and keep it holy: 'For in six days the Lord made heaven and earth... but rested on the seventh day.' But, in the later text, they observe it in order to 'remember that you were a slave in the land of Egypt and the Lord your God brought you out from there...' (Deut. 5:15). Does Exodus 20 record the Torah that was broken? Or is the canon of Torah telling us that the written Torah will itself change through Israel's transmission of it? Or, we might also ask, does the Torah that, as the rabbis later say, stood with God at creation refer not to the written verses themselves, but to the relations among them? And, if the Torah refers to relations *among* the verses, would we map the written Torah not as some discrete series of words and verses (ab...n), but as an indefinite set of relations among these relations (aRb, bRc,...nRn)? On such a view – *were* we to entertain it – to know the Torah would mean to know these Relations.

In fact, the biblical scholar Michael Fishbane based his inductive study *Biblical Interpretation in Ancient Israel* on the observation that virtually every biblical verse interprets some other biblical verse. He calls the phenomenon 'intra-biblical interpretation': the way, for example, that Deuteronomy 4:16b–19 ('be careful... not to make for yourselves a sculptured image...: the form of a man or a woman, the form of any beast on earth...') reapplies to the laws of image-making the creation imagery of Genesis 1:14–27 ('Let us make humankind in our image'). Fishbane suggests that we can, per hypothesis, reconstruct the ways in which a passage (like Deut. 4) interprets another one (like Gen. 1). In this case, 'the Deuteronomist offers a form of aggadic exegesis that establishes a distinct rhetorical nexus between the themes of creation and idolatry..., reinfor[cing] the Israelites'... [theological claim] that idolatry is a sin against the creator and his transcendence'.[4] Fishbane's study suggests that almost every passage of written Torah can be re-read as interpretive commentary on other passages.[5] The teachings of Torah, in other words, appear first as interpretive judgements about other teachings, rather than as judgements about the world-itself beyond the text. Noting that these judgements can be collected into groups of judgements, or types, Fishbane labels each type a rule of interpretive judgement, or logos. For example, there are logoi of prophetic prediction, of legal inference, of historical application, and so on.

In these terms, we could recharacterise the written Torah as a collection of revealed logoi, or, to use the English term, revealed reasonings. The scriptural logoi would, in this sense, refer to the identities of the relations revealed in scripture; to adopt such logoi as rules of reasoning would, then, be to reason scripturally, or to engage in scriptural reasoning.

3. The rabbis' Oral Torah as reading between the verses

Redescribing the Torah this way makes it much easier to account for the fundamental hermeneutical claim of the rabbis in both Mishnah and Talmud. The rabbinic sages claim that their midrashic re-readings of the

---

[4] Michael Fishbane, *Biblical Interpretation in Ancient Israel* (Oxford: Oxford University Press, 1985), p. 322. To take another example from the Ezra narrative, Fishbane notes how Ezra is portrayed as law-interpreter as well as Torah-teacher. 'Ezra was informed by his princes that "the people of Israel, and the priests, and the Levites have not *nivdalu*, separated themselves from the people of the land whose abhorrent practices are like those of the Canaanites,... the Ammonites, the Moabites, the Egyptians, and the Amorites" (9:1)' (p. 114). In response, Ezra mourns (9:4) and then later agrees with his princes' proposal to expel all foreign wives and separate the Israelites from the peoples of the land (10:11). Fishbane notes that the proposal makes deliberate allusion to Deut. 7, 'wherein the Israelites are prohibited to intermarry with the local population' (p. 116). It appears that the princes want both to associate their new commonwealth with the Israelites' first settlement of the land and also to add more recent enemies (Ammonites and Moabites) to the old Deuteronomic list. In this case, the Bible extends an earlier conception of national holiness to a new setting while also revising the details of the older law. If Ezra reforms the Torah text, it appears he also extends and reforms Torah law.

[5] In similar fashion, Tikvah Frymer-Kensky examines ways in which verses of the Five Books of Moses reinterpret other verses, for example in which Moses himself restates God's words. She suggests that the Written Torah problematises any notion that individual verses have the status of revealed text independently of their relation to the whole of the Written Torah. See, for example, Frymer-Kensky, 'Revelation Revealed, The Doubt of Torah,' in P. Ochs and N. Levene, eds., *Textual Reasoning: Jewish Philosophy and Text Study at the End of the Twentieth Century* (London: SCM, 2002; Grand Rapids: Eerdmans, 2003), pp. 68–75.

written Torah are continuous with the revealed text, no matter how much the literal words of the midrashim appear not only to differ from, but at times even to 'uproot', the literal texts of the Bible ('uprooting', *l'aker*, is their own term for what some of their readings may appear to do!). Consider, for example, what some consider the emblematic claim of the Mishnah for scriptural authority: the first verse of *Pirke Avot*, the 'Chapters [or Ethics] of the Fathers':

Moses received the Torah on Mt. Sinai, handed it over to Joshua, who handed it over to the elders [and, thence to . . .] the prophets . . . to the men of the Great Assembly (the first Legislature after the return from Babylonian exile), to . . . the rabbinic sages. (*Avot* 1:1)

The text suggests the claim that here, after the Destruction of the Temple in 70 CE, and after the Dispersion of 135 CE, the sages of the Mishnah still speak the authoritative words of the Torah as given to Moses. The text could not, however, refer only to the literal words of Moses' Torah, since it leaves out of the chain of transmission the priests and priestly scribes who, according to the biblical record, preserved those words and stored them in the Temple. Yet, the text also claims to refer to the Torah of Moses, and no other. How is this apparent contradiction to be resolved? The dominant interpretation, common to both modern historians and classical commentators, is that the text refers to the Oral as well as Written Torah. But does this mean one Torah or two?

The dominant contemporary reading is symbolised by Jacob Neusner's memorable label for the rabbis' religion: 'Judaism of the Dual Torah'. This is a Judaism that lends equal authority to the Written Torah, *torah she b'khtav*, and the Oral Torah, *torah she b'al peh*, as it appears in the rabbinic teachings of Mishnah and Talmud and in the teachings that subsequently interpret them, from the Gaonic period to today. In this contemporary view, the first verse of *Pirke Avot* is about the Oral, not the Written, Torah, teaching that there is an independent, parallel, chain of transmission that lends the rabbis' own interpretations *effectively* comparable legal authority to what is offered from the text itself (*d'oraita*). I say 'effectively comparable', because laws based explicitly on the Written Torah are clearly privileged. But such laws are typically vague, or in need of further definition when applied to the contexts of actual life in any time period; the definition comes by way of rabbinic readings, and these draw on the authority of the Oral tradition.

Halivni offers a different reading. He recognises, to be sure, the rabbinic distinction between Oral and Written Torah, but he argues that our verse is neither about the Oral Torah as it is typically understood, nor the Written

Torah as *it* is typically understood. He argues, instead, that the Oral Torah originally referred to the rabbis' *corrective* reading of the received text of Written Torah: a reading that, where necessary, corrected the community's imperfect tradition of what the Written Torah says. Thus, he argues, the *tannaim* did not originally recognise the Oral Torah as a second revelation on Sinai, but only as the source of their judgements about how to repair imperfections in the reception of the Written Torah. Halivni's account of these judgements complements Fishbane's account of the biblical logoi: the Oral Torah reads the Written Torah, alone, but between its verses. If it read only the individual verses, the Oral Torah would remain in an enclosed semantic universe. The things of the world, for example, would correspond, one for one, to the words of Torah, and when Isaiah says, 'Israel shall inherit the land for ever', then Israel could not also be 'in exile'. If, however, Torah is revealed in relations *among* its verses, then the relations of things in the world would correspond to the relations among these verses, and 'Israel in exile' may, at a certain time, correspond to 'Israel in the world to come' as 'Israel in the land' may correspond to 'what Israel inherits for ever'.

Halivni suggests that, through the *amoraic* (Talmudic) period and even more so in the medieval period, rabbinic interpretation gradually turned away from such relations towards the words themselves. The Oral Torah then came to refer to a second, independent, revelation at Sinai that gave prophetic, scribal, and, later, rabbinic interpreters direct knowledge of how God would want them to correct or expand the apparent plain sense of the Written Torah. Halivni argues that this later development should *not* be a model for our understanding of *Pirke Avot*, *nor* for contemporary rabbinic practice itself.

4. The Written-and-Oral Torah as a model for Jewish scriptural studies today

Halivni argues that the modern historian's model of the Dual Torah as two separable *torot* inherits an understandable but nonetheless troubling tendency in late rabbinic and medieval commentary. This is a tendency to insulate rabbinic judgements from criticism or reinterpretation by attaching to them the authority of Mosaic revelation. An independent 'oral' Torah might appear, on first glance, to designate a portion of the tradition that is freed from the fixity of a written code and, thereby, opened to rabbinic creativity. Halivni argues that such appearances are misleading. In his reading, such creativity is made possible only by the tradition of a single Torah, whose written form remains unchanged, but whose proper meanings are articulated through the interpretive activities of the sages of each generation. These sages seek to make use of all exegetical sciences and tools at their disposal, since their goal is not to endow any particular *method* of reading with divine sanctity,[6] but to *search out* (*l'drosh*) the actual meanings of the texts as they are received by a given generation. This searching out represents the practice of Oral Torah as an inseparable dimension of the Torah received by Moses, and it enacts what we might label three rules of Oral Torah as it is received by each generation: (1) The Written Torah is God's Word to Israel. (2) This Word makes explicit demands of Israel only by way of the 'searching out' that is authorised by the sages of each generation. (3) This searching out is, in this way, touched both by the holiness of divinity *and* by the finitude and fallibility of the *human* hand. According to these rules, there is no way for the people of Israel to live lives of holiness without also risking the human error of interpretation. This risk does not imperil religious faith, because religious faith calls each member of Israel to live out the interpretations of each generation's sages, *except where those interpretations can be shown*, through recognisable means of argumentation, to lead to errors in practice, which are errors in the reception of Torah.

For Halivni, the trend toward belief in a separate Oral Torah militated against the fallibilism of this understanding of Oral Torah. If a separate Oral Torah was revealed to Moses, then particular rabbinic sages can claim that *their* Oral Torah was revealed and, therefore, as holy and unquestionable as the received words of the Written Torah. Halivni speculates that, by raising the more human and tentative Oral Torah to the status of a complementary revelation, later rabbis protected themselves against their own diminished trust in the hermeneutical process and their fear of criticism from competing interpreters. This is, indeed, the kind of self-protection he observes today in right-wing Orthodoxy. He notes, for example, the custom of some heads of traditional rabbinic schools (*roshe yehivah*), and some chief rabbis of Israel, to accord their own subjective opinions the infallibility of divine legislations.

For Halivni, the academy's historical and literary sciences enhance the work of rabbinic interpretation, since they enable scholars to sift out those aspects of the received tradition that clarify the commanding voice of Torah in any given generation and those that do not. This means that Halivni shares in two dimensions of modern Jewish scholarship: the inductive, historical, studies that have dominated the field for over a century and the intra-textual, literary, studies that have gained attention in the past few

---

[6] In different terms, they would not suppose that such sanctity would imply rigidity of method.

decades. It also means, however, he parts company with the tendency of Jewish academicians to limit their interest to these two dimensions alone.

Writing after the Shoah, he believes that his historiography must also contribute to the work of renewing and repairing the text traditions of Judaism after another time of Destruction. He does not criticise his colleagues who put all their professional energies into plain-sense historiography, but he is critical of those who criticise him for pursuing what they call 'subjective' (or 'communal' or 'religious') interests in addition to his plain-sense work. In reply, he notes that he carefully delimits the portions of his inquiry that are strictly inductive and those that go beyond induction. He divides the latter, moreover, into two additional parts: extra-academic work that is devoted to community-specific theology, and the dimension of his academic work that we have labelled 'depth historiography'. Re-embodying the integrative activity of Israel's Written-and-Oral Torah within the context of academic studies, depth historiography is guided by two rules:

- offer no theory that is contradicted by the plain-sense evidence of text and history, *and*:
- of the theories that are not thereby disqualified, choose the one that speaks most 'truly' to the end of renewing Judaism today, after Destruction.

Following the first rule, Halivni applies the relatively context-free methods of plain-sense science to the study of Judaism's sacred sources. Following the second rule, he shows how, within the bounds of academic practice, scholars may also answer context-specific demands that are voiced within those sources. At least three demands direct Halivni's depth scholarship. One demand is to identify *who* he is as he stands before and interprets this literature at this time. Then, *if he is a member of Israel's Covenant, as well as an academic scholar*, the second demand is to identify the condition of Israel at this time. Then, *if this is a time after Destruction*, the third demand is, in addition to whatever else he seeks to study, *also* to ask how these sources speak *to* Israel at such a time.

These sources speak to Halivni by drawing his attention to a series of narratives of Israel's life after Destruction that introduce a prototype for Israel's life after the Shoah. One, as noted earlier, is the biblical account of Ezra. Another is the biblical account of Moses' work after the Exodus, and another is the rabbinic account of the work of Rabbi Akiva and his peers after the Destruction of the Second Temple. Reading *between* the verses of all these accounts, Halivni perceives[7] a model for his own work of re-reading

---

[7] This kind of perception belongs to the category of what Charles Peirce calls 'abduction', or warranted hypothesis-formation.

the received texts of Talmud after the Shoah. Summarised very briefly, the model portrays Moses, Ezra, and R. Akiva as each participating in a religious and social renewal that also accompanies a major transformation in the hermeneutical axes of Judaism. According to the Talmudic account, for example, Ezra uses the textual and rhetorical tools of Persian-Jewish culture to re-teach the Written Torah that he receives out of the fires of destruction as something different in appearance from what his forebears saw before those fires. R. Akiva makes comparable use of Greco-Roman-Jewish literary technologies. Sharing in this pattern, Halivni adopts the historical-critical tools of European-Jewish scholarship to reform his religious community's received traditions of Oral Torah: reforming what he believes are both redactional maculations within the Talmud and hermeneutical maculations in rabbinic tradition as a whole. In this way, his depth reading of Ezra provides a vivid scriptural model for renewing and reforming the entire tradition of Written-and-Oral Torah after a time of terrible loss.

Some of Halivni's Orthodox colleagues contend that, by adopting academic historiography as an instrument of Jewish textual renewal, he has subjected rabbinic discourses to the methods of a non-Jewish culture. One of Halivni's responses is that the rabbinic sages appear to have done the same with the hermeneutical technologies of their time. Another response has been to criticise the efforts of ultra-Orthodox leaders to identify their own rabbinic rulings with 'the Oral Torah that was revealed to Moses on Sinai'. For Halivni, as noted earlier, these efforts at self-legitimation contradict the rabbis' fallibilism as well as their attentiveness to the demands of the day. According to a verse in Mishnah *Berachot*, 'this [time after Destruction] is a time to take emergency actions for the sake of God', which means a time to extend the work of interpreting Torah in ways previously unseen. For Halivni, the present time after Destruction is a time to extend the self-imposed limits of both poles of modern Jewish scholarship: the poles of plain-sense science and of ultra-Orthodox fideism.

A THIRD MODEL FOR THEOLOGICAL AND RELIGIOUS STUDIES AFTER MODERNITY

As a prototype for theological studies, Halivni's depth historiography suggests how, after modernity, the academic study of theology can participate confidently in the literary and historiographic sciences, while at the same time contributing confidently to the reformatory study of particular traditions of scriptural religion. This means that, on the one hand, tradition-based theologians should have no reason to feel threatened by plain-sense historiography. As long as they recognise marks of the human hand in their received traditions of textual commentary, then historical criticism provides a tool for separating those marks from the 'voice of Sinai' as they now hear it at this time and place. It means, on the other hand, that academic scholars of religion should have no reason to define the academy as 'off limits' to the study of particular traditions of theology. In Halivni's terms, scholars need only distinguish between 'depth historiography' and 'community specific theological work'. The latter belongs outside the academy, within communities that *test* the practical efficacy of depth historiographic claims. But the academy provides the appropriate place for *introducing* those claims as imaginative hypotheses about how the plain-sense evidence may or may not point beyond its boundaries.

Halivni's model thereby speaks, as well, to the relation between Theology and Religious Studies in the academy. In his terms, both Theology and Religious Studies would include plain-sense scholarship (historical, literary, and so on). Both would also foster imaginative reflection that pointed beyond the limits of the plain-sense studies. They would differ in the potential (but not immediate) uses of this reflection. Theology might offer its reflections as *potential* (or conceivable) contributions to the life of some set of religious communities, but abstracted as yet from any actual contribution of this kind. Religious Studies might offer its reflections independently of any such use, or as potential contributions to the prosecution of some other field of academic inquiry (semiotics, anthropology, history, and so on). So characterised, Theology and Religious Studies should enjoy a peaceful co-existence.

Many departments of religion, however, remain under the influence of the binary patterns of the modern study of religion. This means that they either house two warring sub-factions or promote only one. What approaches to religion might allow for more productive relations? The study of scripture after modernity suggests the following rules:

(1) Disallow the prosecution of either Theology or Religious Studies according to the modern models of either reductive science or exclusive orthodoxy.
(2) Protect the legitimacy of plain-sense studies of various kinds.
(3) But be sure that a department is not limited to only plain-sense studies. Protect the performance of depth studies.
(4) And maintain intellectual exchange and dialogue between plain-sense and depth studies on all levels.

We close with two viable and visible illustrations of how these rules may be enacted.

Religious Studies as comparative traditions

The study of comparative religion frequently serves as a flash point for conflict between binary models of Theology and Religious Studies. On the one side, one school of comparativists identifies religions as the variety of human responses to some extra-linguistic event of 'religious experience'. In this view, since religious experience lies outside of language, no scripturally based tradition has direct access to it, and all such traditions represent comparable efforts to construct beliefs and practices in response to a reality that lies beyond their ken. If there is no privileged religious construction, there is, nonetheless, a privileged practice of comparative religious studies. Phenomenology merits this status because it brings with it no presuppositions other than the primacy of experience and the capacity of humans (particularly after Kant) to exhume and compare the elementary categories of their own individual or collective constructions. On the other side, some scholars of theology argue that religions are simply incomparable. In this view, the truths of a religion are strictly internal to its particular discourse and history, and so-called 'comparative' studies represent only a form of colonialism: an effort to reduce all such discourses to the analytic terms of some socially dominant discourse.

Wary of either approach to comparative religion, the University of Virginia Department of Religious Studies has nurtured a third approach. The Department devotes most of its teaching to tradition-specific studies of the Abrahamic, Asian, and some African religions. Each tradition is studied, for the most part, in its indigenous terms, and most undergraduate and graduate students work in more than one tradition. While the Department also offers many courses in Western traditions of philosophic theology and the philosophy of religion, little comparative work is offered according to the 'religious experience' model discussed above. Instead, faculty members are beginning to develop a comparative approach that emerges out of dialogues among practitioners and scholars of the various traditions themselves. This approach begins with each tradition's claim to *house* the divinity's self-presentations within its own sacred literature. It invites students to examine *how* two or more traditions claim to read and interpret such self-presentations and then to compare patterns of reading and interpretation that may appear within or across the various traditions. These comparisons are to be tested against scholarly accounts of each tradition *and* against actual dialogues among practitioners of the several traditions. The Department has introduced a new graduate programme to foster the practice and study of such dialogues. Named 'Scripture,

Interpretation and Practice', the programme bases its central vision on the work of the Society for Scriptural Reasoning (SSR): an association of Jewish, Christian and Muslim scholars whose contribution to the study of comparative traditions emerges from ten years of dialogue in scriptural theology.

Theology as scriptural reasoning

The purpose of SSR has been to foster a 'third model' of academic scriptural theology that avoids the intellectual reductionism of strictly plain-sense studies of scripture as well as the religious reductionism of orthodox theologies that eschew the plain-sense sciences altogether. Members of the SSR have found that this purpose is best served by promoting circles of Jewish, Christian and Muslim text scholars and theologians who bring both their sciences and their faiths to the table while they engage together in extended periods of scriptural study. After examining text-historical studies of some set of Qur'anic and Biblical verses, each circle devotes two to three conferences a year (along with intervening email exchanges) to intense discussion of the theological force of these verses when placed in dialogue one with the other. The society labels the interpretive activity that emerges through this dialogue Abrahamic 'scriptural reasoning' (SR). SR refers to the patterns of reasoning which are prompted by faithful-and-scientific studies of all three scriptural traditions, which are disciplined by contemporary practices of hermeneutics, and which – as of this date – appear to be generating effective guidelines for the study of scripture, theology and comparative traditions after modernity. I will close this essay by illustrating a few of these guidelines. This sampling is drawn from the work in progress of the Scriptural Reasoning Theory Group, an SR circle sponsored by the Cambridge University Faculty of Theology:[8]

(1) Study is a group as well as an individual activity. Good scholars display social as well as strictly intellectual virtues. These include extending hospitality to fellow learners, listening, and speaking to the heart as well as the mind.

(2) The primary intellectual virtue is reading well.[9] Group study should focus, first, on a religion's primary scriptural sources, as they appear

[8] This listing is stimulated by the work of the Jewish philosopher/theologian Steven Kepnes, who is currently composing 'A Handbook of Scriptural Reasoning'. Kepnes is a member of the SR Theory Group.

[9] And also observing well. In this essay, we are examining the study of scriptural traditions, but the Third Model could also be applied to the comparative study of non-textual religious practices, in which case we might speak more generally of 'observation' and not only 'reading'.

to have been received by their early reception communities and as they are scrutinised by text-historical scholars. Group study should focus, secondly, on the ways these sources are received by contemporary communities of practitioners.

(3) Group study should address at least two different scriptural sources and scriptural traditions. After introductory instruction by specialists and representatives of each tradition, all scholars/students should contribute equally to the work of discussing and interpreting all of the sources. This work should move gradually through all appropriate levels of study: from philological, semantic and rhetorical studies, to intra-scriptural readings, to comparative interpretations of the source texts' societal, ethical and theological implications.

(4) Comparative interpretations should be stimulated by a range of interests: from formal studies of hermeneutical and narrative patterns, to ethical and theological dialogue among the traditions studied, to the implications of such studies for addressing contemporary intellectual and societal debates.

CHAPTER 8

Worship

Eamon Duffy

I want in this chapter to explore the relationship between history, theology, and Christian practice in worship. I want to do this not by way of generalisation, but by scrutinising the mythopaic power of a particular reading of Christian history and its impact on theology, and, more especially, the way in which one such exercise of the historical imagination actually served within twentieth-century Roman Catholicism to reshape the fundamental and constitutive act of the Christian community, the celebration of the liturgy. In the process, I hope I will illuminate something more general about the interaction between theology, liturgy and history so as to contribute to the overall theme of this book about the nature of our discipline, in honour of Nicholas Lash.

Specifically, I want to consider the seminal work of the Austrian Jesuit liturgical scholar, Josef Andreas Jungmann. Jungmann spent a lifetime teaching at the University of Innsbruck, but he also played a key role in the establishment of anglophone liturgical scholarship at Notre Dame. He was a key player in the series of international congresses on Liturgical Studies which throughout the 1950s prepared the ground for the liturgical revolution inaugurated by Vatican II. Above all, he was one of the principal draughtsmen of *Sacrosanctum Concilium*, Vatican II's momentous constitution on the liturgy, and subsequently wrote the official commentary on it. As a scholar, he is best known for his magisterial study, *Missarum Sollemnia*,[1] in its thousand-page English version entitled *The Mass of the Roman Rite, its origins and development*, first published in 1948, and generally recognised as the most authoritative single study of the origins and evolution of the Roman Mass.[2]

---

[1] Josef A. Jungmann, *Missarum Sollemnia. Eine genetische Erklärung der römischen Messe* (Vienna: Herder, 1949).

[2] *The Mass of the Roman Rite: its origins and development* (2 vols; New York: Benzinger, 1951–5). On Jungmann more generally, including a bibliography of his writings, see Joanne M. Pierce and Michael Downey, eds., *Source and Summit: Commemorating Joseph Jungmann SJ* (Collegeville, MI: Liturgical Press, 1999).

As all this suggests, Jungmann's influence on the shape of modern Roman Catholic worship was enormous, and it was rooted in wide and deep historical scholarship. That of course meant that it was rooted in a *particular* set of historical constructions: the historian does not neutrally stumble over evidence and in the process uncover the buried outlines of the past. The writing of history is an imaginative act involving intuition and hypothesis as well as patient documentary scrutiny. Jungmann was a great and formidably learned historian: yet, as is well known, not all his historical intuitions have turned out to be 100 per cent sound. One of the most familiar ceremonies of the post-conciliar Roman Rite is the offertory procession, in which lay people bring the eucharistic elements to the altar as an expression of the congregation's involvement and self-offering in the eucharistic sacrifice. We owe the prominence of this ceremony in the new Roman Mass, essentially, to Jungmann, who was convinced that such a procession had been an important feature of the primitive Roman Rite, and of the great Eastern liturgies, but one which had been allowed to atrophy as part of the medieval clericalising of the liturgy. It now appears, however, that he was utterly mistaken in this supposition, and that there is in fact no warrant for supposing that an offertory procession of this sort was ever a feature of the Roman Mass. Its honoured place in the modern liturgy therefore may, and no doubt does, make perfectly good liturgical sense, but its historical warrant appears to be a simple case of scholarly guesswork running ahead of the evidence.

That is an example of a mistake over a simple matter of fact. The historical errors that matter, however, are rarely simply about facts, but about a take on facts. In what follows I want to suggest more seriously that, for all its profundity and power, central aspects of Jungmann's account of the Christian past are in many respects just as problematic. I want to argue that his account of the history of liturgy, for all its scholarship, was in crucial respects tendentious or at any rate simplistic, and that as a consequence Jungmann inadvertently contributed to a sense of alienation and dislocation within the doctrinal and liturgical tradition of Catholic Christianity which is deeply troubling, and which has had devastating effects on Catholic apprehension of the meaning and value of tradition. And since the liturgy is the principal vehicle for the transmission of the tradition, this is a serious matter, which takes us to the heart of questions about the nature – what liberal Protestants used to call the essence – of Christianity itself.

I shall focus my discussion on Jungmann's seminal essay 'The defeat of Teutonic Arianism and the Revolution in Religious Culture in the early Middle Ages'. This lengthy piece, 100 pages in its English version, first appeared in the *Zeitschrift für katholische Theologie* in 1947, but it was republished on the eve of the momentous debates on the Liturgy at the Second Vatican Council in 1960, as the first essay in Jungmann's enormously influential *Liturgisches Erbe und pastorale Gegenwart*, a 1960 collection badly translated into English as *Pastoral Liturgy* in 1962.[3] The article, which I shall call for short 'Teutonic Arianism', has been widely recognised as Jungmann's most important single essay, a position-paper encapsulating the essence of his life's work, and a powerful manifesto for the Conciliar and post-Conciliar transformation of the liturgy in which he was to play so central a role. A recent American *Festschrift* commemorating the twenty-fifth anniversary of his death was in fact structured around discussion of 'Teutonic Arianism' as its point of reference.[4]

It is not hard to see why. Jungmann's essay is a historical tour de force, a whistle-stop survey of the whole course of Christian history in the West, which he seeks to illuminate by the application of a single hypothesis. That hypothesis is essentially a primitivist tale of ancient kerygmatic and liturgical purity regrettably overlaid by the Church's unavoidable but distorting preoccupation with the refutation of heresy. The heresy in question is the Teutonic Arianism of the essay's title, reaction to which Jungmann saw as the decisive element in shaping the theological context, ethos and configuration of worship in the West from the fourth down to the nineteenth centuries. His story is structured round a series of contrasts. According to Jungmann, the early Christian liturgy was essentially corporate public worship, '[i]n which the people's Amen resounds, as St Jerome tells us, like a peal of heavenly thunder'. There was in early Christianity a close connection between the people and the altar, and the clergy spoke and acted not as a discrete guild, but for and to the people. Christian worship was informed by a sense of the high Christian dignity of the baptised, and accordingly universal lay communion formed the climax of every celebration of the Mass. By contrast, the liturgy in the Middle Ages and Baroque period became a clerical preserve. The people, whose primary religious sense now was of their own sinful unworthiness, were silenced and reduced to the role of spectators, the Mysteries were veiled from a community conceived of as profane, and lay communion became a rarity.

The exclusion of the laity, Jungmann believed, was matched by or rather was the outcome of a corresponding theological decline. The early liturgy, he argued, was dominated by the Easter motif, indeed at first Easter was the Church's only feast. The liturgy was understood as a sacramental renewal

[3] Josef A. Jungmann, *Pastoral Liturgy* (New York: Herder and Herder, 1962).
[4] Pierce and Downey, eds., *Source and Summit*, esp. pp. 7–20.

of and entry into Christ's mediatorial work, the worshipping Church's participation in the triumph of the Church's head and high priest, who is most characteristically depicted in early Christian liturgical art as the risen and ascended Lord, his humanity as youthful and perfect. By the end of the Middle Ages, by contrast, the Easter theme has been overlaid not merely by the ever-growing dominance of Christmas and the festivals of the saints, but above all by the all-absorbing thought of the suffering and death of Christ. The Paschal and eschatological character of the Eucharist has been forgotten, and it is no longer celebrated in front of images of the ascended Lord, but of the crucifix, on which Christ hangs defeated and dead. Christian piety has become historically bound, essentially commemorative, and the liturgical entry into the redeeming and transforming power of the priestly work of Christ has given way to the subjective devotional recollection of past, completed action, as a motive for present behaviour. Moralism and exhortation ousted the eschaton. As Jungmann wrote: 'in the early period mystery predominates – the world of grace, what is objective and corporate: in the Middle Ages the emphasis is laid more and more upon human action and moral accomplishment, upon what is subjective and individual.'

The motive force for this transformation, according to Jungmann, was a desire to refute the Arianism which was the religion of the Teutonic tribes who dominated the Church in the West from the end of antiquity into the high Middle Ages. Spain was the principal focus of this struggle, for in Spain the Arian debates reverberated longer than anywhere else, into the sixth century. Because of the crucial role of Spain in the formation of early medieval theology, in particular the impact of Spanish theology and liturgical texts in the Frankish church, the 'bellicose' preoccupation of Spanish Christianity with the refutation of Arianism left a permanent mark on the Christianity of the medieval West, long after the Arianism which had elicited it had been forgotten. Against the Arian demotion of Christ to the status of a creature, the Church insisted on exalting him ever higher within the Godhead. The figure of Christ is increasingly absorbed into the Trinity, a Trinity no longer conceived in economic terms and as the source of the dynamic of salvation and the experience of the Church, but abstracted and absolutised. Accordingly prayer is increasingly offered to Christ, rather than through him: he rather than the Father becomes the object of liturgical address. His ascended humanity continues to be confessed, but is identified now simply with the divine nature. It recedes from us and from the liturgy, and his high-priestly and mediatorial role is forgotten or obscured. A tension arises in the Church's perception of Christ: as his divinity is increasingly stressed, his humanity is indeed revered, but is increasingly conceived not as glorious and triumphant, but as wounded and weak. The medieval Church sees the humanity of Christ as it suffered on Calvary, an object of compassion and a trigger for emotion – amazement, sorrow, thanksgiving, repentance . Even the resurrection and ascension are accommodated to the master-theme of the passion – as Jungmann wrote, 'they bear more the character of vanquished suffering than the beginning of glory'. Thus the central icon of the Middle Ages is not the gloriously exalted manhood of our great high priest, the first-fruits of them that sleep and the beginning of the new creation, but the crucifix, the dead Christ, God made visible so that he might also be made vulnerable.

The consequence, Jungmann thought, was the disappearance of the conception of the Church as the Body of Christ.

For Christ can only be described as Head of the Church in his glorified humanity. It is only of his humanity that the faithful can become members through baptism, so that they form one Body with him, that they indeed corporately become his body. It is well-known how little the thought of the Church as the Body of Christ flourished in the Middle Ages.

Jungmann saw this collapse of a sense of the corporate reflected in the very nature of Gothic architecture and art. The house of God, he wrote, 'begins to be split up into a multitude of chapels, in which the separate guilds, separate families even, have their own guild or family altar and their own worship'. That collapse into privatisation was, he thought, equally visible in the 'monstrous elaboration' of the liturgies of the late Middle Ages, which, however, lacking a sense of the liturgy as the means of participation in the whole Paschal mystery, had diminished to mere external activity carried out to prescribed rules. 'Indeed, we might well say that it had become a lifeless civil act.' He sees ironic significance in the fact that it was in 1517, the year of the outbreak of the Protestant Reformation, that the Papacy finally put the capstone on this privatising and evacuation of the communal dimension of the liturgy by conceding that the faithful might fulfil their Sunday obligation by attending any Mass, in place of the main parish liturgy.

I hope my very compressed account of Jungmann's essay conveys some sense of its remarkable sweep and force. He did not of course *invent* his argument: it is a massively learned piece of work, which draws heavily on the writings of others, among them Ildefons Herwegen, the influential abbot of that great power-house of the German Liturgical Movement, the monastery of Maria Laach, and the argument was widely shared by other liturgists: a similar account, for example, informs Gregory Dix's *The Shape of the Liturgy.*[5] Indeed, in many ways the importance of Jungmann's essay lies not so much in its originality, but in the fact that it encapsulates a powerful reading of the Christian past which had already or was about to become the received version among most protagonists of the liturgical movement. *Mutatis mutandi*, it is also the view of the Christian past which informed the *Nouvelle Théologie*, and similar historical constructs underlie the theological work of Congar and others.

And the construct was, of course, designed to be a platform for specific action. As he wrote in the preface to his enormously influential *The Early Liturgy to the time of Gregory the Great*, 'History is a precious corrective of mere speculation, of subjective hypothesis. True knowledge of our present liturgy is knowledge based on the solid rock of historical facts; it is by studying the past that we can best learn how to shape the future.'[6]

If the liturgy had become historicised and rubricised, if it had lost hold of the ascended humanity of our great high priest and become trapped in a lugubrious devotionalism, if it had ceased to mediate to the laity a sense of active participation in the risen life of Christ and their own baptismal dignity, then all that must be changed. The restoration of the vernacular, the simplification of rites by the removal of medieval elaboration, the reordering of churches round a single altar, the revision of all the texts of the liturgy to restore a sense of the Christian life as participation in the trinitarian economy, the redirection of Christian worship so that it was clearly offered to the Father through the Son in the Spirit, were all implicit in Jungmann's essay. And, within fifteen years of the appearance of the essay in volume form, all these reforms had been achieved, at least in principle, in the *Missa Normativa*. Rarely has an elaborate historical argument played so spectacularly direct a role in restructuring the fundamental framework of Christian experience.

But we need to note at once some remarkable and a few disturbing features of Jungmann's argument. The first and worst of these is the heavy racial essentialism which underlies it: among the elements he borrowed from the school of Maria Laach was the notion that there was a distinct and abiding Germanic spirit which found permanent theological expression in medieval Catholic theology. The Teutonic peoples were 'caught up in a vortex of becoming rather than in the classical sense of being',[7] and this

---

[5] Gregory Dix, *The Shape of the Liturgy* (London: A&C. Black, 1945).

[6] Josef A. Jungmann, *The Early Liturgy to the Time of Gregory the Great* (London: Darton, Longman and Todd, 1959), p. 8.

[7] The words are Regis Duffy's, in 'Lands rich in wine and oil': culture and conversion', in Pierce and Downey, eds., *Source and Summit*, p. 244.

cultural and ethnic distinctiveness he thought had decisively shaped the whole of Western theology. In some senses, his essay is therefore conceived as an exploration of the struggle between the Roman and German races. Jungmann was writing in 1947, and drawing on writings which issued from Maria Laach before the First World War. I think I need not labour the problematic character of such an emphasis on race for a modern historical analysis. But in any case, Jungmann's account of the nature of the conversion of the Germanic peoples and his pessimistic conviction of the centrality of a residual Arianism within it can be challenged on purely historical grounds: what he saw as the adaptation of Christianity to pagan and heretical German ways of thinking – a process which involved compromise and distortion – is just as plausibly understood as a far more organic process of inculturation, not a distortion but the legitimate expression of the Christian faith within Germanic culture.

This is not the place to explore the minutiae of that particular debate: it does however alert us to the radical pessimism of Jungmann's theological analysis. The argument of 'Teutonic Arianism' turns on the central contention that, almost from the beginning, the embodiment of the authentic Christian message in liturgy was not merely shaped but distorted by the struggle with heresy. Jungmann seems to privilege the Christianity of the first three centuries: after the conflict with Arianism begins, however, its successive cultural expressions become increasingly off-beam. In the process, the content of the liturgical *kerygma* is contaminated. The ills of the liturgy spring, in a word, from a defective Christology, itself the product of a set of overemphases devised as correctives to heresy.

These are remarkable contentions for a conservative Austrian Jesuit in Pius XII's church. Jungmann was at some pains to distance himself from any notion that he was offering a fundamental doctrinal critique – he repeatedly insisted that these distortions were matters of ethos, style, emphasis, which never amounted to deviations from the faith. Yet these protestations do nothing to soften the devastatingly wholesale character of his critique of the liturgical tradition, and his fundamental analysis does not seem to me very different from that offered in the historical work of liberal Protestants like Harnack, and, behind Harnack, the liturgical and institutional historians of the Enlightenment. On this account, the history of Christianity is a history of decline and progressive misunderstanding.

In Jungmann's hands, it is in essence a primitivist argument, designed to buttress a call for a return to ancient purities, which, by peeling away accretion and elaboration, will reveal and restore the authentic lineaments of Christ's mediatorial work and its application in the work of the liturgy.

Just how deep-seated this degenerate vision of Christian history was in Jungmann's writing can be seen from a revealing passage at the beginning of his book *The Early Liturgy* which makes his assumptions explicit:

The Liturgy of the Catholic Church is an edifice in which we are still living today, and in essentials it is still the same building in which Christians were already living ten or fifteen or even eighteen and more centuries ago. In the course of all those centuries the structure has become more and more complicated, with constant remodellings and additions, and the plan of the building has been obscured – so much so that we may no longer feel at home in it because we no longer understand it. Hence we must look up the building plans, for these will tell us what the architects of old really wanted, and if we grasp their intentions we shall learn to appreciate much that the building contains and even to esteem it more highly. And if we should have the opportunity to make changes in the structure or to adapt it to the needs of our own people, we shall then do so in such a way that, where possible, nothing of the precious heritage of the past is lost.[8]

Jungmann's use of an architectural metaphor here – the liturgy as a noble building whose ground-plan and aesthetic logic have been disguised and deformed by later accretion – determines the logical outcome of his argument – the need for a restoration which clears away later development. Had he chosen an organic metaphor – the liturgy as a plant or animal which grows to maturity – the rhetorical direction of his argument would be reversed. Jungmann, however, hoped that the liturgical movement would not merely explore and explain the riches of the liturgy, but would provide the expertise and rationale for a far-reaching revision and reform, involving the 'restoration' of the original or primitive purity of the Roman Rite, freeing it from later accretions and corruptions which had obscured its real nature, and which mean that 'we no longer feel at home' in the liturgy. He was certainly sincere in his declared intention to preserve entire 'the precious heritage of the past', but he had very clear and, as it turned out, quite limited notions of just what constituted 'precious heritage', as opposed to accretion and debasement.

I shall return to that issue in a moment: but first I want to register the fact that key elements in Jungmann's historical analysis are open to serious question. For a late-medievalist like myself, one of the most glaring of these is Jungmann's negative assessment of the character of late medieval religious life. Jungmann was writing in the age of Josef Lortz and Hubert Jedin, an age in which, for the first time, major Catholic historians were effectively conceding the Protestant case for the decadence of late medieval Christianity, and, in so doing, accepting their analysis of the roots of the Reformation.

[8] Jungmann, *Early Liturgy*, p. 2.

This was, no doubt, a major step forward in the ecumenical movement, and an advance on the vulgar slanging match that passed for Reformation debate in earlier ages: it is rather less certain that it advanced the cause of historical understanding very much. Jungmann's section on the liturgical life of the late medieval Church simultaneously recognises its apparent abundance and vitality, and offers a devastatingly negative account of its religious worth as hectic, overblown, and spiritually vacuous – 'a mighty façade, and behind it – a great emptiness'.[9] Jungmann was convinced that the eucharistic faith of the late medieval Church had narrowed to a preoccupation with sacrifice and presence: the Church had lost hold of the fact that the celebration of the eucharist is what constitutes the Church: the body of Christ is not simply or even primarily the thing which lies on the altar, but the union of head and members joined in the celebration of the heavenly and earthly liturgies. He therefore reiterates the notion that '[i]t is well-known how little the thought of the Church as the Body of Christ flourished in the Middle Ages', and for confirmation of this produces a round-up of the usual suspects – the individualism of the German mystics, the non-ecclesial character of movements like the *Devotio Moderna*, and the fissiparous character of late medieval religious organisation, where, as he sees it, sectional interests like guilds challenge or erode the fundamental unity of the parish.

Though there are still some historians who would accept Jungmann's account, they are a good deal thinner on the ground than they used to be, and I believe this aspect of his analysis to rest on a fundamental misunderstanding of late medieval Christianity. It is extremely misleading – and unhelpfully elitist – to deduce the character of the Christianity of that era from the distinctive characteristics of unrepresentative movements like the *Devotio Moderna*, but in any case I think Jungmann takes a superficial, and unnecessarily negative, view of the religion of the laity and non-elite clergy on the eve of the Reformation. I have set out my critique of this aspect of Jungmann's writing elsewhere.[10] I can only indicate here the main thrust of that criticism. Examination of the actual practice of late medieval eucharistic piety demonstrates that late medieval Christians understood perfectly well the social character of the eucharist, and the interaction between the eucharistic elements and the creation and maintenance of charity and justice in the community . An instance here is the famous account of the Corpus Christi Day riots at St Alban's Abbey in 1381, during the Peasants' Revolt.

---

[9] Jungmann, 'Teutonic Arianism', p. 78.
[10] Eamon Duffy, 'Lay appropriation of the sacraments in the late middle ages', in G. Turner and J. Sullivan, eds., *Explorations in Catholic Theology* (Dublin: Veritus Publications, 1999), pp. 209–32.

The abbots of St Albans had established a monopoly on the milling of flour locally, forcing the commons to get their flour from the Abbey mills, and in a naked assertion of power had confiscated the millstones from privately owned mills and floored the monastery parlour with them. The commons broke into the Abbey on Corpus Christi day, dug up a circular millstone, and, in a parody of the distribution of holy bread at the end of the Mass, broke up the stone and distributed it as a token of the restoration of right order in the community. This symbolic action drew heavily on lay experience of eucharistic and para-liturgical ceremonies, and seems to me an overwhelmingly eloquent example of a profound and sound eucharistic theology which is manifestly not exhausted or dominated by the themes of presence and sacrifice.

Moreover, Jungmann's insistence that the Gothic church, with its transepts, aisle and side-chapels, reveals a fractured community, begs the very question it purports to address, and bears the marks, if not of the totalitarian age in which he was writing, at least of the Enlightenment search for a unified social order. It will certainly not stand up to close examination of the way in which late medieval religious buildings, with their corals and enclaves of the semi-private as well as their shared spaces, actually worked. That there were privatising tendencies in late medieval Christianity is certain, but anyone who has studied the parish communities of pre-Reformation England must be struck by the extent to which private interests, like those of local elite families, or the guilds, were in fact woven into and accommodated by the collective life of the wider community . The work of a historian like Clive Burgess on the city of Bristol, for example, has demonstrated how the concern for personal salvation, and for the display of conspicuous wealth, certainly ministered to private ambitions and the desire for prominence, but simultaneously fostered a huge growth in the provision of corporate religious services understood as benefiting both the provider and her immediate family, and the wider community, with little or no sense of opposition or contradiction between these interests.[11] The late medieval Church recognised the reality of social complexity, the presence within the community of tensions and competitive forces: in giving religious expression to such sub-groups within the single overarching reality of the faith, however, it did not in any straightforward sense perpetuate division, but performed what John Bossy has called 'the social miracle',[12] holding together what otherwise might have

---

[11] Clive Burgess, ' "For the increase of Divine Service": Chantries in the Parish in late medieval Bristol', *Journal of Ecclesiastical History* 36 (1985), pp. 48–65.
[12] Bossy's views are best expounded in his *Christianity in the West 1400–1700* (Oxford: Oxford University Press, 1985).

broken apart. In fact the attempts of both reformers and counter-reformers from the sixteenth century onwards to weld the diversities of late medieval communities into a single unit regimented round the parish altar or the parish pulpit – a development Jungmann would certainly have approved – is viewed by John Bossy as an authoritarian and secularising move, which contributed to the exclusion of the social reality of the people from the formal and symbolic structures of the Church, and thereby contributed to the process of alienation from them which we call secularisation. On this reading the diversities of late medieval sub- or supra-parochial organisations and liturgical opportunities, the Gothic complexity Jungmann saw as decadence, should not be seen as denials of community, but rather as the form in which the matching complexities of community were organised, ritualised and recognised: they do not fragment but articulate the social order of the late medieval Church. There is a direct analogy here with John Milbank's argument about the nature of 'complex space' in Christian social teaching. Milbank defends 'gothic complexity' over against 'enlightenment simple space' because he perceives Gothic, in this sense, not, as Jungmann does, as an instance of the Germanic negation of true liturgical community, but as the expression of a genuinely organic understanding of the nature of community.[13]

Jungmann's pessimistic account of the condition of late medieval religion need not, then, be taken at face value. But there is more at stake here than this or that mistaken emphasis, a matter of getting the facts wrong or out of focus. The whole structure of Jungmann's analysis, and the remedial course of action which flows from it, turns on the assumption and assertion of a radical process of 'kerygmatic distortion' over a millennium and a half of Christian preaching and praying. He is at pains, it is true, to make it clear that he does not consider that the tradition had lapsed into heresy – as he says at one point, discussing the lavish use of the *communicatio idiomatum* that permitted medieval Christians to talk of God being born of the Virgin or dying on the Cross, 'no one is going to see dogmatic error in such phraseology'. Nevertheless, Jungmann argues for a radical and persistent distortion within the tradition arising from the 'popular simplification of the Christian message, accommodated to the primitive spirituality of these people and their less than sketchy instruction'.[14] As a consequence, he views medieval Christian worship as essentially adrift. 'What remains firm,' he wrote, 'is on the fringe. To begin with faith is not disturbed, but the things men are living by are fragments of faith, peripheral things.'[15]

[13] John Milbank, 'On Complex Space', in *The Word Made Strange* (Oxford: 1977), pp. 268–92.
[14] Jungmann, 'Teutonic Arianism', pp. 41, 43. [15] Ibid., p. 79.

There are many reasons why I think so pessimistic a reading of the unfolding of the Western medieval Christian tradition, as a steady drift away from the centre to the periphery, should be rejected, not least that it is so wholesale. If Jungmann is right, mainstream Christianity was on a downward slope from the outbreak of the Arian controversy onwards. But we can see some of the flaws in his analysis more clearly if we go to the heart of it, and consider what he has to say about the liturgy as an expression of the Easter faith, and, in particular, if we consider what he has to say about the role of art in the liturgy.

For Jungmann, what characterises the church art of the early Church, and gives it paradigmatic authority for later ages, is its firm grasp on the resurrection: in early Christian basilicas Christ is portrayed in the fullness of his completed work, standing or enthroned among the apostles or the four living creatures, emphatically the Christ of Easter, Resurrection, Pentecost and final consummation – as he is to be seen in the apse mosaics at San Cosmo e Damiano or Santa Prassede in Rome, or in San Vitale in Ravenna. And by contrast:

there are no representations of the Crucifixion in the ancient churches . . . the Cross, yes, but in stylised form as the Cross of glory, the tropaion as a victory sign erected after the victory . . . The Cross is the King's throne; instead of the thorns there is a kingly crown on his head; the linen cloth has become a regal robe; at his feet the Church looks up, full of trust, while the synagogue turns away in shame [sic!].

Thus, in ancient Christianity 'the basic redemptive fact, the Easter fact, was present to the Christian mind in a different, much more intense way, and this arose out of the liturgy'.[16] Correspondingly, Jungmann views the liturgical emergence of the crucifix, on which Christ is portrayed as suffering or dead, as part of the descent into subjectivity and individualism which characterises the Middle Ages, and as a slackening of the Church's grasp on the Easter fact: behind such realism lies a decline from the passion as redemptive mystery to the passion as sad story.

Anyone who went to the millennium 'Seeing Salvation' exhibition at the National Gallery in 2000,[17] and who noticed the overwhelmingly passive and suffering character of the person of Christ in work after work in that exhibition, will recognise that Jungmann is right in identifying a profound transformation of Christian representations of the person of Christ in the course of the Middle Ages. But there are many reasons why I think we

---

[16] Jungmann, *Pastoral Liturgy*, pp. 361–2, an expansion of his remarks in 'Teutonic Arianism'.
[17] The catalogue of the exhibition was published as Gabrielli Finaldi, ed., *The Image of Christ* (London: National Gallery Company Ltd, 2000).

should resist Jungmann's account of this process of change as a whole as one of decline into subjectivity. For a start, the emergence of the Gothic crucifix certainly cannot be accommodated within a hypothesis about the triumph of Teutonic Arianism: representations of the cross with the dead Christ were not the product of Germanisation, but came to the West from Byzantium. But quite apart from any questions of provenance and origin, can we really accept the simplistic view that triumphant images of the crucified are necessarily more authentic expressions of the Easter fact and Easter faith than representations of the suffering of the Cross? This is not a question that can or ought to be considered in the abstract: so the point may be made by reference to some famous images, a series of crucifixes, all northern Italian, and painted within a hundred miles and a hundred years of one another. The first is the Romanesque crucifix of the twelfth century presently displayed in the basilica of Santa Chiara in Assisi, formerly in the church of San Damiano: this is the crucifix which is supposed to have spoken to Francis and told him 'rebuild my church, which as you see is in ruins'.[18] This crucifix conforms to most of Jungmann's criteria for correct liturgical representation of the Easter mystery. Christ is portrayed on it emitting streams of water and blood from his side wound – which of course happened after his death, according to John: but his eyes are open, gazing into a future which he commands, and he stands tranquil and untroubled, his arms open to embrace. Details of the Johannine passion narrative in particular are alluded to in the group of witnesses gathered under his outstretched arms, but he is also surrounded by angels, and in a mandorla above his head is a representation of his triumphant ascension to heaven, blessed by the hand of God above. Here is an unequivocal expression of the Easter mystery.

Consider by contrast the marvellous crucifix by an anonymous Umbrian master of 1260s or 1270s, kept in the treasury of the Basilica of St Francis at Assisi.[19] We are here in a different world, of mourning, lamentation and woe. The body of the crucified hangs, gracefully certainly, but equally certainly mortally: his head sags on his right shoulder, his eyes are closed in death. Crucifixes of this sort often had an upper terminal disc with an image of *Christos pantocrator*, an allusion to the paschal victory, but even where they are present they do not, I think, outweigh the overwhelming

---

[18] Rona Goffen, *Spirituality in Conflict: Saint Francis and Giotto's Bardi Chapel* (Pennsylvania: Pennsylvania State University Press, 1988), fig. 20: web image available at http://san-francesco.org/santachiara/crocifisso_eng.html.

[19] Reproduced in G. Morello and L. B. Kanter, *The Treasury of St Francis of Assisi* (Milan: Electa, 1999), p. 61. Available as a web image at http://www.artnet.com/magazine_pre2000/reviews/stern/stern4-19-1.asp.

impact of this type of crucifix's emphasis on the death of the crucified. We have here still an image from the Johannine crucifixion narrative: Mary and John stand on either side in the left and right terminals, Mary wrapped in the grief which formed the theme of many of the most characteristic devotional texts of the Middle Ages, such as the *Stabat Mater*, while the beloved disciple stands in the sorrowing contemplation of the mystery from which his Gospel will issue. The characteristics of this poignant work are developed further in the even more marvellous crucifix Cimabue painted for Santa Croce in Florence, and which was ruined in the floods of 1966, or in the wonderful Rimini crucifix painted by the young Giotto.[20]

In these crucifixes the humanisation of the crucified has progressed even further, accentuated by the transparent loincloth derived from eleventh- and twelfth-century Byzantine representations, and which seem to have been designed to emphasise the incarnate humanity of the Logos. These great works can stand as emblems of a whole world of imagery: they become the current coin of liturgical representation, and established the crucifix type which still dominates Western iconography, almost a millennium on.

It is of course a value judgement, but it seems to me that any one of these latter representations of the dead Christ is incomparably more eloquent than the San Damiano crucifix, and, although I think Jungmann would have considered the Romanesque cross more correct and liturgically satisfactory, I doubt if he would have disagreed about which of these crucifixes is the greater work of art. But I would want to press this issue, beyond taste to theology, and to insist that the comparison does more than establish a hierarchy of artistic worth. Could we not also argue that there is a *theological* depth to these Gothic crucifixes which is lacking in the more tranquil and affirmative Romanesque representation? It is, it seems to me, naïve and simplistic to assume that the depiction of Christ as dead and defeated obscures the Paschal mystery: rather, it acknowledges and gives expression to aspects of it which resonate with universal human experience of death and diminishment. The Paschal mystery is present here precisely in the depiction of the sleep of the second Adam, from whose side pours water and blood, and from whose heart is born the Church, prefigured in the sorrowing mother who is Israel and the woman of the Apocalypse as well as the historical Mary, and in the beloved disciple, archetypical witness of the contradictory glorification of the Son of Man in death. Jungmann saw in such emotive imagery a symptom of a decline into subjectivity:

---

[20] The pre-flood image at Santa Croce is available as a web image, at http://www.kfki.hu/~arthp/ html/c/cimabue/crucifix/index.html. For Giotto's Rimini crucifix, http://www.artchive.com/ artchive/G/giotto/giotto_crucifix.jpg.html.

might we not with at least equal plausibility argue that what we witness in this development of the crucifix is an incalculable gain in depth and resonance, as the universal human experience of suffering and death is more firmly located in the heart of the redeemer's work? A eucharist celebrated before such an image, it seems to me, is not less but more deeply Christian; in it the Easter faith is differently but just as profoundly figured forth.

One could go on indefinitely testing the viability of Jungmann's argument against the concreteness of other medieval liturgical art. The people of thirteenth-century Siena took Duccio's *Maesta*, surrounded and backed as it is with representations of Christ's passion, and set it above the main altar of their cathedral. According to Jungmann, the Church of the thirteenth century, preoccupied with the theology of presence, did not properly understand the constitutive relationship between the celebration of the eucharistic Corpus Christi and the experience of the social Corpus Christi: yet how could one have a more overwhelming representation than this of the incarnation as the constituting element of the community of the redeemed? Jungmann saw the growing emphasis on the incarnation and infancy of Christ as in some sense a deflection from the centrality of the paschal mystery: Duccio's great altarpiece, it seems to me, silences that sort of analytic oversimplification.

This is more than just an attempt to rescue later medieval art for the liturgy. If the point I have been pressing here has any weight, it seems to me to count against Jungmann's whole argumentative strategy: his narrative of the progressive diversion of Christian worship and Christian profession from the primitive mainstream, under the pressure of heresy, collapses; the story we tell is not one of progressive deterioration and complication, to be rectified by a recovery of primitive emphases and simplicities. Instead, the evolution of Christian worship and Christian doctrine can be viewed more tranquilly as a legitimate process of acculturation, the gathering of new emphases and deepening nuances as the mystery of the incarnation unfolds itself in time. Or, to express the matter in less pietistic terms: it is not clear to me why we should privilege the very earliest cultural expressions of Christianity over its later stages.

Yet precisely such a privileging of the supposed primitive essential features, '*das Wesentliche*', of the Roman liturgy, in fact determined the shape of the reforms of the Catholic Mass and other rites implemented after the Vatican Council, and ensured that that reform would take the form of a stripping down and reduction towards a supposed earlier simplicity. The thrust of Jungmann's argument, that is, required the enactment of a dislocation within the tradition, seeking contact with deep tradition by breaking with recent tradition – which in some cases meant not merely the critique but the repudiation of centuries of liturgical praxis. History here was being used not as a delicate scalpel, tracing the successive elaborations of tradition, but as a bulldozer, ripping away more than a millennium of development in pursuit of foundations.

The gains from this process, in terms of greater intelligibility and active involvement, I do not doubt and need no underlining, but they were undoubtedly achieved at a cultural cost which it will take generations properly to assess. My point here is that in a community which understands itself as shaped and constituted by the perpetually renewed enactment of the tradition – for what else is the gathering of the Church but the recitation of the institution narrative of the Mass? – in such a community so radical a break with recent tradition – even when carried out in the name of deep tradition, maybe most of all when carried out for that reason – constitutes a problem.

All of which amounts to a cautionary tale, I suppose, about just how careful we have to be in pressing history into the service of theology. Jungmann of course never doubted that '*das Wesentliche*', the essence of the Roman Rite, had never been lost, but had persisted under the accretions of the Gothic and Baroque ages. He was no iconoclast, and his last publications reveal an alarm at the iconoclastic direction that much liturgical reform was actually taking in the 1970s. The effect of his critique, however, was to locate the essence of that rite in its earliest expressions, not in its historical unfolding. The defects or at any rate the presuppositions of this primitivist historical method are visible now, I think, because of a change in the way in which historical theology is practised nowadays: we are less eager to tell cautionary tales, and religious historians work less often to the Enlightenment agenda, so strong in the Jansenist liturgical reformers of the seventeenth and eighteenth centuries who were in many respects Jungmann's ancestors, of recovering ancient treasures or unmasking ancient errors from beneath the rubbish and detritus of more recent times. Perhaps one of the benefits of post-modernity is a stronger sense of the immediacy to us of the whole tradition, the conviction that we can engage fruitfully not only with the most remote, but with the whole of the, Christian past.

Section 2: The Practice of Justice and Love

CHAPTER 9

Argument

Nicholas Adams

INTRODUCTION

This essay contributes to what Nicholas Lash calls 'meetings on mutual ground' by looking at one of the practices that is shared across the various disciplines in Theology and Religious Studies: arguing. Arguing takes its place alongside other basic practices like describing or entering into dialogue, and probably should not be considered independently of them. These practices might be said to fall loosely under the category of 'paying attention' (along with textual study, historiography and aesthetic criticism). In what follows I restrict my remarks to arguing, and take for granted the kinds of descriptive and dialogical issues explored and developed by writers like Timothy Jenkins and Peter Ochs.[1]

The primary question that motivates this essay is: 'What do theologians hope to achieve by arguing with each other and with non-theologians?' I shall investigate this topic as a Christian theologian. More particularly, the influence of the work of Nicholas Lash and his understanding of the inter-relationships between tragedy, prayer and theological argument will be evident in what follows. I hope that the kinds of issue discussed here will, however, readily suggest possible ways of tackling the subject from within other religious traditions and, perhaps, from perspectives that are not immediately congruent with the major faith traditions of the contemporary world. Is argument any good? This question has Platonic and Aristotelian dimensions. If Platonic, then the task will be to find out whether, and in what ways, argument is associated with The Good. If Aristotelian, then the task will be to ask: 'Good for what? For what purposes?'

First, the Platonic. I want to suggest that argument is indeed associated with The Good. To say that argument is associated with The Good is to

---

[1] For models of description and dialogue see, respectively, Timothy Jenkins, *Religion in English Everyday Life: An Ethnographic Approach* (New York: Berghahn Books, 1999), and ch. 8 of Peter Ochs, *Peirce, Pragmatism and the Logic of Scripture* (Cambridge: Cambridge University Press, 1998).

say that in some way God wills us to argue. To find out whether God does will us to argue I turn to the Old Testament.[2] It is a mark of many of the prophets and kings that they encounter God head-on, and enter into debate with God. Whether one looks at Jacob's wrestling in Genesis, David, Job or Psalms, it is apparent that being God's people entails arguing with God. The particular part upon which I shall focus is the book of Job, as in the Christian tradition it expresses some of the most important and difficult aspects of argument with God.

Second, the Aristotelian. If argument is good, what is it good *for*? This question presupposes some task which argument might be good for addressing. Theologians argue with each other and with non-theologians. The fact that they do so suggests a purpose is served by argument. Looking at the book of Job, I shall suggest that argument is good for two things, among others: legitimation and the embrace of pain.[3] By legitimation I mean things like defending or challenging some state of affairs, or defending or challenging someone's right to occupy some territory. By the embrace of pain I mean a response to pain which both acknowledges its reality and tries to live in a way that does justice to it rather than ignoring it or playing down its significance.

In this discussion I shall look at two Christian readings of the book of Job: Karl Barth's reading of Job as 'true witness' and Thomas Aquinas's exposition on the book of Job.[4] It might be said that to look to the book of Job for help in understanding argumentation with God is, from two important perspectives, a mistake. From the first, God's interactions with Job are unsatisfactory simply because there is, apparently, little visible or audible action by God for most of the book. Jacob's struggle with the stranger, in Genesis 32:25, might be a better model for a more obviously engaged struggle between God and a human being.[5] From the second, our arguments with God are not best understood in the kind of unmediated encounter that Job exemplifies, but more indirectly, in arguments *with each other*. Janet Martin Soskice, in her essay on 'Friendship' in this collection,

---

[2] The term 'Old Testament' is problematic, not least because of its associations with Christian supersessionism with respect to Judaism. Despite this problem, no consensus has emerged over a suitable alternative. I use 'Old Testament' whilst acknowledging the difficulties in doing so.

[3] Legitimation and the embrace of pain are the two principal features of Old Testament theology, according to Walter Brueggemann in *Old Testament Theology* (Minneapolis: Fortress Press, 1992), pp. 1–44.

[4] Karl Barth, *Church Dogmatics* IV.3.1, ed. G. W. Bromiley and T. F. Torrance, trans. G. W. Bromiley (Edinburgh: T&T Clark, 1961), pp. 383–8, 398–408, 421–34, 453–61; Thomas Aquinas, *Literal Exposition on the Book of Job*, trans. A. Damico, interpretive essay by M. Yaffe (Atlanta: Scholars Press, 1989).

[5] Suggested by Diana Lipton, in the discussion following this paper's oral delivery.

indicates this well in her understanding of human friendship *as* friendship with God, and in her striking reading of Schleiermacher on the creation narrative, where it is *human* companionship that enables humanity to relate to God. These objections are not fatal, however. The method used here exemplifies a process of what Peter Ochs, in his essay on 'Scripture' in this volume, calls 'scriptural reasoning'. In order to investigate the goodness of argument, Job will be read as *already mediated* in a tradition (by Barth and Aquinas) and already read precisely for this kind of investigation (into argument). In other words, it is the place of Job as a text in an already interpreting tradition, rather than the book of Job 'cold', as it were, that I shall discuss: Job already understood as exemplary of human argument with God. I shall interrogate the part of the tradition of reading Job, rather than Job itself, to aid our inquiry.

I propose also to look at actual practices of argument. My two examples will be John Milbank's *Theology and Social Theory* and Peter Ochs's *Peirce, Pragmatism and the Logic of Scripture*.[6] Both Milbank and Ochs are interested in argument, and both exhibit self-awareness about how they address theologians and non-theologians. Because both Milbank and Ochs say they are writing one text for two kinds of readership (theologians/social theorists and theologians/philosophers respectively), and are open about how they wish to be read by these different kinds of reader, they are excellent subjects for an inquiry into the character of argument. I shall compare them.

THE GOODNESS OF ARGUMENT

The subtitle of Walter Brueggemann's *Theology of the Old Testament* is 'Testimony, Dispute, Advocacy'.[7] The main thrust of Brueggemann's work is to help the reader notice that the character of Old Testament theology is not dogmatic (which he suggests is what Christian readers tend to desire) but disputatious. Brueggemann has a contemporary agenda in arguing this. He suggests that the character of Christian theology depends significantly on how secure the Christian community is in its surrounding culture.[8] He notes that in situations where Christian life and thought is securely part of culture, the community's theological argument tends to be dogmatic: its

---

[6] John Milbank, *Theology and Social Theory* (Oxford: Blackwell, 1990); Peter Ochs, *Peirce, Pragmatism and the Logic of Scripture* (Cambridge: Cambridge University Press, 1997).

[7] Walter Brueggemann, *Theology of the Old Testament: testimony, dispute, advocacy* (Minneapolis: Fortress Press, 1997).

[8] Brueggemann finds the impetus for recovering conflictual interpretations in the work of Barth and its effects on Walther Eichrodt and Gerhard von Rad. See ibid., pp. 16–20, 27–38. On the character of theology and its cultural setting see also pp. 61–71, and p. 82.

thrust tends to be towards generating orthodoxy. But where Christianity's legitimacy is contested in a culture, and is one voice competing with other voices who are in conflict with it, it cannot afford to be dogmatic, and it certainly cannot afford to expend its energies on enforcing orthodoxy. On the contrary, it must be marked by testimony, dispute and advocacy, where it recognises the claims made elsewhere in the world and counters them by its own different claims. Israel's theology was forged in this second, conflictual, cultural situation. Christian theology has had its conflictual history (most obviously in its early years), but much modern theology was produced at a time when Christianity was deeply and safely embedded in its surrounding culture. Today that has changed, and Christianity finds itself in a similar situation to Judaism. Consequently, Christians can learn a great deal from the conflictual responses of Old Testament theology. Brueggemann argues, in effect, that the contemporary situation of Christians means that a full-blooded re-engagement with Old Testament theology, with its rich resources for thinking through the theological nature of disputatious testimony, is timely and necessary. The contemporary situation to which he refers is pluralist, post-modern and problematic: it calls for arguing.

Central to Brueggemann's presentation of Israel's rhetoric is the embrace of pain, and the tension of this embrace with struggles to legitimate social structures. I want to draw out one small aspect of this theology. I want to focus particularly on *argument* as the embrace of pain. Israel's embrace of pain can be discovered, as Brueggemann shows, in a number of key texts. One can point to Psalms, or Lamentations, Isaiah 53, or Job. Because I want to highlight the significance of argument, rather than other forms of lament, I intend to look at the book of Job, a text where the embrace of pain is expressed argumentatively.

BARTH ON JOB

Job famously speaks the truth about God. When the Lord turns his attention to Eliphaz, the first of Job's friends, he expresses his wrath: 'for you have not spoken of me what is right, as my servant Job has' (Job 42:7). This truth, however, cannot be specified exactly. Job's speech is a testimony to his suffering, mingled with bitter contradiction. He asks: 'Why hast thou made me thy mark?' (Job 7:20), but acknowledges the impossibility of this question: 'Who will say to him, "What doest thou"?' (Job 9:12). In his more reflective arguments, Job is forced to give up and admit that he does not know. 'I cannot answer; I must appeal for mercy' (Job 9:15).

Job is important for us because he shows not only that argument is quite understandable under the circumstances, but that argument is *required*.

Karl Barth took some pains to explain why Job's complaint is required by God, and not simply understandable under the circumstances. Barth's interest in Job is, characteristically, as a Christological type (*CD IV.3*, p. 385).[9] He treats the story primarily to illuminate the nature of Jesus Christ as true witness to God.

Barth has a problem which he attempts to solve dogmatically. The problem is this. On the one hand, Job understands God's freedom and expresses his commitment to obeying God. At no point does Job curse God (although he freely curses his own birth). Job makes no attempt to constrain God, or try to judge God. He knows God is free to dispense good and to dispense evil. And Job knows that he himself is free to accept both good and evil, according to God's will. But on the other hand, Job's correct knowledge of God is sharply at odds with his experience of suffering, *and he complains*. Barth characterises this conflict as the result of a deficit in *Job's intellectual competence*: between Job's knowledge and his ignorance (*CD IV.3*, p. 401).

Barth's conclusion, at the end of his second discussion of Job, is that Job experiences the contradiction between God's goodness and Job's suffering as pain, and is right to articulate this pain, but wrong to express this in the form of an argumentative claim. It is wrong because it attempts, arrogantly, to force God to conform to Job's expectations. Job's dogmatic error is to subordinate his evaluation of God's sovereignty beneath his understanding of God's goodness, whereas the dogmatically correct response is to recognise their identity.

Barth exerts himself hard to argue his point. The character of Barth's prose in this section is striking: it twists and turns many times, with long sections in which very little of substance is said, as if he were taking in breath ready for the next difficult effort. Along the way he makes some remarkable discoveries. I want to draw attention to some of Barth's intermediate reasoning, as it is much more interesting (and messy) than his final view.

At times, Barth himself seems to tire of dogmatic insistence. For example: 'Materially, however, Job's final word is to be found neither in the question nor request, nor even in the protestation, but in his constant sighing, which is both painful and angry and even scornful, at the obvious incongruity and impotence of all these forms of complaint, and especially of his protestation

---

[9] References are to Barth, *Church Dogmatics* IV.3.1.

of innocence' (*CD IV.3*, p. 403). Barth wants not only to attend to Job's sighs, but to make theological sense of them. Dogmatic neatness might attribute the sighs to Job's ignorance – his ignorance about the extent of God's dealings with him. But this is unsatisfactory. Barth's attentive reading of the text suggests to him that Job's complaining is presented, in the book of Job, as right. This blocks any simplistic dogmatic assertion. Barth thus suggests the following:

> . . . it is in the name of God that he complains against God, i.e., against the strange form in which God encounters him, rejects him, disputes against him, and persecutes him as an unjustly disowned and ill-treated servant. Even though from the very outset he knows that he has neither competence nor power to mount this attack, yet he presses it to the bitter end. This is the remarkable and indeed honourable complaint of Job in all its rights and wrongs. (*CD IV.3*, p. 405)

Barth sums up: '[Job] would not have been obedient if he had not raised this complaint and carried it through to the bitter end in spite of all objections' (*CD IV.3*, p. 406).

This is perhaps the profoundest part of Barth's discussion: he has found a way to say that Job is right to argue with God. Barth adds something extraordinary. He suggests that Job is right to argue, but that his arguments are inadequate. Barth forbids cherry-picking amongst the text, applauding Job here, castigating him there. He also rules out focusing upon passages of reflection where Job is obviously right: because at these moments Job is not complaining, but reasoning. It is the complaining, rather than the reasoning, which is both right and wrong.

Using Brueggemann's categories, Job's complaint is right insofar as it embraces pain, but wrong insofar as it makes a bid for legitimation. Barth makes a definite separation between the two. This is dogmatically neat, and later on I wish to make such a separation problematic.

What, then, is learned by attending to the character of argument between God and Job? We learn from Barth that argument is not only 'understandable under the circumstances' but positively required. We do not learn why it is required. In God's judgement of Job in the concluding chapters, God both silences with overwhelming questions and blesses his servant Job, who spoke what is right concerning the Lord. We are never told in the text when Job spoke what was right or when he spoke what was wrong. In summary, *it is good that Job argues with God, but his arguments aren't any good.*

To say that Job is right to argue but that his arguments aren't any good is rather confusing. I think that some (not all) of this confusion arises because Barth identifies the contradictions with Job's intellectual shortcomings.

Barth thinks, in essence, that Job makes a *dogmatic* mistake: Job fails to acknowledge that God's sovereignty matches God's righteousness. I think it is possible to do better than this. To help show how, I turn now to Aquinas's commentary on Job.

AQUINAS ON JOB

Commentaries are never just commentaries. They are commentaries for particular communities at particular times, addressing particular questions. Barth's remarks on the book of Job were directed to a church in danger of assimilating to a secular society which worshipped something other than God, at a time when many churches had done precisely that; a church asking what it means to be a true witness to God in the face of suffering and pain.

When Aquinas wrote his *Expositio super Job ad litteram* in the mid 1200s, he was writing for a church in which theology was being taught boringly. Martin Yaffe has indicated that there is a strong similarity of purpose between the *Summa Theologiae* and the *Exposition* on Job.[10] The *Summa* was for teaching students of theology how to argue philosophically as well as answer theological questions correctly. There was no shortage of theological learning in Aquinas's time, but theologians were not equipped adequately to reason their learning through in ways that address the practical problems of everyday life. Aquinas's *Summa* was intended to introduce his readers to philosophy. His *Exposition* on Job betrays these interests too. Aquinas's Job is a man who is perfectly equipped with sound theological learning. His speeches to Eliphaz, Bildad and Zophar are perfectly correct (that is, they are not corrected at any point). It is Job himself – his whole life – who is corrected by God. 'The "history" of Job is thus the history of a man who is perfectly wise in the divine truth as taught by the Church, yet who must reconsider the possible sinfulness involved in professing that truth to others in society.'[11] It is not Job's learning that is corrected but the shortfall between his doctrinal wisdom concerning God and his practical understanding. 'Thomas' exposition induces the student or professor of Christian theology vicariously to re-examine the wisdom he would profess. Learning from Job's example, Thomas' reader too must approach that wisdom in a fuller way than his merely academic education may have provided him with until now.'[12]

---

[10] See Martin Yaffe, 'Providence in Medieval Aristotelianism', in L. Perdue and W. Clark Gilpin, eds., *The Voice from the Whirlwind: Interpreting the Book of Job* (Nashville: Abingdon, 1992), pp. 111–28.
[11] Martin Yaffe, 'Interpretive Essay', in Aquinas, *Literal Exposition*, p. 27.   [12] Ibid.

Yaffe's interpretation of Aquinas on Job is compelling. Aquinas is motivated, in effect, by the question: what good is theology? Just as Job discovers that his knowledge is not adequate to confront God, so the student of theology must discover that the purpose of theological learning is the assistance it offers in living God's own life and acquiring a deeper wisdom. 'Considered pedagogically, Thomas' exposure of the practical shortcomings of Christian theology would be impossible without his protreptic Aristotelianism, understood as the ongoing "love of wisdom", rather than the mere dogmatic profession of wisdom.'[13]

There is a similarity between Barth and Aquinas. For both of them, Job is right to argue but his arguments are no good. For Barth, however, the mistake lies in the lack of fit between Job's understanding of God's goodness and his attempt to force God to express this goodness in accordance with Job's expectations. For Aquinas, by contrast, it is not so much that Job makes a dogmatic mistake, as that he needs to learn a practical wisdom that matches his intellectual knowledge. Moreover, this practical wisdom will enable Job *to communicate his intellectual knowledge better and more truthfully.* Aquinas's Job is taught not more information (he has enough), but how to live. Whereas Barth bids for dogmatic correctness, Aquinas's interpretation has only just begun when one grasps its meaning: once one understands that theology is for learning how to live, the real task then lies, precisely, in learning how to live.

So what is the real problem in lived life that motivates our current inquiry into Job? What situation requires this reading, which stresses that it is good to argue, but our arguments are no good?

I suggest argument has been too heavily associated with issues of legitimation, and has insufficiently included the dimension of the embrace of pain. That is, theological argument has tended to be used to legitimate various practices and beliefs. It has tended much less to be understood as a guide for learning how to live. It is difficult to defend this here, but for corroboration I would point to the way Theology is taught in universities. The syllabus where I teach in Edinburgh, for example, is biased heavily towards giving students intellectual knowledge of Christian doctrine, together with some background to the philosophies which inform it. If students want to learn about how to live (which we call 'Christian Ethics and Practical Theology'), then this is taught in a completely different set of courses, in which one often encounters almost no doctrine at all (some of us are slowly trying to change this practice). I suspect that this is not exclusively a

---

[13] Ibid.

Scottish problem. Like Aquinas and Barth, we need to teach doctrine in a way that makes plain that its purpose is to aid learning how to live. Job could not convert his friends simply by dogmatic argument. In the end, what was required was that he pray for them. For Aquinas, the study of theology helps one to imitate this practice.

MILBANK'S ARGUMENT

Our result thus far is modest: it is good for us to argue with God, but (following Barth) our arguments will be no good. It is good for us to argue because (following Aquinas) that is how we learn how to live and share in God's own life.

I now want to develop the theme of legitimation and pain a little. Job's argument is not only a bid for legitimation, but also a struggle to embrace pain and admit it as a part of his relationship with God. Job knows that he is required to argue, and comes to understand that this is not because he is able to advance good arguments, but because by doing so he learns how to live with God. I want to turn now to some examples of argument to find out what their authors think argument is good for.

John Milbank's *Theology and Social Theory* opens with an acknowledgement that its claims are addressed not universally, but to particular audiences. 'This book is addressed both to social theorists and to theologians.'[14] Milbank acknowledges that different readers will be able to accept different aspects of his work, and he recognises that there are different levels in his discourse. Milbank says that he proposes to do two things: (1) identify metaphysical issues where there is significant overlap or competition between theological and sociological writing; (2) expose the impossibility of adjudicating between them, in order to show that Christian theological claims are no less 'valid' than non-Christian. In short, he proposes to place obstacles in the way of those who want to use words like 'valid' in allegedly neutral ways.

Milbank's two aims serve two purposes: to advance a sceptical relativist argument for social theorists, by challenging attempts to legitimate their enterprise (via 'genealogy' à la Nietzsche); and to advance a positive argument for theologians, by offering a theology that handles the metaphysical issues (identified in (1) above) in a way more habitable for Christian life and thought than is found in much sociological writing. Milbank places in question the idea that the disciplines are distinct. Rather, there are

---

[14] Milbank, *Theology and Social Theory*, p. 1.

competing versions of a series of common metaphysical interests. Some locate their founding principles in empiricism or reason or history (or some combination); others acknowledge their source of revelation in what is made known by God.

So how does Milbank go about this 'exercise in sceptical relativism', as he puts it? Simplifying greatly, the structure of his argument is repeated at each stage. First, he establishes his competence to speak on a subject, by rehearsing the salient points in a particular thinker's project; secondly, he exposes the antagonistic revelation to which it makes appeal; thirdly, he suggests that the telos of this 'pagan' or 'heretical' revelation is nihilistic; fourthly, he articulates the orthodox Christian position; fifthly, he suggests that the telos of this orthodox revelation is not nihilistic but harmonious and peaceful.

How does this relate to his two audiences, the social theorists and the theologians? Milbank uses one complex voice to address two constituencies. He does not prejudge what his potential reader will be able to accept. He suggests that a social theorist, for example, can at least see the theoretical possibility of the Christian perspective. He has also drawn attention to the fact that there is limited scope in a book like *Theology and Social Theory* for developing the kinds of rhetoric that would give this perspective persuasive force.[15]

We have a sufficient understanding of Milbank's argumentative strategy.[16] In the terms of my earlier discussion, his project falls within the ambit of legitimation. That is, Milbank is concerned to challenge various attempts at legitimation by certain sociologists and to relieve his theological readers of any fears they might have about the legitimation of theology. Milbank does not, of course, promote legitimation: rather he shows the pointlessness and danger of attempts at legitimation that do not acknowledge their dependence on God. In effect he says 'No More Legitimation'. I want to draw attention to the fact that this insistence appears to be an intellectual matter, a matter of right knowledge. To be sure this points towards a practice, but this practice is not taught. It is only ever presupposed as possible. We shall return to this.

The other point to notice is that Milbank does not offer different styles of delivery or different modes of address for his two readerships: they are offered the same material on identical terms.

---

[15] John Milbank, personal communication with the author.

[16] To substantiate the general remarks made here would require more attentive engagement with Milbank's discussion of particular figures, e.g. Durkheim, Nietzsche and Augustine: see Milbank, *Theology and Social Theory*, pp. 61–8 (Durkheim), 280–9 (Nietzsche), 389–92 (Augustine).

OCHS'S ARGUMENT

I want to contrast this with Peter Ochs's *Peirce, Pragmatism and the Logic of Scripture*. Ochs and Milbank, it should be said immediately, have a great deal in common. Like Milbank, Ochs addresses his book to two constituencies, this time philosophers and theologians. And like Milbank, Ochs differentiates between stages in his argument. There are some instructive differences of emphasis and style, however. Unlike Milbank, Ochs develops different styles of address for his different readerships. And unlike Milbank, Ochs advances his argument not only for purposes of legitimation but also as part of an embrace of pain.

There are a number of aspects of C. S. Peirce's work that make it attractive to Ochs's theological interests. I want to single out two. First, the kind of pragmatism developed by Peirce is intended to address what he calls 'real' doubts rather than 'paper' doubts. That is, Peirce sees the philosopher's task to be one of responding to problems that are thrown up in the course of life rather than attempts to provide imaginary solutions to imaginary problems. Second, Peirce's pragmatic method entails identifying and correcting errors in previous work rather than starting from scratch. That is, Peirce takes traditions of thought seriously, rather than thinking he must develop a universal logic within which to frame his thinking.

Ochs has different strategies for appealing to two different kinds of reader. The first he calls the 'general reader'. This means the kind of reader who might open a book on the philosophy of Peirce. In order to address the general reader, Ochs gives an account of Peirce's philosophy, traces its internal developments, draws attention to problems and inconsistencies which Peirce himself works through, notes some inner contradictions, and offers interpretations of what Peirce's work is intended to perform. Ochs calls all of this a 'plain-sense' interpretation. The plain-sense interpretation of a text is one that any general reader could reasonably be expected to produce, given the same degree of careful engagement with the philosophy.

The second he calls 'Dear Reader'.[17] Dear Reader is addressed directly in the second person, partly because the claims made from this point onwards are not intrinsic to the matter in hand (that is, Peirce's philosophy) but arise from some other situation, in this case the particular Jewish or Christian tradition from which Dear Reader comes. Dear Reader is not offered only plain-sense interpretations: Ochs accommodates what might interest members of particular communities of interpretation.

[17] Ochs also calls this person the 'pragmatic reader', meaning someone who interrogates the texts in question in the light of particular questions extrinsic to those texts.

Ochs thus differentiates between the general reader and Dear Reader. The general reader is offered plain-sense interpretations. Dear Reader is offered other, 'pragmatic', readings. Ochs does not forbid the general reader from continuing with the argument, but he makes it plain that the general reader is not invited to evaluate the argument once it ceases to function at the level of plain-sense interpretations: '[general] readers may want to limit their critical evaluations to the previous chapters and read this one only the way ethnographers or tourists might observe a foreign society'.[18]

We have here evidence of a refinement that contrasts with Milbank. Milbank differentiates between two kinds of reader (social theorists and theologians) but does not develop different modes of address. Ochs differentiates between the 'general reader' and 'Dear Reader' and uses different modes of address in order to acknowledge that different readers will find different kinds of argument persuasive, and will have differing limits to their critical evaluation.

This, however, is only one of the two points I want to make. The second is that Ochs does not limit the scope of argument to legitimation. He also defines pragmatic interpretation as a process of healing broken forms of life.[19]

The clearest place where this happens is the discussion of 'Rabbinic Pragmatism'.[20] Ochs rehearses the work of Hermann Cohen, Martin Buber, Franz Rosenzweig and Max Kadushin, and presents the work of each as a correction and repair of previous thinking. In each case, the question which motivates the philosophers is the question of human suffering and how to direct knowledge towards addressing this suffering. In the case of Cohen, for example, Ochs revisits the origins of Cartesian philosophy. Drawing on Cohen, Ochs suggests that the source of Cartesian philosophy is a complaint about the scholastic Church tradition from which it emerged. The best way to address Cartesian philosophy is to hear it as a complaint and then to try to diagnose the problem. However, Cartesian philosophers and their opponents both read the complaint as a claim. This is a mistake, because if Cartesian philosophy is read as a claim, then it makes sense to try to examine whether it is a good claim, and whether it is coherent. But if it is a complaint, then it is not logical coherence that is of prime importance, but the situation that motivates the complaint. In effect Ochs suggests that the pragmatist asks: 'What's wrong?' rather than 'Justify your position'.

Ochs's approach maps well onto the issue of legitimation and embrace of pain explored here. For Ochs, philosophical argument has a number

---

[18] Ochs, *Peirce*, p. 247.   [19] See, esp. pp. 253–4.   [20] Ibid., pp. 290ff.

of purposes. Cartesian argument can be heard as voicing some kind of suffering. Ochs suggests that readings of Cartesian philosophy that treat it as a claim mistake an attempt to embrace pain for a bid for legitimation. If people's attempts to voice their pain are mistaken for claims (particularly if those who voice their pain dress it up precisely as a bid for legitimation) then that pain can never be properly addressed and it will keep recurring despite the most ingenious philosophical responses. For Ochs, philosophy is partly a response to suffering.

<h3 style="text-align:center">RECAPITULATION</h3>

It is time to relate these two dimensions. The first was to examine Job's arguments, and discover that Job is right to argue with God, but that his arguments are no good. He is right to argue because he knows who God is, and his suffering is not consonant with this knowledge. His arguments are no good because his suffering is not a problem to be solved, but a life to be lived faithfully. The second was to compare Milbank's mono-vocal concern with legitimation with Ochs's multi-vocal concern with legitimation and the embrace of pain.

I want to bring these together by returning to the interpretation of Job by Thomas Aquinas, which I want to read in the light of Ochs's therapeutic pragmatism. Aquinas's interpretation of Job is an attempt to explore the relationship between two different kinds of wisdom: intellectual wisdom and practical wisdom. For Aquinas, Job's journey is one of discovering that his intellectual wisdom, which is perfect, is one-sided. It needs to be complemented by a practical wisdom: he must repair his life.

Job's doubts are not paper doubts; they are doubts as real as his dead sons and his boils. Yet he attempts to confront them *intellectually* and, indeed, *judicially*. He calls for his accusers, and he argues his defence. He attempts to remedy his doubts by asking for *more knowledge*, in this case knowledge of his guilt which he currently lacks. The knowledge he seeks is knowledge in the service of legitimation, in this case the legitimation of his righteousness.

What God requires, however, is for Job to know not *that he is righteous* but *how to live*. In naming him 'my servant Job' God makes plain that knowledge is required not for legitimation (he already *is* 'my servant Job') but for repairing his life. Job's life needs repairing because his practical response is, wrongly, to seek intellectual answers, and to answer his comforters intellectually. And, interestingly, the repair of this life is not achieved by Job. Job does not suddenly acquire miraculous practical knowledge at the end. Rather, God repairs his life, and Job then lives it, by praying for the friends who let him down.

In Ochs's terms, the plain sense of Job leads one to discover that argument with God is good, but the arguments are no good. Aquinas's pragmatic reading seeks to interpret this with an extra-textual concern: a concern with the benefits of philosophy and wisdom, as Yaffe shows. One of the striking features of Aquinas's *Literal Exposition* is its length: like Barth's *Church Dogmatics* it is far longer than the communication of propositions requires. The textual practices of Aquinas and Barth suggest that their wisdom must be learned by time-consuming companionship rather than by being plundered for quotable material. This companionship teaches the reader to argue theologically rather than providing facts to be memorised.

I want to extend this to concerns that are shared by those interested in the future of the study of theology and religions. The extra-textual question, with respect to which I want to interrogate Aquinas's reading of Job, is 'What good are our arguments with each other and, more widely, with our colleagues in other disciplines?'

The tendency of Aquinas's Job is to answer that our most important arguments are poor for providing new information or yielding intellectual knowledge. We have learned this too from Milbank: attempts at legitimation are fruitless and instead of squandering the resources of the Christian tradition in pursuit of social *theory*, Christians should instead practise a peaceful and harmonious social *life*. I said before, however, that Milbank never teaches this practice, he only ever insists, *intellectually*, on its possibility. If Milbank is wrong it is only in the sense that Job is wrong, but it is here that there is work to do. I want to try to start repairing this lack here.

Our most important arguments are not mainly for providing new information, any more than God's answer to Job provides Job with information that hitherto he lacked. Rather, just as God heals Job and restores his life, the purposes of our argument must be therapeutic. They will, despite everything, involve legitimation and new information. After all, it will be difficult to argue for social justice, better prisons, the cancellation of world debt, non-proliferation of nuclear weapons or green energy without *arguing for or against* these things. Yet, at the same time, the arguments will be no good. Doubtless there are manifold occasions for problem-solving in these areas, but the more reports into bad prisons or global warming there are, the more it is apparent that the practical difficulties are of a certain sort. They are not primarily technical difficulties whose root is ignorance (although this too) but the recalcitrance of governments and corporations. If you like, the kind of argument called for is less like mathematics and more like campaigning. It calls for repentance as much as for engineering.

So what is argument good for? It is good for teaching each other how to live. That is how God argues with his servant Job. Argument entails legitimation and the embrace of pain. If it is allowed only to do the first then the second will come back to haunt us, as it does in debates over healthcare, where people refuse to be ill or vulnerable or handicapped, and where the fit are encouraged to despise the unfit. In this respect, knock-down arguments are problematic: at best their bids for legitimation succeed in knocking people down.

So what are the real doubts, as opposed to paper doubts, that stimulate this paper? It is the question about what theologians hope to achieve by entering into argument with each other and with non-theologians. I used Milbank and Ochs as my examples because they both hope to reach out, beyond theological faculties, by doing good philosophical thinking. There is something slightly shocking and embarrassing about the idea that debate in the university should be for teaching each other how to live. To my mind the amplitude of this embarrassment is a gauge for showing how far universities have strayed from their true vocation.

The conclusion of this inquiry? The matter does not call for a neat, closed solution. But it seems to me that good *philosophical* places to look are the work of philosophers like Cohen, Buber and Rosenzweig, whom Ochs discusses, or Benjamin, Bloch, Adorno, Habermas, Foucault and Levinas, all of whom exemplify engagement with both legitimation and the embrace of pain. These philosophers, in various and different ways, recognise that philosophy is always unfinished because there remains suffering in the world. Some of the figures mentioned last are also influenced by Marx, and remain unsatisfied until the world is not only described but transformed by philosophy. With philosophers like these, those who study and practise theology can surely do business. I hope I have clarified a little the role that argument plays in this transformation of the world which, unlike Marx's belief in revolution, I describe as the task of teaching each other how to live. And unlike the philosophers, but like Milbank and Ochs, I do not believe this teaching resides autonomously in nature or aesthetics or reason, but is something that God teaches us first. That might mean arguing is an aspect of love. But doubtless one can argue about that.

CHAPTER 10

Reconciliation

John W. de Gruchy

A few years ago I supervised the Master's dissertation of a Catholic priest.[1] His research focused on how reconciliation was understood amongst the members of his large sprawling parish of six congregations located on the Cape Flats and composed of so-called 'coloured' people, a community to which he also belonged. He wanted to compare their understanding of reconciliation with that expressed in various documents produced by the Southern African Catholic Bishops' Conference. The way in which the bishops understood reconciliation was in keeping with traditional Christian teaching, though contextually related. But this was not the case amongst the members of my student's parish. For them reconciliation had to do with recovering their identity as 'coloured' people. Whenever their priest preached on the need for reconciliation in South Africa, exhorting them to become reconciled to other ethnic groups, they heard him say that they should recover their own self-respect. This understanding of reconciliation has, on reflection, a certain logic, for how can South Africans overcome the legacy of apartheid and create a genuinely just and sustainable society unless those who were previously oppressed and who still suffer from the indignities of the past regain respect for their own identity? By the same token, there can be little chance for reconciliation in South Africa unless those of us who were privileged by apartheid because of our skin colour renounce an immoral past and seek to develop a fresh identity as members of a new country in search of transformation.[2]

The need to recover respect for personal identity, or the need to shed the shackles of the past whether as victim or oppressor, is not normally what theologians think about when we hear the word 'reconciliation'. Nor is that what reconciliation commonly means. Yet precisely because we take

---

[1] Basil John Hendricks, 'The Notion of Reconciliation as Part of the Emerging Coloured Identity' (Master's diss., University of Cape Town, 1996).
[2] See Kadar Asmal, Louise Asmal and Ronald Suresh Roberts, *Reconciliation Through Truth* (Cape Town: David Philip, 1996), pp. 51f.

the meaning of 'reconciliation' for granted, we tend to employ it without much critical consideration. Indeed, the contemporary debate about 'reconciliation' in South Africa and elsewhere has generated as much heat as it has light, with cliché and slogan too often replacing careful analysis and reasoned use. We thereby fail to recognise the extent to which its use is historically and contextually constructed; we also fail to appreciate its layered set of possible meanings and the extent to which the term evokes expressions of hope and hurt, of anticipation and disillusionment, amongst many people in conflict situations. By contrast it may evoke little thought or comment amongst people in places where social order is taken for granted and 'reconciliation' is bland and even banal. In much popular secular and theological usage, reflected in the rhetoric of pulpit, parliament, and the press, it has become, as Rowan Williams puts it, 'a seductively comfortable word, fatally close to "consensus".'[3] Yet, as the South African Truth and Reconciliation Commission soon discovered as it set about its task in 1996, reconciliation carries a far more complex meaning in contexts such as South Africa where it has become a highly contested term in public life, and where its achievement remains elusive.

All this may lead us to conclude that the word 'reconciliation' is so overloaded with significance in some contexts and so emptied of meaning in others that it is no longer useful. However, as long as 'reconciliation' is ingrained in popular rhetoric and academic discourse and, more importantly, expresses the longings of many, it is necessary to clarify its use and ponder its significance. But we need to do so aware that 'reconciliation' cannot be understood properly apart from the context in which it is used, and therefore in the light of the history of its usage. Certainly, reconciliation as now used in South Africa embraces a whole complex of inter-related ideas that go to the heart of social reality, and the same is undoubtedly true in Northern Ireland or Burundi, to name but two other places. Hence the remarkable fact that so many people from different parts of the world are presently engaged in various research projects on reconciliation in post-apartheid South Africa.

Critical reflection on the theme of reconciliation serves an additional purpose, one that relates to the future of the study of Theology and Religious Studies as well as the connection between these two fields of inquiry. There are many factors that need to be taken into account in this regard, many of them explored in other essays. However, it is surely self-evident that the future of both Theology and Religious Studies depends to a large

---

[3] Rowan Williams, *On Christian Theology* (Oxford: Blackwell, 2000), p. 266.

degree on their ability to contribute meaningfully to the public debate about issues that affect the common good. The debate on reconciliation in South Africa provides a significant example of how both theological reflection from within the Christian tradition and perspectives derived from the study of religion can, in tandem, contribute critical insight and do so in discussion with other disciplines as well. The extent to which this is already taking place can be gauged from the wealth of material that is being published on the theme both in South Africa and further afield. What follows is an attempt to contribute to that debate, and hence to the future of our disciplines.

THE RHETORIC OF RECONCILIATION

The rhetoric of reconciliation in contemporary South Africa reflects the divisions and conflicts within its public life. As such it sometimes obfuscates material reality, foreclosing the issues that really divide, and cynically exploiting both hope and disillusionment. But the rhetoric of reconciliation also demonstrates the extent to which the debate has been theologically shaped, reflecting as it does the conflict between different versions of Christianity that have contributed to the making of modern South Africa. Originally, this had to do with two very different theological traditions, that of Afrikaner neo-Calvinism which gave legitimacy to racial segregation and then to apartheid, and the more liberal theology of the white-dominated English-speaking churches. For the former, national salvation lay along the path of ethnic and cultural separation; for the latter, reconciliation was an ideal to be striven for, but what that meant in concrete political terms was uncertain. For both, the Christian doctrine of reconciliation was inextricably bound up with social reality and thereby politicised, whether through its denial in support of apartheid, or the painfully slow recognition that racial segregation and Christianity were incompatible. It was not until the publication of *The Message to the People of South Africa* by the South African Council of Churches (SACC) in 1968 that the churches were challenged to acknowledge this incompatibility in unambiguous terms.

The *Message* categorically stated that 'separate development', as apartheid was euphemistically called, was a false gospel. Whereas the gospel of Jesus Christ reconciled people to each other, apartheid drove them apart. The ensuing debate about the *Message* embroiled not only the churches but also politicians, reaching even into the chambers of parliament. It soon became evident that while many understood reconciliation as a private affair between God and the individual with, at most, some consequences for interpersonal relations, for others it had far-reaching social and political implications. The debate around the *Message* was, however, largely one between white Christians, reflecting the theological divide between conservative and liberal. It was only subsequent to the rise of Black Consciousness and the emergence of Black theology that its parameters radically shifted. From this perspective reconciliation between white and black South Africans was regarded as impossible as long as apartheid existed. Those who sought reconciliation were, in fact, undermining the cause of liberation; hence the word itself was politically suspect. Hence, too, the refusal to countenance P. W. Botha's reformist policies in the 1980s.

Botha's reformist rhetoric appeared reconciliatory, but his policies were divisive and soon plunged South Africa into turmoil and a State of Emergency. One Christian response to this crisis was the National Initiative of Reconciliation (NIR) launched in September 1985 by African Enterprise, an evangelical para-church organisation. The NIR managed to gather together a wide range of Christian leaders, including white Dutch Reformed church leaders and SACC representatives. Its 'Statement of Affirmation' clearly acknowledged the connection between reconciliation as a theological concept and the struggle for justice. The struggle for justice and the ministry of reconciliation were not equated, but neither were they separated.[4] At the same time, many involved in the NIR regarded reconciliation as a gift that could be appropriated here and now between people, and therefore as a means and not only an end contingent upon the demise of apartheid.

A more radical response was that expressed in the *Kairos Document* a few weeks later. For the Kairos theologians, reconciliation was not a means to an end, but rather the end product of the struggle for justice. Justice and the ending of apartheid were preconditions for reconciliation. Recognising that the basic difference between Christians in South Africa was not primarily denominational or confessional, but political and economic, the *Kairos Document* perceived that the Church itself was a site of the struggle against apartheid. The *Kairos Document* not only attacked the 'state theology' of those who gave their support to apartheid, but also opposed what it named the 'church theology' of the mainline multi-racial churches, accusing them of promoting 'cheap reconciliation':

In our situation in South Africa today it would be totally unChristian to plead for reconciliation and peace before the present injustices have been removed. Any such plea plays into the hands of the oppressor by trying to persuade those of us who are oppressed to accept our oppression and to become reconciled to the intolerable crimes that are committed against us. That is not Christian reconciliation,

[4] See the essays in Klaus Nürnberger and John Tooke, eds., *The Cost of Reconciliation in South Africa* (Cape Town: Methodist Publishing House, 1998).

it is sin. It is asking us to become accomplices in our own oppression, to become servants of the devil. No reconciliation is possible in South Africa without justice.[5]

Thus, rejecting the rhetoric of reconciliation, the *Kairos Document* called for direct Christian participation in the struggle, including acts of civil disobedience in resistance to government tyranny.

Heated controversy around the meaning of reconciliation once again ensued within the churches,[6] as state repression against Christian activists associated with the *Kairos Document* intensified. Much of the discussion reminded one of Dietrich Bonhoeffer's attack on the way in which the Lutheran *sola gratia* had been reduced to cheap grace within the German Evangelical Church during the Third Reich.[7] The fundamental problem was the prevailing notion amongst many white Christians and church leaders that they could be neutral, acting as agents of reconciliation without being engaged in the struggle for justice as its prerequisite.[8] But even churches and church leaders who had rejected apartheid and who were engaged in the struggle to end it, such as Archbishop Tutu, were unhappy about the way in which 'Church theology' and reconciliation were, in their terms, caricatured and criticised. Clearly there was hesitation about the ideological abuse of such a key doctrine of Christian faith, whether by those who used it in defence of their supposed neutrality, or those who rejected it as counter-productive to the struggle.

At first glance it may appear ironic that it was precisely at this time that the imprisoned Nelson Mandela began to explore the possibility of negotiations and set off down the path of reconciliation, thereby opening up a new and necessary front in the struggle.[9] Secret talks between Mr Mandela and the National Party government were under way, then, at the very time when the *Kairos Document* was being written.[10] Those who were engaged in the liberation struggle, and who came to know of these talks, were at first concerned that Mandela had sold out and become engaged in an exercise

---

[5] *The Kairos Document* (Johannesburg: Institute for Contextual Theology, 1986), p. 9, art, 3.1.

[6] *Journal of Theology for Southern Africa* 58 (March 1987); John W. de Gruchy, 'The Struggle for Justice and the Ministry of Reconciliation' Nürnberger and Tooke, eds., *Cost of Reconciliation*, pp. 166-80.

[7] Dietrich Bonhoeffer, *The Cost of Discipleship*, rev. ed. (New York: Macmillan, 1960). pp. 35ff.

[8] Tony Balcomb, *Third Way Theology* (Pietermaritzburg: Cluster Publications, 1993).

[9] I have explored this more fully in John W. de Gruchy, 'The Dialectic of Reconciliation: Church and the Transition to Democracy in South Africa', in Gregory Baum and Harold Wells, eds., *The Reconciliation of Peoples: Challenge to the Churches* (Maryknoll: Orbis, 1997), pp. 16–29.

[10] The remarkable story of these talks is told in Nelson Mandela, *Long Walk to Freedom: The Autobiography of Nelson Mandela* (Johannesburg: Macdonald Purnell, 1994). See also Alistair Sparks, *Tomorrow is Another Country: the Inside Story of South Africa's Negotiated Revolution* (Cape Town: Struik, 1994).

of cheap reconciliation, the very temptation against which the *Kairos Document* warned. But Mandela had not served such a long term in prison for the sake of selling out the birthright of the oppressed. As far as he was concerned there could be no negotiated settlement unless the government was prepared to accept the goal of a non-racial democratic society. There could be no reconciliation without liberation and justice. Until that was accepted in principle he would stay in prison, the armed struggle would continue, and sanctions would remain in place. Nevertheless, the fact that Mandela initiated the talks, and the way in which he entered into them, indicates that he was committed to pursuing the path of reconciliation as an integral part of the process of achieving the goal of liberation. It had become abundantly clear to him that there was no alternative other than a protracted civil war.

Given this history of the contestation of reconciliation, it is perhaps not surprising that reconciliation became such a central political focus when apartheid finally crumbled. The Interim Constitution approved late in 1993 as the basis for the election of a new democratic government had a final clause on National Unity and Reconciliation. It included these words:

The pursuit of national unity, the well-being of all South African citizens and peace require reconciliation between the people of South Africa and the reconstruction of society.

... there is a need for understanding but not revenge, a need for reparation but not for retaliation, a need for ubuntu[11] but not for victimisation.

On Friday 21 October 1994, the South African Parliament approved a bill establishing a Truth and Reconciliation Commission to enable the country to pursue these goals. Clearly reconciliation was now seen as part of the process of national reconstruction; equally clearly it was regarded as contingent upon the perpetrators of oppression's 'telling the truth' about their misdeeds, and the victims' receiving reparation. Thus reconciliation became the key word in speaking about how we should deal with the past and in defining national goals for the future. As President Mandela said on receiving the Report of the TRC in February 1999: 'The quest for reconciliation was the spur that gave life to our difficult negotiation process and the agreements that emerged from it.'[12] But this did not mean

---

[11] A Xhosa word which means human solidarity.
[12] Quoted in Mxolisi Mgxashe, 'Reconciliation: A Call to Action,' in Charles Villa-Vicencio and Wilhelm Verwoerd, eds., *Looking Back Reaching Forward* (Cape Town: University of Cape Town Press, 2000), p. 218.

that there was consensus either on its meaning or on how it could be achieved.

A comparison of truth commissions in various parts of the world has shown that while in South Africa reconciliation was, from the outset, regarded as essential to the process and necessary to its outcome, most of the others did not understand their task in this way.[13] One major reason for this was the extent to which the TRC vision arose out of religious and specifically Christian conviction. The debate about reconciliation within the TRC itself and as generated within the wider South African public would undoubtedly have been different if the Commission had been chaired by a judge rather than an archbishop, by a politician rather than a pastor and father confessor. But that was not the case. In addition the majority of the Commissioners were devout Christians, and some were clergy and theologians. This certainly made it difficult for those of other faiths, or secularists with a forensic mindset, to reach consensus on several issues related to our theme. For those who belong to other religious traditions, the particular way in which Christians speak about reconciliation may be appropriate within the life of the Church, but it does not necessarily relate to their understanding of the word. And for those who are secular in outlook, and for whom politics is primarily about justice, power relations, and economic forces, the use of such a specifically theological term is highly problematic unless its theological meaning and its political usage are clearly distinguished.

During the work of the TRC it soon became clear that, irrespective of its Christian meaning and its specific sense of national reconstruction, the rhetoric of reconciliation had become highly politicised. It even became possible to determine a person's political commitments by examining the way in which he or she used the term. Those who wanted to forget the past spoke of the need for reconciliation as though it were coterminous with moral amnesia, a particular failure of the apartheid ruling class. Hence F. W. de Klerk and others emphasised the importance of letting 'bygones be bygones', which explains in part their opposition to the TRC. Right-wing conservatives and many pan-Africanists to the left, for different reasons, spoke of reconciliation as an impossible dream. For them, the TRC was a waste of time and money, even though they were ideologically at opposite ends of the spectrum. Those in the mainstream of the new dispensation, as represented by Nelson Mandela and Desmond Tutu, spoke of reconciliation as a meaningful challenge, opportunity and goal.

[13] Priscilla Hayner, 'Same Species, Different Animal: How South Africa Compares to Truth Commissions Worldwide', in ibid., p. 41.

The rhetoric of reconciliation, and the use of the word to describe the work of the TRC, is undoubtedly pretentious at one level because it seems so distant from reconciliation as reality. Would it not have been better, some might then ask, to refer to the TRC as the Commission on Truth and National Reconstruction? That would have avoided any theological problems and made the task of the TRC seem more manageable. But that description would not have carried the same weight nor had the same significance. It would have become yet another 'five year plan', akin to economic development programmes. The use of the word 'reconciliation' gave depth to the process even though it was very difficult to define precisely or impossible for the TRC to achieve. National reconstruction, it was rightly seen, requires economic transformation and the overcoming of poverty, but it required even more the overcoming of the hostility which colonialism and apartheid had generated: it required reconciliation between oppressors and victims. In short, reconciliation was a synonym for national reconstruction of a certain kind – national reconstruction in which a nation was born and gained its soul. But how does this relate to the Christian understanding of reconciliation as a gift of God's grace, and the ministry of reconciliation to which the Church is called in the world? Clearly the two are not identical, and to confuse them will inevitably lead to obfuscation of the issues. But equally clearly the two cannot be kept in separate compartments, for then the rhetoric loses touch with reality.

THE REALITY OF RECONCILIATION

For ecumenical pioneers during the First World War, J. H. Oldham being a good example, reconciliation summed up both their hopes for the world and their understanding of the churches' role in seeking to overcome the hostility between Germans and the Allied nations. This was also the context in which the Fellowship of Reconciliation was founded by Christians committed to a pacifist resolution of the conflagration. But it is clear from these references that there was no consensus on precisely what reconciliation meant and even less on how it was to be achieved. Oldham's political realism, which recognised the need to engage in war, was not the same as the pacifism of the Fellowship of Reconciliation, and both rejected the eschatological interpretation of reconciliation amongst German theologians for whom reconciliation was beyond human agency and realisation.[14] It is

---

[14] See Keith Clements, *Faith on the Frontier: A Life of J. H. Oldham* (Edinburgh: T&T Clark, 1999), pp. 137ff.

surely noteworthy that three groups of intelligent, well-trained, Christian theologians disagreed so much in their interpretation of this key concept, leading to such different political responses to the crisis that was shaking Europe to its core. Yet there is truth in each of their perspectives, and we need each to understand the full meaning of reconciliation and the way in which it becomes a reality.

The word translated 'reconciliation' (*katallasso*) in the New Testament appears infrequently, and then chiefly in the Pauline literature.[15] Yet it is widely understood in Christian theological tradition as a key concept for describing the core meaning of the gospel. A Scottish divine of an earlier generation, James Denney, spoke of it as 'the inspiration and focus of all' doctrines of the Christian faith.[16] And, of course, this was the central theme of volume IV of Karl Barth's *Church Dogmatics*. Clearly, then, the meaning of 'reconciliation' within Christian theology is more significant and multi-layered than the infrequent use of the Greek word in the New Testament would suggest. It is, in fact, the key symbol for the overcoming of the legacy of human sinfulness and the hope for the restoration or recapitulation of all things.[17] Reconciliation has to do with our personal relationship to God and to others, but from a Pauline perspective its scope is far greater. It has to do with God's breaking down of the wall of hostility between Jew and Gentile and, by inference, between other ethnic groups, between rich and poor, male and female, thereby bringing into birth a new humanity through the ignominy of the cross. According to the Pauline gospel, this is both a given reality and an eschatological hope. And it is to this reality and hope that the Church is a sign and witness in the world. The importance of this ministry of reconciliation in many contemporary contexts of conflict is widely acknowledged, and may be regarded as the most significant role which the Church can fulfil within society.[18]

The issue at stake for us is making the connection between reconciliation as a given reality of God's redemptive grace, and political concern and action, between the ministry of reconciliation within societies torn apart by conflict, and reconciliation as an eschatological promise. How does national reconstruction, as in South Africa, relate to the Christian conviction that reconciliation is something given by God ('the middle wall of hostility

---

[15] *The Theological Dictionary of the New Testament*, ed. Gerhard Kittel, vol. 1, trans. Geoffrey Bromiley (Grand Rapids: Eerdmans, 1977), pp. 255ff.

[16] James Denney, *The Christian Doctrine of Reconciliation* (London: James Clarke, 1959), p. 6.

[17] Article on Reconciliation in *The New International Dictionary of New Testament Theology*, ed. Colin Brown (Exeter: Paternoster Press, 1978), pp. 145ff. 1.

[18] See the collection of essays in Baum and Wells, eds., *The Reconciliation of Peoples*.

has been broken down'), which we can now appropriate whether or not we happen to be Christian believers? What is the connection between the religious, or specifically Christian, understanding of reconciliation and the secular, forensic, or political meanings? How does reconciliation overcome past hostilities and enable future peaceful relationships? If reconciliation is a process and a goal, how do means and ends relate? Does reconciliation require that differences between people need to be overcome, or that differences need to be respected and enhanced? How do oppressors and victims, along with the many bystanders, become reconciled? How is reconciliation to be understood within the framework of a multi-faith context? And how does reconciliation in South Africa relate to the broader concerns of the region, of Africa, and of the world at large? Such questions repeatedly surfaced during the work of the TRC in South Africa, and the responses reflected the range of perspectives, persuasions and experiences that one would expect in any diverse society, especially one with our historical legacy.

Clearly, reconciliation as a gift of grace that restores our relationship with God and anticipates the restoration of all things cannot be equated with reconciliation as a political policy and objective. But neither can these be separated as though they belonged to different spheres, the one religious, the other secular. There is undoubtedly an ultimacy to the first which is not true of the second, hence the need for distinguishing between them. But there must equally be a connection, else the gospel would be irrelevant to the world in which we live. The connection is surely that which Karl Barth recognised between justification and justice, and Dietrich Bonhoeffer between the ultimate and the penultimate.[19] God's will is not only the reconciliation of individual persons to God, nor is it an eschatological promise without present significance. God's will, if one may speak so boldly, is the overcoming of human alienation and the restoration of human community within society. This being so there is a fundamental connection between Christian witness and political endeavour and struggle. Ultimately our justification before God and therefore our reconciliation with God is dependent on God's grace; penultimately it is inseparable from our daily relationship to others and the exercise of social responsibility in pursuit of the common good.

The fact of the matter is that in both theological and secular use reconciliation is properly understood as the overcoming of hostility between

---

[19] Karl Barth, *Community, State, and Church: Three Essays*, Introduction by Will Herberg (Garden City, NY: Doubleday (imprint: Anchor), 1960), pp. 101ff. Dietrich Bonhoeffer, *Ethics* (New York: Macmillan, 1965), pp. 120ff.

people, whether as individuals or groups of one kind or another. It signals the healing of broken relationships. Thus the word is appropriately used within a variety of contexts, from marriages in crisis through ethnic and religious strife to international conflict. Reconciliation has to do with the breaking of barriers of hostility that historically and often violently divide people, communities and nations. It has to do even more with the restoration of relationships once such hostility has been overcome. Reconciliation has to do with our relationship to the individual as well as to the corporate 'other' from whom we are alienated and estranged, normally to such a degree that healing can only be achieved at considerable cost to both parties. Though it must be stressed that reconciliation is not necessarily something that occurs between parties of equal power, or between parties that are equally guilty, and therefore the dynamics involved are more complex and costly than those associated with conflict management. Reconciliation, as we have come to recognise in South Africa, is seldom 'a symmetrical process of mutual absolution'.[20] Reaching consensus may be part of what is involved, but reconciliation is more than achieving consensus. It is achieving a sustainable and genuine peace between former enemies, not least in situations where the playing fields are uneven given the legacies of the past and hopes for the future. Thus within my own context reconciliation means specifically the overcoming of racism and other forms of divisive and oppressive discrimination. The task of national reconstruction would be severely hampered, if not impossible, if at the same time there was not an attempt at deconstructing the apartheid soul and mind. Reconciliation has to do with the overcoming of the legacy of apartheid's hostile divisions as the *sine qua non* of constructing a just social order. Thus, to quote from Mandela's speech on receiving the TRC Report, reconciliation was the 'search for a nation at peace with itself and the building of a better life for all'.[21]

This brings us to another sense in which the word 'reconciliation' is used in Christian tradition, namely to the process of personal conversion within the life of the Church, associated with the confession of sin and the sacrament of penance.[22] From this perspective reconciliation has to do with a fundamental reorientation of life, *metanoia*, a change of heart and mind which demands acknowledgement of the truth and repentance followed by acts of reparation. At the same time, this presupposes the

---

[20] Asmal, Asmal and Roberts, *Reconciliation Through Truth*, p. 49.
[21] Quoted in Mgxashe, 'Reconciliation: A Call to Action', p. 218.
[22] Regis A. Duffy, article on Reconciliation in Joseph A. Komonchak, Mary Collins and Dermot Lane, eds., *The New Dictionary of Theology* (Dublin: Gill and MacMillan, 1987), pp. 830–6.

reality of God's grace and forgiveness, and the possibility of being forgiven by those who have been wronged. Without this the reality of reconciliation remains elusive within the experience of both the individual and society.[23] Reconciliation is, in fact, a shared and painful spiritual and ethical journey in which the truth is laid bare, hostility overcome, and fresh commitments made for putting wrongs to right. Understood in this way reconciliation becomes a journey enabled by grace and motivated by love and hope. It is the appropriation of the gospel promise, connecting our own personal and social journey to that of the grand narrative of redemption.

From this evangelical perspective reconciliation is far more than an idealist concept open for debate and logical clarification. It is a story to be lived and a story to be told. After all, for the Christian, reconciliation is not a concept or an idea but a story, a good news story. For this reason narrative becomes the appropriate discourse for expressing the reality of reconciliation experienced, and at the same time for uncovering the chasm between expectation and reality that remains to be bridged. The most potent accounts of the work of the TRC were not those that engaged in philosophical or political analysis, but those that told the story of what happened or did not happen during the process and how this impinged on the life of both individuals and the wider community.[24] By reflecting on such stories we begin to discern what reconciliation might concretely mean within a particular context, and we are able to relate them to the paradigmatic story of God's reconciliation of the world in Jesus Christ.

Allow me, then, to recount what happened during a doctoral seminar at the time of the Truth and Reconciliation Commission. Having heard about a PhD student at another university whose dissertation was on the TRC, we invited her to give an account of her work in progress. A middle-aged woman, working in sociology, she was engaged in research around the so-called 'Heidelberg Tavern Massacre' which occurred in 1993, a year before the first democratic elections. The Heidelberg Tavern is located not far from the University of Cape Town and at the time attracted a fair number of students and other young people. One evening four masked men burst into the tavern and fired several rounds of AK47 bullets into the crowd. Many people were injured and a number killed. Later the men, young black men, were arrested and sentenced to life imprisonment. During the TRC

---

[23] On the political significance of forgiveness, see Donald W. Shriver, *An Ethic for Enemies: Forgiveness in Politics* (New York: Oxford University Press, 1995); Gregory L. Jones, *Embodying Forgiveness: A Theological Analysis* (Grand Rapids: Eerdmans, 1995); Geiko Müller-Fahrenholz, *The Art of Forgiveness: Theological Reflections on Healing and Reconciliation* (Geneva: World Council of Churches, 1997).

[24] Antjie Krog, *Country of My Skull* (Johannesburg: Random House, 1998).

they applied for amnesty on the grounds that they were members of APLA (the armed wing of the Pan Africanist Congress) and that the shootings had been politically motivated. They did not believe that liberation had yet been achieved and therefore that reconciliation was possible. Our visiting sociology student's research centred on these four men. During their trial, which she attended, she asked permission to speak to them during an intermission. They were obviously wary of this white woman, but reluctantly agreed to talk. They asked her why she was interested in them. Her reply shattered both my seminar group and the accused. 'My daughter', she said, 'was killed in the massacre, and I want to find out whether or not we can become reconciled to each other!' From that time on she developed a close relationship with the young men, visiting them in prison, and eventually embarking on a programme of counselling together with them. Her research highlighted how personal, costly and traumatic genuine reconciliation can be, and how difficult it is for people coming from such vastly different backgrounds to find ways to achieve it.

Stories of this kind powerfully demonstrate the reality of reconciliation as a costly but graced journey, as well as something that can be experienced and expressed here and now, even though it can never be fully realised. It is an experience of reconciliation that is deeply embedded both in the gospel and in the realities of the South African political struggle. It is at the same time personal and social, a process and a goal, both religious and political. Indeed, the story just told confirms the idea that reconciliation is a God-given gift which we can appropriate here and now even though its full realisation must always lie in the future. Desmond Tutu, as chair of the TRC, worked on this assumption, understanding his role as consonant with his priestly vocation.[25] He was essentially a minister of reconciliation, reflecting the Pauline conviction that God has 'reconciled us to himself through Christ, and has given us the ministry of reconciliation' (2 Cor. 5:18ff.). As an ambassador of God's reconciliation, Tutu appealed to and entreated victims and oppressors to be reconciled. God has reconciled us in Christ so it is eminently possible for us to be reconciled. What was required was the willingness of those who are guilty to confess their sin and be willing to make amends, and the willingness of those who have been wronged to forgive their oppressors. Hence it was sometimes, though by no means always, possible for victim and oppressor to find each other during the TRC proceedings. If this were not the case then reconciliation would either be

[25] See Michael Battle, *Reconciliation: The Ubuntu Theology Of Desmond Tutu* (Cleveland: Pilgrim Press, 1997).

so cheapened as to become meaningless from a Christian perspective, or it would become so eschatological, so beyond present possibilities, that it would have no political significance at all.

It was far beyond the mandate and the capacity of the TRC to bring about the reconciliation of South Africa. What it did was to create space and opportunity, within the broader task of national reconstruction and the struggle for justice, for the deeper processes of forgiveness, confession, repentance and reparation, and therefore reconciliation. That is an ongoing process tied to the challenges demanded for national reconstruction, a process that must by its very nature be unending, for the tasks do not diminish with the passing of history. Yet, along the way, reconciliation can be and is experienced; there are signposts that encourage that conviction and sustain that hope. And there are stories to tell to help us understand what reconciliation can and does mean, and how its rhetoric can become reality in the service of national healing and reconstruction.

A POSTSCRIPT ON THE FUTURE OF THEOLOGY AND RELIGIOUS STUDIES

As intimated in my introductory remarks, reconciliation is not only a matter of considerable urgency within societies torn apart by conflict, but it is also a subject that demands the combined interdisciplinary attention of those engaged in theological and religious studies. Reflecting back over the contents of this essay it should be evident how these cognate disciplines contribute both appropriate methods for studying the issues, complementary insights in understanding them, and common approaches to dealing with them.

Those of us who have been engaged in the struggle for justice and reconciliation in South Africa as theologians have often been located within Departments of Religious Studies, to the immense benefit of our work. This in itself speaks loudly about the need for such co-operative interaction. It is not simply the case that this brings us into daily contact with religionists of other faiths, or of no particular religious commitment, for that is not the primary consideration here. Rather, it has to do with the differing perspectives and approaches of theology and religious studies to issues in general and to the problem of reconciliation in particular.

From a Christian theological perspective, reconciliation has a very particular history and meaning. As I have sought to demonstrate, it is of fundamental importance that such a perspective is taken seriously in a context such as ours. However, if that is the only approach to understanding reconciliation, then it is clearly inadequate in a multi-cultural and secular environment. Those who approach the subject in terms of religious studies certainly see reconciliation through a different set of lenses, and thus provide a different but equally necessary phenomenological perspective. An illustration of such co-operation and interaction can be seen in the work done by the Religion and Social Change Unit in the Department of Religious Studies at the University of Cape Town. Virtually all of the research emanating from that Unit provides evidence of how the disciplines inform and enable one another. One example that relates directly to the theme of this paper must suffice. I refer to the research report produced at the request of the Truth and Reconciliation Commission on the 'faith community hearings'.[26] There can be little doubt that a purely theological approach to the subject would have been inadequate. But it is equally the case that theological insights which arise out of the perspectives of particular faith commitments were necessary. It is in co-operation of this kind at the level of both research and teaching that the future of the two fields of academic endeavour are most likely to flourish.

[26] John W. de Gruchy, James C. Cochrane and Steve Martin, eds., *Facing the Truth: South African Faith Communities and the Truth & Reconciliation Commission* (Cape Town: David Philip, 1999).

CHAPTER II

Friendship

Janet Martin Soskice

According to Cicero, the 'one thing in human experience about whose advantage all men with one voice agree, is friendship...'. Some men hold virtue in contempt, others disdain riches or political honours, but 'concerning friendship all, to a man, think the same thing... that without friendship life is not life at all'.[1]

That friendship is one of life's greatest goods is as near a universal sentiment as one is likely to find, yet, as a topic for philosophy, friendship is nowadays neglected. It was not always so. Western Christian writings on friendship are heavily indebted to Cicero, who is himself already indebted to the Greeks. In the fourth century Ambrose and Augustine are wholehearted in their endorsement of Cicero – Augustine finds his definition of friendship cannot be bettered. Writing in the same vein in twelfth-century England, Aelred of Rievaulx cites Cicero almost word for word: 'Friendship is mutual harmony in affairs human and divine coupled with benevolence and charity.'[2]

Indeed, despite some fretful indications that one *should* be able to carve out a distinctly Christian position on friendship – Aelred insists, for instance, that 'Tullius [Cicero] was unacquainted with the virtue of true friendship, since he was completely unaware of its beginning and end, Christ' – Aelred rarely moves far in form or in substance from his pagan master.[3] In this he and other Christian writers were no doubt encouraged by Cicero's own natural theology, notable in the way his definition continues. 'I am inclined to think that with the exception of wisdom no better

---

[1] Cicero, *Laelius on Friendship*, trans. W. A. Falconer, Loeb Classical Library, vol. XX (Boston, MA: Harvard University Press), 1923, xxxiii.86.

[2] Aelred of Rievaulx, *Spiritual Friendship*, trans. Mary Eugenia Laker SSND (Kalamazoo: Cistercian Publications, 1977), p. 53. The Ciceronian definition he cites reads: 'For friendship is nothing else than an accord in all things, human and divine, conjoined with mutual goodwill and affection (*benevolentia et caritate*), and I am inclined to think that, with the exception of wisdom, no better thing has been given to man by the immortal gods' (*Laelius on Friendship*, vi.20).

[3] Ibid.

thing has been given to man by the immortal gods' (Cicero, *On Friendship*, vi.20). Aelred corrects such sentiments only by changing the plural, 'gods', to the singular, 'God'.[4]

Cicero writes so well and with such warmth that it is not surprising that his sentiments should resound across the ages. Friendship cannot exist except among good men (iv.18). It contains nothing false or pretended, it arises not from need or desire for material gain but from love. In friendship the two are equal, indeed the friend is 'another self', for: 'What is sweeter than to have someone with whom you may dare discuss anything *as if you were communing with yourself*?' (vi.22).

The Greek and Latin literature provides lists of templates, types and taxonomies of friendship. In the *Nichomachean Ethics* Aristotle gives a threefold classification of friendships, again much used by Christians, based on pleasure, on mutual advantage, or on shared concern for that which is good. All three have their merits but the third is the best. In Aelred we see what is recognisably the same three more sharply distinguished into carnal, worldly and spiritual friendships – the first two, in his monastic setting, entirely eclipsed by the third.[5]

We get lists of qualities a friend must have. Cicero would have us seek good men, loyal and upright, fair and generous, free from all passions, caprice and insolence, with great strength of character (v.19), frank, sociable, sympathetic (xviii.65), candid, affable, genial, agreeable, wholly courteous and urbane (xvii.66). This list of desiderata surely must limit the number of likely candidates to be anyone's friend.

In our own time friendship is more frequently discussed by social scientists than by philosophers or theologians. Sociologists, psychologists and anthropologists study 'friendships', treating them often as a 'natural' phenomenon in a sense which was not Cicero's – that is, as biological, adaptive and functionally effective. Christian writers, on the other hand, seem to take more interest in the more powerful concept of 'love'. Some of the most stirring sayings of the New Testament concern love – 'love your enemies', 'God is love'. If God is love, then why look further for affective relationships? Love is, indeed, all you need. By comparison friendship is love's pale echo.

Notoriously, some Christian theologians have tried to contrast *agape* and *philia*, privileging the first as the truly Christian form of love – a love

---

[4] See, too, Cicero's reproach to those philosophers (probably Stoics) who would say that friendship is a need and a weakness: 'Why, they seem to take the sun out of the universe when they deprive life of friendship, than which we have from the immortal gods no better, no more delightful boon' (*Laelius on Friendship*, xiii.47). Aelred, again, can cite directly ('Tullius speaks beautifully on this point . . .'), changing only 'gods' to 'God', *Spiritual Friendship*, p. 81.

[5] Ibid., p. 61.

which knows no bounds and loves without cause or concern. We need to be cautious of such 'taxonomies of love', for in the classical literature, and most noticeably in the Latin, love and friendship flow into one another.[6] Cicero several times makes a point that is more than etymological – *amicitia* derives from *amor* – and, in the Greek of the New Testament, *agape* and *philia* overlap in use. Etymology apart, it seems fundamentally mistaken to suppose that we can honour love only by disparaging friendship. The latter is not so much love's competitor as a particular manifestation of it. Friendship is best considered not in contrast to love's gold standard but rather as what friendship 'is' distinct and in itself.

Friendships, again following Cicero, are particular and partial. You are friends with particular people and not with everyone, and this gives friendship a different scope from love within the Christian lexicon. You should love your neighbour and even your enemy. We cannot be *friends* with everybody without evacuating all meaning from the notion. Cicero marks this as a difference between friendship and relationship (*propinquitas*): goodwill can be removed from a relationship but not from friendship, since 'if you remove goodwill from friendship the very name of friendship is gone...' (v.19).

Friendship is reciprocal – it involves at least two. A lover may have a beloved but we can readily think of circumstances where love is not returned. Love can be unrequited or, plausibly, may be a love for someone, past or present, with whom we are not personally acquainted (like Thomas Aquinas or Nelson Mandela). Although we may doubt whether we can *love* our enemies (*not* a sentiment to be found in Cicero), the New Testament enjoins us to do so with no suggestion that they will love us back. We also read there that it was not we who first loved God, but God who first loved us. So love, like hatred, need not be reciprocal or symmetrical: I can love without being loved, have an enemy without being one.

I can love without being loved, but friendship is quite different. I might say I love Nelson Mandela, but I cannot say that he is one of my friends. I cannot say, except in a deliberately contentious sense, 'I am *his* friend but he is not mine.' To be a friend is to have a friend. Yet if love is divine then friendship is, in its fundamental aspect, human. Friendship demands a certain distance as well as an intimacy between the one and the other. Christians can and do speak of the love flowing between the three persons of

---

6 One thinks here especially of Anders Nygren but also of Kierkegaard. On this and for many other insights see Gillian Clark and Stephen R. L. Clark, 'Friendship in the Christian Tradition', in Roy Porter and Sylvana Tomaselli, eds., *The Dialectics of Friendship* (London, New York: Routledge, 1989), pp. 26–43.

the Trinity but it would be unwise, in trinitarian terms, to say that the three 'persons' are friends of each other: that would be a sentiment dangerously near to tritheism, although we might be able to say 'the Trinity is friendship' much as one says 'God is love'.[7]

Friendship, I suggest, is fundamentally a creaturely and more specifically a human good. There are of course many 'goods' for us which cannot be predicated of God. It is good for us to eat, laugh, swim and play musical instruments. It is good for us to breathe, walk and have red blood cells. All these are creaturely goods and, the Christian doctrine of the Incarnation apart, good for God only insofar as we are God's creatures and what is 'good' for his creatures is, in a sense, 'good' for God.

Not all creatures have the same goods. It is good for a bird to have feathers but not for a snake; good for a rabbit to have furry, mobile ears but not for a fish. We need then some anthropology, some concept of the human being, to understand friendship as a distinctly human good. Here I confess myself to be suspicious of those anthropologies that undergird aspirational theories of friendship like that of Cicero – friendships springing from nature rather than from need. I have my doubts concerning this winnowing of men in a search for the truly virtuous, for the flash of soul upon soul. I hesitate over this search for men loyal and upright, fair and generous, free from all passions, caprice and insolence, frank, sociable, sympathetic, candid, affable, genial, agreeable, wholly courteous and urbane (xvii.66). Aelred at least makes our task a little easier, in a departure from Cicero, by listing not *what to seek* in a friend but *what to avoid*. We should avoid the irascible, the fickle, the suspicious, the garrulous, the angry, the unstable, the avaricious and the ambitious (*Spiritual Friendship*, 3:14 passim). Now all this is very good advice and, let us hope, advice that could be pursued in a twelfth-century Cistercian cloister, but, we may ask, this side of eternity, where could one find such a friend? Even more daunting, how could one be such a friend? Do these directives not presuppose superhuman self-knowledge, as well as a preternatural insight as to the inner workings of our neighbour? I want an anthropology at once more earthly than Cicero's and, at the same time, more genuinely divine.

C. S. Lewis, an Oxford don and important populariser of the Christian message in the mid-twentieth century, published an influential little book, *The Four Loves*, in which he devoted a chapter to friendship. There he, improbably, provides an anthropology which grounds friendship in the

---

[7] When Ivo, in the dialogue, asks Aelred, 'Shall I say of friendship what John, the friend of Jesus, says of charity: "God is friendship"?' (cf. John 4:16), Aelred replies that while this is unusual and does not have the sanction of scripture, 'what is true of charity I surely do not hesitate to grant to friendship...' (*Spiritual Friendship*, pp. 69–70).

primal horde. Speaking throughout of 'male friendship' – since he believes friendship will in most societies and periods be between men and men or women and women – he provides a little creative ethnography: 'In early communities the co-operation of the males as hunters or fighters was no less necessary than the begetting and rearing of children . . . Long before history began we men have got together apart from the women and done things. We had to.' He continues: 'Palaeolithic man may or may not have had a club on his shoulder but he certainly had a club of the other sort,' a sort of 'early sacred smoking-club'.[8]

From this basic 'clubbableness', as Lewis terms it, friendship arises on the basis of shared insight, interest and vision. Modern friends 'will still be doing something together, but something more inward . . . still hunters, but of some immaterial quarry . . .'[9] This, he tells us, is 'the luminous, tranquil, rational world of relationships freely chosen'. Friendship on his account is the least organic of loves and thus differentiated from the tugging of the guts and the fluttering of the diaphragm that characterise *Affection*, which we have for our young, and *Eros*, which we have for the opposite sex.[10] Women are to all intents and purposes ruled out of this happy band. Friendships between the sexes easily and quickly pass into erotic love (even within the first half hour, according to Lewis!) unless, of course, the two are lucky enough to be physically repulsive to one another.

Thus, 'it will be clear that in most societies at most periods Friendship will be between men and men or women and women. The sexes will have met one another in Affection and in Eros but not in this love.'[11] Even with his own wife or lover, then, a man will share Affection and Eros but not friendship.

Lewis's manly friendship is highly streamlined:

You become a man's Friend without knowing or caring whether he is married or single or how he earns his living. What have all these 'unconcerning things, matters of fact' to do with the real question, *Do you see the same truth?* . . . No one cares two-pence about anyone else's family, profession, class, income, race or previous history . . . This love (essentially) ignores not only our physical bodies but that whole embodiment which consists of our family, job, past and connections.

---

[8] C. S. Lewis, *The Four Loves*, 1960 (London: HarperCollins, 1998), p. 60. This continues: 'What were women doing meanwhile? How should I know? I am a man . . . I can trace the pre-history of Friendship only in the male line' (p. 61). He does not explain how he knows what *men* were doing in prehistoric times.

[9] Ibid., p. 62. It will be apparent that this is Lewis at his most insufferably 'donnish'.

[10] Ibid., p. 56. Lewis goes out of his way to distance this real manly friendship from homosexuality: 'Hrothgrar embracing Beowulf, Johnson embracing Boswell (a pretty flagrantly heterosexual couple) . . . ', p. 59.

[11] Ibid., p. 68.

Whereas 'Eros will have naked bodies', friendship is 'an affair of disentangled, or stripped minds'.[12]

Lewis's account of friendship is recognisably Ciceronian but without Cicero's human warmth. Cicero is at least willing to speak of friendships, not albeit of the highest kind, between children and their parents, or between a man and the nurses and slaves who tended him when a child, and even between animals and their young. Lewis takes to an extreme the Ciceronian ideal of a friend as 'alter ego'. And it is important to see that what is unsatisfactory about friendships with women on this account is not their sexual allure, something which troubled Ambrose and Augustine when it came to the question of friendships with women, but the fact that women will not share the same interests and activities as us – they are not like 'us', for 'they (men and women) will seldom have had with each other the companionship in common activities which is the matrix of friendship'.[13] What of the emotional world of these 'stripped minds'? How, we wonder, would Lewis react if another 'stripped mind' arrived at the club and told him that his child had been knocked off a bicycle and was mortally ill? Blustering silence? – 'terribly sorry, old boy, didn't know you were married – had offspring – that sort of thing . . . but let's get on with translating Beowulf'. How can we love someone or be friends with someone in their distinct particularity without knowing what they love? Stripped of all distinctiveness the other is an 'alter ego' only in a parodic sense – a mirror in which I see myself reflected.[14] It is not the exclusivity of this vision which should concern us, for friendship must always be particular, but rather that it rules out as a possibility friendship with one who is distinctively other. No doubt Lewis's practice was better than his theory but there is something sterile and self-regarding about Lewis's sketch of friendship here, something which took a terrific blow when he fell in love with an other who was an American, a Jew and a divorcee.[15]

It is not surprising that, despite being the most 'spiritual' of the four loves in his reckoning (that is, the least biological), friendship has, for Lewis, little directly to do with God. He does not want to speak of God as a friend. Surprisingly, for a writer so committed to the Bible, he does not mention any of the biblical passages which speak of friendship with God. On the contrary it is better, he says, to speak of God as father or as husband, language that cannot be taken literally. Nor can Lewis speak of

---

[12] Ibid., pp. 66–7.   [13] Ibid., p. 68.

[14] Lewis's sketch, while not homosexual, is certainly 'hommosexual' in Luce Irigaray's sense – a panegyric of love between same and same.

[15] Lewis writes of this movingly in *A Grief Observed*, originally published under a pseudonym in 1961.

God as 'friend' since a friend is for him, by definition, another self, an *alter ego*, and God must be further away, holier than that. There is no room for friendship with the genuinely other and as such not for friendship with God.

This distortion may allow us to see, amongst the gold, some iron pyrite in Cicero's famous account of friendship which is, after all, not in the least egalitarian. The highest form of friendship is found between men (it is taken for granted by Cicero – not between men and women) who are virtuous and wise, with common goals and aspirations, and enough wealth so as not to need the friendship in any material way.[16] The 'alter ego' is an image of the good man's virtuous self.

Aelred's variant is more attractive. His is not a picture of a perfect male society although to some extent he inhabited one. There are no women in his circle, but he is happy to speak of the creation of Eve from the very stuff of Adam and as his equal as a most beautiful inspiration as to what charity and friendship might be. Nonetheless his account of spiritual friendship retains some of the static features that limit Cicero's. What, were it ever achieved, would friendship have been like between monastic paragons? Would it be like the friendship of angels or of celestial spheres whose movements were so perfect they neither needed to be, nor could be, tuned? And is it not the case that *sub specie aeternitatis* we bump along – fragile, forgetful and all too human in our failings?

Let us come at this from a different starting point, not Cicero but the book of Exodus:

Moses used to take the Tent and pitch it outside the camp, at some distance from the camp. He called it the Tent of Meeting. Anyone who had to consult Yahweh [the Lord] would go to the Tent of Meeting... Whenever Moses went out to the Tent, all the people would rise ... the pillar of cloud would come down and station itself at the entrance to the Tent, and Yahweh would speak with Moses ... Yahweh would speak with Moses face to face, as a man speaks with his friend. (Exod. 33)

The Lord would speak with Moses face to face, *'as a man speaks with his friend'*.

Friendship, I have argued, is not an affective bond which may or may not be required. It is not, as Aristotle knew, a 'virtue' from which some other may or may not benefit, but *a relationship*. In this relationship 'the other person enters in not just as an object who receives the good activity,

---

[16] In our time this is why it is not enough to put too much weight on the power of 'discussion' if we have not first considered who is, and is not, in fact present as a discussion partner – who is present at friendship's table?

but as an intrinsic part of the love itself'.[17] An anthropology adequate to
friendship would be an anthropology of the at-least-two, the one and the
other who may reach out to include a third and a fourth. I suggest we might
look for such an anthropology to the writings of Martin Buber and of his
friend and associate, Franz Rosenzweig – to Buber's 'dialogical principle'
and to Rosenzweig's philosophy of 'speaking thinking'. For both Buber and
Rosenzweig the human being was essentially a 'speaking' being.

While ample and perplexed consideration has been given to the question
of how it is that God may speak to us (for instance in revelation), far less
has been paid to the fact, equally mysterious and wonderful, that we speak
to each other. We take our capacity for speech for granted, but no other
animal speaks one to another in the elaborate, diffuse and unpredictable
way we do. No other animal makes a promise or, in the truest sense, tells
a lie.

I am particularly fond of a passage in his *Speeches* where Schleiermacher
pauses to reflect on Adam alone in Eden. As long as Adam was alone, he
says, God addressed him in various ways, but Adam did not understand
for he did not answer. Adam's paradise was beautiful but he could not fully
sense it. He did not 'even develop within his soul'. Naming the animals
brought no solace to Adam but only greater dereliction. It was not until
there was another human being that his silence was broken and Adam
could, for the first time, see the glory of what lay about him and praise its
Creator.[18] Schleiermacher turns this mythical reverie to an anthropological
observation whose truth is empirical as much as metaphysical. Without
other persons one could not speak. This is true of any individual – no
infant, apart from being taught to speak by other people, could do so. It
is also true of the human race in general: were there only one man there
would not be language; this is Wittgenstein's point in the private language
argument. Language is a social possession and a social phenomenon. Without others we would not have language and without language we would not
be ourselves. In a very real sense we all, except for the most unlucky, come
fully into being by being spoken to. We are brought into full human being
by those others who bring us into language as much as by those who bear
us physically in their wombs. Even our most private thoughts are always

---

[17] Anthony Kenny, *Aristotle on the Perfect Life* (Oxford: Clarendon Press, 1992), p. 43.
[18] F. Schleiermacher, *On Religion: Speeches to its Cultured Despisers*, trans. Richard Crouter (Cambridge:
Cambridge University Press, 1988), p. 119. I discuss this passage at greater length in 'Incarnation, Speech and Sociality in Schleiermacher and Augustine', in M. M. Olivetti, ed., *Incarnation*,
Proceedings of the Castelli Colloquium (Milan: Cedam, 1999).

already framed and formed by the language we share with others, though not fully determined by it.[19]

A sustained meditation on the sociality of speaking is to be found in Martin Buber's philosophy of 'dialogue', presented in *I and Thou* (1923) and developed in other essays. It is mistaken to read Buber as an existentialist, as I was directed to do when first I read him, if we mean by that a lonely, fraught soul on a solitary quest for meaning. Indeed, Buber sets his face against this solitary inversion. He rejects any quest for human identity that begins either with the individual or with the collective 'mankind'. The essence of man, he tells us, begins neither with the individual nor with the collectivity, but only with the reality of mutual relations between man and man.[20]

His 'turn to the other' was attendant on a change in Buber's understanding of 'the religious'. In the essay 'Dialogue', written in 1929 to clarify the dialogical principle of *I and Thou*, he speaks about this change: 'In my earlier years the "religious" was for me the exception. There were hours that were taken out of the course of things. From somewhere or other the firm crust of everyday was pierced . . . "Religious experience" was the experience of an otherness which did not fit into the context of life.'

One forenoon, 'after a morning of "religious" enthusiasm, I had a visit from a young man . . . ' Buber's account of this meeting is sketchy, but while being friendly and even listening attentively Buber felt he had failed to hear this young person. He failed to discern in him an anguish about which he found out only after the young man was dead.

Since then I have given up the 'religious' which is nothing but the exception, extraction, exaltation, ecstasy; or it has given me up. I possess nothing now but the everyday out of which I am never taken . . . I know no fullness but each moral hour's fullness of claim and responsibility. Though far from being equal to it, yet I know that in the claim I am claimed and may respond in responsibility, and know who speaks and demands a response.[21]

---

[19] It interesting to note that both Aelred and Cicero have similar thought experiments to Schleiermacher's. Aelred asks his young monastic colleague if, had he all the possessions, riches and delights in the word – 'gold, silver, precious stones, turreted camps, spacious buildings, sculptures, and paintings', but no companion, he would enjoy all these possessions. Walter answers, 'Not at all.' Aelred then says, 'But suppose there were one person, whose language you did not know, of whose customs you were ignorant, whose love and heart lay concealed from you?' Walter says, 'If I could not by some signs make him a friend, I should prefer to have no one at all rather than to have such a one' (*Spiritual Friendship*, p. 78).

[20] Martin Buber, Foreword to *Between Man and Man*, trans. Ronald Gregor Smith (London: Kegan Paul, 1947), p. vii.

[21] Ibid., p. 13.

Here we have the this-here-now of existentialism, but tied always by Buber to the presence of the other: 'I do not know much more. If that is religion then it is just *everything*, simply all that is lived in its possibility of dialogue.'[22]

The dialogue of which Buber speaks is, of course, more than a speaking *at* one another. It is more than just exchanging pleasantries or pieces of information: '[T]he most eager speaking at one another does not make a conversation (this is most clearly shown in that curious sport, aptly termed discussion, that is "breaking apart", which is indulged in by men who are to some extent gifted with the ability to think.'[23]

This dialogue has equally little to do with those fictitious conversations which pass for religious dialogues 'where none regarded and addressed his partner in reality'.[24] Rather, it is a meeting and a speaking of the open-hearted to the open-hearted: it can even be found, says Buber in apophatic mode, in a certain silence which is nonetheless true communication.

Like the theorists of friendship we discussed earlier, Buber makes a three-fold classification into genuine dialogue, technical dialogue and mono-logue. 'Technical dialogues' are necessary but quotidian communications of the 'please pass the sugar' variety. Monologue, and especially monologue disguised as dialogue, is treated by Buber with contempt. If the basic life of dialogue is a turning towards the other, then the basic life of the monologist is not a turning away from, for to turn away one needs already at least to have *noticed* the other, but rather a 'reflexion' where the other is not met as an other at all but merely as an aspect of the monological self. An example Buber gives is the lover's chat which, far from being an ideal of intimacy, is little more than a dual monologue 'in which both partners alike enjoy their own glorious soul and their precious experience'.[25] (Buber's analysis of this erotic love is rather like that of Mme de Staël – 'égoïsme à deux'.) Just as the verbose do not necessarily speak, the monologist is not necessarily a solitary. He may be in the midst of the social swim, a campaigner for good causes, but never speak 'from being to being' with a fellow man.[26] Nature, for the monologist, is either a glorious state of the soul (an *état d'âme*), or a passive object of knowledge, either completely internalised in his feeling life or completely externalised to the world 'out there'.[27] The one living the life of monologue, above all 'is never aware of the other as something that is *absolutely not himself* and at the same time something with which he

[22] Ibid., p. 14.   [23] Ibid., p. 3.
[24] Ibid., p. 8. Buber, writing in 1929, seemed to anticipate a new dawn of conversations between the faiths – a tragic hope when we reflect that the Shoah followed.
[25] Ibid., p. 20.   [26] Ibid.   [27] Ibid., pp. 19, 20.

nevertheless communicates'.[28] Whereas: 'Being, lived in dialogue, receives even in extreme dereliction a harsh and strengthening sense of reciprocity; being, lived in monologue, will not, even in the tenderest intimacy, grope out over the outlines of the self.'[29]

Religion, if this represents an attempt find union with the One by casting off the dross of 'mere humanity', is the most deceptive retreat for the monologist. 'This person is not nearer but more distant from the God who is turned to men and who gives himself as the *I* to a *Thou* and the *Thou* to an *I* . . . '[30]

It is important to see that, despite his fulsome prose, Buber is not calling for 'universal unreserve'.[31] He is not saying that we must enter into this intimacy with everyone we meet, and indeed he puts some serious questions to Christian interpretations of 'love your neighbour' which decant into an indiscriminate caring. He *is* saying that one must be ready to stand in relation to others and even to meet and be changed by others who are not one's *alter ego* but, rather, 'absolutely not' oneself. Buber's is, in the end, a disciplined and austere religious vision. In it one seeks, not perfection, but just a 'break through' into 'nothing exalted, heroic or holy, into no Either or no Or'. He describes this in a beautiful phrase as the 'tiny strictness and grace of the everyday . . . '[32]

In what is one the most theologically revealing moments in his 'Dialogue' Buber says, 'Only when two say to one another with all that they are, "It is *Thou*", is the indwelling of the Present Being between them.' The 'indwelling of the Present Being' here is the Shekinah, 'the place where the Lord God causes his name to dwell'.[33]

The deeply Jewish nature of *I and Thou* was to some extent concealed from its first audience, partly by Buber himself who wished to give the book a broader appeal, and partly by a readership little attuned to his religious message. As Rivka Horowitz notes, those whose orientation was to social philosophy read *I and Thou* as social philosophy and judged its references to God and religion to be inessential. The truth, according to Horowitz, is the other way around: the social aspects were added to a work 'whose original and primary concern was the attempt, prompted by the disillusion with mysticism, to reformulate the concept and position of religion'.[34]

---

[28] Ibid., p. 20 (my emphasis).   [29] Ibid.   [30] Ibid., p. 25.

[31] Buber's expressionist style does not please all readers, yet one can see why, in an effort to burst through the starched formality of philosophical writings of his day, his writing verges on the vatic.

[32] Ibid., p. 36 .

[33] Ibid., p. 30 . Cf. Deut. 12:11 (see the Translator's note on p. 207).

[34] Rivka Horowitz, *Buber's Way to* I and Thou: *An Historical Analysis and the First Publication of Martin Buber's Lectures* 'Religion als Gegenwart' (Heidelberg: Verlag Lambert Schneider, 1978), p. 29.

The book is the fruit of reflections that absorbed Buber between 1918 and 1923, influenced by his reading of Hermann Cohen and his conversations with Franz Rosenzweig. By 1919 Buber had written a draft of the book and was already describing Jewish teaching as 'two-directional, as a reciprocal relation existing between the human I and the divine Thou'.[35] *I and Thou* came late as a title. Buber had earlier referred to the work as the 'Prolegomena to a Philosophy of Religion' or, more tellingly, 'Religion as Presence'[36] In 1922, and thus a year before the publication of *I and Thou*, he gave a course entitled 'Religion as Presence' (*Religion als Gegenwart*) at a Jewish college.[37] In these lectures he continues his earlier rejection of nineteenth- and twentieth-century religious functionalism and rationalism and the Kantian subordination of religion to ethics. He also rejects, with even more vigour, his own earlier advocacy of mystical experience as a means to counter religious rationalism. Truth lies not in mystical union but in encounter.[38]

Evident in the lectures, though downplayed in the eventual *I and Thou*, is the fact that the template for this encounter is the meeting of Moses with God on Sinai. This is the *God who is present to* Israel, the God who addresses Moses from the burning bush and who is, in turn addressed by him. For Buber, as for Rosenzweig, this moment is of decisive importance. When translating the Bible the two pondered at length over the proper translation of the Hebrew 'name' given to Moses in Exodus 3:14, the name frequently rendered in English language Bibles as 'I AM WHO I AM'. In their opinion, and scholarly opinion both Jewish and Christian is with them on this, I AM WHO I AM is not, in Exodus, a statement of metaphysics. Here is a gloss of Rosenzweig's, expressing a translator's viewpoint the two shared:

[A]ll those who find here notions of 'being,' of 'the-one-who-is,' of 'the eternal,' are all Platonizing . . . God calls himself not 'the-one-who-is' but 'the one-who-is-there,' i.e. there for you, there for you at this place, present to you, with you or rather coming toward you, toward you to help you. For the Hebrew *hayah* is not, unlike the Indo-Germanic 'to be,' of its nature a copula, not of its nature static, but a word of becoming, of entering, of happening.[39]

---

[35] Ibid., p. 20.   [36] Ibid., p. 22.

[37] These lectures were published for the first time only in 1978 by Rivka Horowitz, in the book mentioned above.

[38] Ibid., p. 30.

[39] 'A Letter to Martin Goldner', in Martin Buber and Franz Rosenzweig, *Scripture and Translation*, trans. Lawrence Rosenwald with Everett Fox (Bloomington: Indiana University Press, 1994), p. 191.

This relationship with the Absolute Thou stands, for Buber, behind all our being present to others: the German *gegenwart* indicates both 'presence' and 'present'. The Absolute Thou is the presence which guarantees that religion cannot be past, but only present. In the lectures, though not in the book, Buber is pleased to identify this presence with the Shekinah.

Rosenzweig is more restrained in developing his philosophy of 'speaking thinking', but the same themes run throughout. This is thinking always done in genuine response to an other and allowing of difference. It is modest in allowing that the other may have something to tell us, yet not fearful. In contrast to the Hegelian pattern where thesis and antithesis sublate one another to be mutually annihilated in synthesis, in dialogical thinking the one and the other are not destroyed by their encounter but become more truly themselves. In contrast with the pretensions of so much philosophy to speak from a timeless nowhere, actual speech is 'bound by time and nourished by time'. Because of this, dialogue 'does not know in advance just where it will end. It takes its cue from others.' Unlike the *faux* dialogues of Plato or of Hume, where the philosopher controls and brings it to a predetermined destiny, 'In actual conversation, something happens.' We are changed. 'Perhaps the other person will say the first word for in a true conversation this is usually the case; a glance at the Gospels and the Socratic dialogues will show the contrast.'[40]

Buber and Rosenzweig provide the foundations for an anthropology of the at-least-two which may assist our reflections on friendship. I have mentioned that I think there is probably too little sustained reflection on friendship today. There is a great deal of idealisation of friendship – we are told that young people take friendship more seriously than they do marriage – but what kind of friendship? Is the ideal put before us that of a friendship that does not disturb us too much? A friend who can be a friend as long as he or she does not make too many demands? While the 'self as solitary cogito' characteristic of much early modern and Enlightenment philosophical writings has been subjected to damning philosophical criticism, what might be called the 'popular' modern self (that is, the notion of self placed before us by advertising, media, governments and even of some philosophy) is still fundamentally autarchic after the eighteenth-century

---

[40] Franz Rosenzweig, 'The New Thinking: Philosophy and Religion', in Nahum N. Glatzer, ed., *Franz Rosenzweig: his life and thought* (Indianapolis, Cambridge: Hackett Publishing Company, 1998), pp. 198–9. I am warmed by Rosenzweig's suggestion that the Gospels, and he must mean their accounts of Jesus, show someone who is a 'speaking thinker', someone who is actually hearing and responding. Christianity has not proved so good at this.

pattern. This is a picture of the self as fully self-ruling and self-possessed, dipping into association with others only where this suits a private end. Cicero would more likely call this *propinquitas* than *amicitia*.

Within an anthropology of the 'at-least-two' the friend is not a blank sheet for the free play of my emotions or my virtues. Nor are the friends aligned in symmetrical but static perfection. I am becoming myself in and through who I am for others and who they are for me.

Who can be my friend? Not *everyone*, certainly not everyone at once. Friendship is a relation with particular persons and not with generic humanity. But if we cannot be friends with everyone, we should not dismiss the unCiceronian possibility that we might be friends with almost *any one*. Buber prompts us to consider the possibility that a friend may come as a surprise, a grace. Friends cannot after all be mechanically generated. Like the divine You, there is a sense in which the human you encounters me by grace. And because friendship is not based on shared perfection in virtue and is not static, within this way of thinking there is room to say that we might become the friends of God. Indeed that this is what we should aspire to – in the words of Nicholas Lash, a 'creaturely dependence relearned as friendship'.[41]

Friendship, according to one classical tag, either finds or makes equals. If we consider what is entailed in friendship – reciprocity, equality, respect – it is no mean thing to hope that we may become a friend of God. C. S. Lewis was very nearly right to sense an unacceptable presumption in claiming God as our friend – very nearly right but not entirely faithful to his scriptures.

Were I here trying to devise a Christian theology of friendship I might develop this along the lines of being made friends of God in Christ ('I call you my friends'), but that is not my object here. I have been trying in this essay not just to enunciate a position but to practise it. I have been trying to listen to my friends Buber and Rosenzweig and for this purpose I wish to stay with the Mosaic moment of the burning bush, that graced moment of call and address. In any case, God's 'being present' to Israel, immanent in divine transcendence as cloud and fire and tabernacle, is, if I may be so bold, behind what becomes in Christianity the doctrine of the Incarnation.

But this raises a question on the extension of the term 'friendship'. Can I call Buber my friend, or Rosenzweig? It's not clear how the desiderata of equality and reciprocity would work here. Perhaps to think of them as

---

[41] Nicholas Lash, *The Beginning and the End of 'Religion'* (Cambridge: Cambridge University Press, 1996), p. 13.

my friends is to evacuate the term of meaning. We are right be concerned that this precious and intimate notion of friendship should not degenerate into a lazy, generalised benevolence – a 'cheap friendship' along the lines of 'cheap grace'. Yet it does not seem enough to say that I have been trying *to listen to* Buber and Rosenzweig. In a palpable way I feel myself to have *been found* by their writings, addressed from across the years. Like friends they change me and in this analogical way we can speak of friendship.

Can we speak then, analogously, of 'being friends' with the texts of the Parsis or the Buddhists, of standing alongside the natural scientists or the poets? In some sense, are not most scholars of religion and theology engaged in befriending – being alongside particular texts and traditions and trying with imaginative sympathy to listen to them as we proceed *in via*? We cannot be friends with them all but we can learn to love and respect some very much and, in doing so, glimpse the beauty of the others.

I can never be confident that I am hearing Buber and Rosenzweig aright – never certain that I am not reading my own Christian predilections into their Jewish texts, or my twenty-first-century British circumstances into their early twentieth-century German existences. But I am comforted by Buber's own modesty. We are like those illuminated by a passing meteorite which brightly if momentarily illumines the place in which we stand. I find in this modesty a partner to those elements of my own Christian tradition I find most attractive – we are confident but partial . . . on the way, but not yet there.

I hope I will be changed by my friendship, because change is essential to growth. It is to me interesting that it is Buber in his more distinctly Jewish and less generically philosophical moments who speaks to me most. My friend does not need to be my *alter ego*. Indeed I am no friend to her nor she to me if she does not continue to be fully, truly herself. In Gregory of Nyssa's *Life of Moses*, a work addressed to a friend and written as a guide to virtuous life, the template of perfection held out to the Christian reader is the Israelite, Moses. And what more clear testimony, says Gregory, rounding off his argument, of the fact that the life of Moses did 'ascend the highest mount of perfection' than that he is called the 'friend of God'?[42]

---

[42] Gregory of Nyssa, *The Life of Moses*, trans. Abraham J. Malherbe and Everett Ferguson (New York: Paulist Press, 1978), p. 137.

CHAPTER 12

Justice

Maleiha Malik

It seems appropriate to start an essay in honour of Professor Nicholas Lash by citing the words of a former theologian at Cambridge as the basis for my discussion. In 1917 John Wood Oman, who from 1907 to 1935 was Professor of Systematic Theology and Apologetics at Westminster College, observed in his book *Grace and Personality* that 'If the infallibilities have been overthrown by inquiry and reason, they cannot be raised again by affirmation or even by the strongest conviction of their utility.' He went on to note that behind this question of the infallibilities lies a deeper question about whether we, in the face of history and experience, maintain the conception of God and man on which it rests.[1]

This strikes me as a particularly apt observation for discussions about faith, politics and justice because it identifies two key ideas. First, the observation raises important questions about political advocacy and therefore the appropriate contribution of a theological or religious perspective to contemporary politics. Second, it suggests that there is a relationship between activity in the public sphere and the concept of the self. This essay explores these general ideas by examining one way in which theology and religious studies can relate to contemporary issues of justice and politics. In this essay the wider term *faith perspectives* is used to capture not only the formal and theoretical aspects of theology and religious studies but also the more practical way in which faith operates within the lives of individuals. The other noteworthy feature of Professor Oman's writing in *Grace and Personality* is his recognition of history and experience as limiting factors on our analysis. This realism is, in my view, a most attractive framework for analysis. These limits include rooting political theory in the 'here and now'.[2] More specifically, it means that political analysis and activity in the

---

[1] J. Oman, *Grace and Personality* (Cambridge: Cambridge University Press, 1917).
[2] M. Oakeshott, *The Politics of Faith and the Politics of Scepticism* (New Haven: Yale University Press, 1996).

conditions of contemporary Europe are dependent upon a field of historic possibilities. In the past a range of political responses may have been appropriate that is no longer either available or appropriate. The range of action in contemporary politics may have contracted in some direction but it has expanded in other ways. Any discussion of the role of faith perspectives in contemporary politics must respond to these new realities.

Perhaps the most important feature of the 'here and now' of contemporary Europe are social conditions that include a deep diversity of belief which is simultaneously different, reasonable and sometimes conflicting.[3] As John Rawls has noted, this diversity in contemporary liberal societies reflects the fact that there are many comprehensive conceptions of what it means to lead a good life. Rawls labels this social condition *reasonable pluralism* and he states:

A modern democratic society is characterised not simply by a pluralism of comprehensive religious, philosophical, and moral doctrines but by a pluralism of incompatible yet reasonable comprehensive doctrines. No one of these doctrines is affirmed by citizens generally. Nor should one expect that in the foreseeable future one of them, or some other reasonable doctrine will ever be affirmed by all, or nearly all, citizens. Political liberalism assumes that, for political purposes, a plurality of reasonable yet incompatible comprehensive doctrines is the normal result of the exercise of human reason within the framework of the free institutions of a constitutional democratic regime. Political liberalism also supposes that a reasonable comprehensive doctrine does not reject the essentials of a democratic regime. Of course a society may also contain unreasonable and irrational, and even mad, comprehensive doctrines. In their case the problem is to contain them so that they do not undermine the unity and justice of society.[4]

In the context of the present discussion this diversity of conceptions of the good is relevant in a number of ways. It is assumed that the faith perspectives that we are concerned with fall within the class of Rawls's reasonable comprehensive doctrines that should be accommodated within a liberal democracy. In addition, the fact of reasonable pluralism will mean that faith perspectives (religious doctrines) must co-exist with conceptions of the good that are not based on faith. In some cases faith perspectives will have to co-exist with doctrines that are generally sceptical about faith and religion (atheist or agnostic) or are specifically sceptical about a particular

³ For a more detailed discussion of these issues see the discussion in M. Malik, 'Faith and the State of Jurisprudence', in *Faith and Law: Essays in Legal Theory* (Oxford: Hart Publications, 2000). Parts of this chapter draw on and are a revised statement of the arguments in that chapter.
⁴ J. Rawls, *Political Liberalism* (New York: Columbia University Press, 1993), p. xvi.

faith (e.g., anti-Jewish, anti-Muslim, anti-Hindu approaches, etc.). Finally, the fact of reasonable pluralism will mean that there is diversity within faith perspectives. No one faith perspective or religion can claim priority over another: Jewish, Christian, Muslim, Hindu and Sikh perspectives will have *equal and valid* claims in the public sphere. Moreover, the State will treat all interpretations of faith perspectives by insiders that are within the limits of being 'reasonable comprehensive doctrines' as equally valid. So, no particular version of a faith perspective will be given priority over another in the public sphere. Within this essay the fact of reasonable pluralism provides the most pressing limit on our analysis. Reasonable pluralism is the most salient fact about the 'here and now' which will influence our discussion of the relationship between faith perspectives and contemporary issues of politics and justice.

This essay explores some of these themes by relating them to our contemporary discussions about the relationship of justice to faith. Although the analysis proceeds through a number of inter-related points which are presented in four parts there is a common thread that runs through all these arguments. That common thread is my concern about a vision of politics that takes neutrality as the appropriate starting point for analysis. This is not equivalent to a general dismissal or scepticism about liberalism as the basis for political justice. Liberalism is a permanent fact of the 'here and now' of our times which the present analysis accepts as its starting point. Rather, my scepticism is about a version of contemporary liberalism that veers towards 'neutrality' in both method and substance. Many theorists who remain liberals have questioned this model and traced the consequences that this model has had for our public (and private) lives.[5] There is also a substantial literature on the difference between these visions of liberalism, between perfectionists and anti-perfectionists.[6] It is not my intention to revisit this debate in this essay. Rather, there are a number of aspects of this insistence on neutrality in our discussion of politics – both in theory and practice – that I want to discuss. The first part of the essay takes up this critique of neutrality through exploring its impact on the way in which we theorise about politics. Should political action and our public life be understood in 'empiricist, verifiable and neutral' terms? What are the consequences of using these criteria for those who rely on a faith

---

[5] See for example the work of Charles Taylor in *Philosophical Papers*, vols. I and II (Cambridge: Cambridge University Press, 1985), or of Alasdair MacIntyre in *After Virtue: A Study in Moral Theory* (London: Duckworth, 1985). See also M. Malik, 'Governing After the Human Rights Act', *Modern Law Review* 63/2 (March 2000), pp. 281–93.

[6] See for example Joseph Raz, *The Morality of Freedom* (Oxford: Clarendon Press, 1986).

perspective? In the second part of the essay I move on to suggest that there are alternative methods for understanding belief and conduct which are more amenable to faith perspectives. However, these alternative methods require painful adjustments and concessions. Theorists may need to accept that there is a limit to the degree of certainty that they can demand when the subject matter is faith. Faith perspectives may need to concede that they cannot always insist that their comprehensive doctrine is the 'absolute truth'. In the third part of the essay I ask how liberal politics and institutions can respond to faith perspectives. I then move on to consider in Part IV whether faith perspectives have any contribution to make to our discussions about justice and politics. Do they have any role to play in contemporary political advocacy?

My tentative conclusions are that there are good reasons why liberal politics and liberal institutions should take faith perspectives seriously and in some cases accommodate them. I also suggest that faith perspectives can make a unique contribution in supporting a distinct vision of human agency and political community. Once we move away from a strict adherence to neutrality there is some space for a faith-based viewpoint to contribute to our contemporary discussions about justice and politics. However, this viewpoint must take the limits identified by Professor Oman – of history and experience – as essential limits on analysis and political advocacy. These limits include recognising reasonable pluralism as a permanent fact about the 'here and now' of contemporary Europe. This means that a faith-based perspective is just one among many legitimate points of view that can influence public discussion and action.

PART I

Contemporary liberal theory presents us with a vision for understanding politics that seems incompatible with faith. It seems to require adoption of a neutral 'point from nowhere' as the appropriate perspective from which to undertake analysis. This demand for neutrality requires the theorist to undertake the task of standing back from personal attachments and beliefs before using rationality and the intellect as the sole guide to the truth.[7] This method is not hospitable to faith for a number of reasons.

---

[7] Despite substantial modifications to his theory Rawls's most recent work, *Political Liberalism*, remains committed to the view that the choice of political principles should be from a viewpoint (the original position) which excludes information about a person's comprehensive concept of the good.

There is an inherent tension in any attempt to respond to faith perspectives.[8] Existing concepts and models based on neutrality and rationality are not the ideal starting point for such an analysis. Theoretical analysis which proceeds via precise definition and rational demonstration does not very easily accommodate faith-based arguments. An adequate response to faith requires an understanding of a realm of experience and consciousness which fits uneasily with practical reason and its concomitant model of truth and cognition. Michael Oakeshott suggests that this is an intractable conflict. He characterises reason-based modes of politics as 'the enemy of authority, of the merely traditional, customary or habitual'. For Oakeshott, the 'rationalist is essentially ineducable' in relation to issues of tradition and narrative – which we have characterised as faith – because they require from him an 'inspiration which [is regarded] as the great enemy of mankind'.[9] In addition, and more worrying, is the risk that the effort to articulate, analyse and subject to critical scrutiny a tradition by 'outsiders' may be incompatible with preserving the full meaning of the tradition as understood and experienced by 'insiders'.

Neutrality and objectivity should, at first sight, be an attractive route into understanding faith, especially in the context of reasonable pluralism. These techniques seem to allow the theorist to bypass problems of choice of evaluative criteria. The claim to neutrality and certainty is achieved by avoiding any subjectivity or 'bias' of the theorist, and by focusing on data which can be understood in absolute terms and without reference to the experiences of the subject. In this way the theorist is encouraged to break free of his own perspective and to adopt a neutral point of view as a pre-requisite to study, thereby using a method for the study of human conduct which avoids the dangers of uncertainty, evaluation and subjective interpretation. All of these ensure that faith-based arguments are on an equal footing between each other and in relation to other types of arguments.

However, a closer look at this model suggests that it is not hospitable to faith. The appropriateness and success of this analysis requires that the subject matter is amenable to study using the techniques of neutral

---

[8] See for example the discussion of Stephen L. Carter in 'Evolutionism, Creationism and Treating Religion as a Hobby', *Duke Law Journal* (1987), p. 977. Although Carter's discussion deals specifically with religious belief his discussion in Part II (Liberalism and Religion) could be applied to all faith-based arguments which are relevant to this discussion. Carter quotes Unger: 'Wherever liberal psychology prevails, the distinction between describing things in the world and evaluating them will be accepted as the premise of all clear thought ... The contrast of understanding and evaluation is foreign to the religious consciousness, for its beliefs about the world are simultaneously descriptions and ideals.'

[9] M. Oakeshott, 'Rationalism in Politics', in his *Rationalism in Politics* (London: Methuen, 1962), p. 1.

observation and description: human conduct needs to be made more manageable to inquiry of this type. This is usually achieved through a number of moves. First, this model gives priority to those features of human agency which can be attributed with absolute properties: that is, which can be described without the dangers of uncertainty and relativity. In this way the focus of analysis is steered towards the external conduct of the agent. The importance of inner motivations, beliefs and states of consciousness is ignored or at the very least marginalised.[10] Even where theory gives priority to these internal attitudes they are treated as 'brute facts' which can be stated unproblematically in neutral and objective descriptions, rather than as inherently subjective 'meanings' which need to be understood from the perspective of the relevant subject who experiences them.[11] Second, the appropriate temporal unit for analysis tends to be the basic action. Instead of concentrating on the history of the individual or the origins of the social practice which provide the context within which the act is performed, conduct tends to be studied as an isolated and one-off act.[12] Difficult questions of evaluation and comparison are avoided. On this model there is no problem of distortion of the other; there is merely a description of conduct about which it is not possible to be wrong. No viewpoint is given priority; neutrality and objectivity ensure accurate and unbiased understanding.

[10] Traditionally, John Austin's attempt to develop a 'science of jurisprudence' sought to develop the subject along the lines of the natural sciences. The fact that reflection on the nature of law is concerned with human conduct was not seen to be a significant barrier to the application of description and observation as the appropriate tools for understanding these facts. Contemporary jurisprudence has of course broken free of the naïve assumptions of Austin's model, although the methods and assumptions concerning human agency which underlie this approach continue to present themselves as an attractive option. Arguably, the attraction of Economic Analysis of Law is explained (in part) by the way in which its assumptions concerning human agency (focusing on man as a rational maximiser of desires) successfully avoids questions of motivation. All questions concerning value are either avoided or equated with what people want, using criteria of efficiency that are amenable to calculation. This type of analysis emphasises weighing between values rather than any investigation of a qualitative contrast between them. For a discussion of these features of Economic Analysis of Law see A. A. Leff, 'Economic Analysis of Law: Some Realism about Nominalism', *Virginia Law Review* 60 (1974), p. 451.

[11] Hart's work breaks from the naïve techniques which focus on outward phenomena, towards a method which attends to the inner states of subjects. He states, in relation to understanding law as a rational and empirical science: 'My main objection to this reduction of propositions of law which suppress their normative aspect is that it fails to mark and explain the crucial distinction that there is between mere regularities of human behaviour and rule-governed behaviour. It thus jettisons something vital to the understanding not only of law but also of any form of normative social structure. For the understanding of this the methodology of the empirical sciences is useless; what is needed is a "hermeneutic method" which involves portraying rule governed behaviour as it appears to its participants, who see it as conforming or failing to conform to certain shared standards.' See H. L. A. Hart, *Essays in Jurisprudence and Legal Philosophy* (Oxford: Clarendon Press, 1993), p. 15.

[12] MacIntyre, *After Virtue*, ch. 15.

Neutrality in method requires a move beyond subjectivity and interpretation in favour of building knowledge on brute and verifiable data that cannot be challenged further by an appeal to facts or interpretation. The resulting analysis of social reality is presented as being free of the 'defects' of subjectivity and interpretation. Social and political concepts and structures are presented as a reality that is based on brute data and verifiable facts. What is objectively real must be identifiable using verifiable brute data. An approach based on techniques such as interpretation, which is not built on precise brute data, does not meet the stringent requirements of avoiding subjectivity and non-arbitrary verification. A reading of social reality that is described in terms of its meaning *for the subject* has a limited place in this analysis. This model treats relevant beliefs as yet another fact about objective reality: these attitudes, beliefs and reactions are either treated as brute data to be noted or they are placed in quotes and attributed as opinion, which has a lesser status. Therefore, within this process the fact that an opinion or belief is held by a subject can be noted as a brute fact; but the content of the opinion itself cannot be verified. Any description of meaning which is open to interpretation is kept separate from the analysis: it is not allowed to influence the reading of social reality itself on a more fundamental level.[13]

Once a method that ignores the fundamental importance of intersubjective meanings is applied to the study of human conduct and political action those who seek to maintain a faith perspective are placed at a significant disadvantage. The fact of faith as a motivation for belief and action cannot be expressed in factual and verifiable terms. It is included within a neutral empiricist analysis as just one opinion amongst all the others that are held by various participants. It cannot provide the basis for a valid understanding of our social life because it is not amenable to verification.

So should we move from neutrality in method towards an approach that takes up the perspective of the subject more explicitly? The shift towards understanding conduct from the perspective of the subject is problematic in the context of reasonable pluralism, which we noted is part of the reality of the 'here and now' of conditions in our contemporary world. How is it possible to take into account all the different motivations and beliefs which underlie these different and various faith perspectives? How should we seek to understand a very different faith perspective when we are an outsider to the tradition from which it springs? Neutrality seems to be an

---

[13] C. Taylor, 'Interpretation and the Sciences of Man', in his *Philosophy and the Human Sciences, Philosophical Papers*, vol. II (Cambridge: Cambridge University Press, 1985).

attractive method of analysis not only for (a) those trying to understand any faith perspective; but also for (b) those with a faith perspective trying to understand a different faith tradition. In these circumstances it is tempting to fall back on description and observation, in the hope of avoiding internecine disputes about intention and belief, thereby providing some potential for understanding and consensus through theory. However, any apparent advantages of this 'neutral' method as a way of understanding faith perspectives in these contexts are illusory. Rather than complying with the requirements of neutrality, in the specific context of faith, strict neutrality and an emphasis on verifiable brute data are unlikely to yield a useful and accurate understanding of the other. The 'point from nowhere' neutrality towards which this method aspires as the basis from which to understand is not – from the perspective of faith-based arguments – neutral. What seems to be a neutral starting point, and an objective method, does not facilitate a non-distorted understanding of faith. On this analysis, faith-based conduct which is alien and different is likely to remain inexplicable and will continue to seem irrational to the theorist.

A neutral method ignores the way in which there can be other alternative ways of understanding social reality that are legitimate and have meaning for individuals. What is excluded in particular is a reading of human conduct, social reality and political action that is construed in terms of the meaning that the action has from the perspective of *that agent*, i.e., an inter-subjective meaning. The way in which a neutral method ignores inter-subjective meanings is especially relevant for our analysis. There are certain types of actions that cannot be described merely as facts and that cannot just be attributed as opinion in quotation marks. Faith-based conduct obviously falls within this category. Where the conduct of a person is motivated by faith, and especially by a faith not shared by the observer, the beliefs and actions of the subject will often remain puzzling, irrational and incoherent to an 'outsider' who does not share that faith. The only way to make sense of this type of action is to understand that the belief or action has a certain significance and meaning for the subject. So we can only make sense of contradictory and seemingly irrational belief or action when we come to a better understanding of why the agent engaged in that action. However, a neutral method cannot give inter-subjective meanings the kind of status that this analysis would suggest because they cannot be presented in factual and verifiable terms. Inter-subjective meanings cannot be allowed to taint our reading of social reality.

There are other ways in which this method is inappropriate when it comes to faith-based arguments. Its focus on external conduct and the basic action is likely to distort the full value of these practices as experienced by participants. What is missed altogether – or at the very least rendered marginal – are the crucial motivations and inner states of consciousness which underpin these types of beliefs and conduct. Understanding these actions fully will require reference to their meaning, as understood and experienced by the participants. A descriptive method often ignores these altogether. Where they are considered, these aspects are treated as facts to be described: by merely noticing that a belief is held or by delineating causal connections between beliefs and conduct and attributing these to specific individuals. These techniques are not ideal for analysing inner states from the perspective of the subject who experiences them, which is of critical importance in this context. In addition, the emphasis on the basic action and a historical analysis of the conduct of the agent will altogether miss the importance of placing these features within the agent's history and background. The action may take on its meaning in the context of the whole of the life of the agent; or it may be linked to a longer narrative tradition or social practice that gives the act its justification, meaning and significance. Attention to the act, without any reference to inner states and this wider temporal context, is therefore likely to miss important features of faith-based conduct.

Recent post-modern scholarship tells us that this problem arises whenever we seek to understand a tradition as outsiders by applying evaluative criteria, which is often a universally applicable standard external to that tradition. In fact, one of the main concerns of the advocates of the 'politics of recognition' in contemporary liberal democracies has been to expose as delusory and ethnocentric the claim to neutrality made by methods that claim to be purely descriptive (and universalist) accounts.

The alternative to ethnocentrism is to avoid evaluation altogether, thereby side-stepping the need to choose criteria. Some post-modern scholarship, particularly the work of theorists who invoke Nietzsche, and work derived from the writing of Foucault and Derrida, argues for the importance of 'diversity' as a value and often insists that any evaluative criteria used are ultimately derived from existing power structures.[14] To impose evaluative criteria from the outside is, for example, to do 'violence' to the other. On the whole, these theories avoid the problem of choice of evaluative criteria in one of two ways: by arguing either that there are no evaluative criteria to apply in this context or that all evaluative criteria are equally valuable.

---

[14] See, for example, I. M. Young, *Justice and the Politics of Difference* (Princeton: Princeton University Press, 1990), esp. ch. 4.

Neither of these is ideal for understanding faith-based arguments. The first claim – which denies the legitimacy of applying evaluative criteria – sits uneasily with faith-based arguments. Although these types of arguments rely on narrative and tradition, and often invoke their own criteria for legitimacy, they remain committed to the position that these are valuable and true options. This first strategy, which seeks to avoid evaluation, is unlikely to provide a useful model for understanding the full implications of the claims made by those who rely on faith. The second option, which concedes that all evaluative criteria are equally valid, seems to be more attractive. It coheres with the claim to respect and recognition which is sought. However, on closer examination this strategy is also problematic. If all positions are granted 'equal respect' without any inquiry into what they are or why they are valued, then – arguably – this is a 'hollow' version of recognition. The respect and recognition sought – and the argument that there should be a better understanding of faith-based arguments – require some attention to the claim by insiders that these have value. An endorsement on demand, without any investigation or appreciation of the true value of the faith for 'insiders', does little to advance understanding in this context. In any event, rather than being an act of respect and recognition, an automatic grant of approval on demand could be construed as an act of condescension.[15]

PART II

To gain a better grasp of faith, what is required is an approach that explicitly shifts the focus from external conduct to the inner motivations and beliefs underpinning this conduct. Those theorists who insist that it is an essential rather than a contingent fact about human beings that they not only desire and act, but also undergo a process of reflection about their conduct, provide some of the resources for this shift in analysis.[16] This alternative method forces us to notice that not only do human agents have first order desires (about what they want), they also have second order desires (where they rank these desires according to evaluative criteria). In this way, some desires

[15] C. Taylor, *Multiculturalism and the Politics of Recognition* (Princeton: Princeton University Press, 1992), p. 70.

[16] See for example C. Taylor: 'What is Human Agency?' in his *Human Agency and Language, Philosophical Papers*, vol. 1 (Cambridge: Cambridge University Press, 1985), p. 15; H. Frankfurt, 'Freedom of the will and the concept of a person', *Journal of Philosophy* 67 (1971), pp. 5–20. I. Murdoch discusses these issues at length in *Metaphysics as a Guide to Morals* (Harmondsworth: Penguin, 1992). See also M. Oakeshott, 'On the Theoretical Understanding of Human Conduct', in his *On Human Conduct* (Oxford; Clarendon Press, 1990), p. 1.

and actions of the agent are ranked by him according to his conception of value as being lofty, noble and an aspect of an integrated way of living, whereas others are deemed to be unworthy, base and associated with a fragmentary life. These second order desires necessarily entail not only a quantitative assessment of what and how much is desired, but also a qualitative assessment of whether these desires fit in with the agent's sense of what makes his life valuable. This method presents a more attractive way of capturing all the data relevant for an understanding of faith perspectives which gives special weight to these features of human agency.

Once this different view of human agency is accepted, it becomes clear that a full understanding of conduct cannot rely solely on observation and description. Reflection – motivations, beliefs and intentions – cannot be communicated in certain, absolute and objective terms. This emphasis necessarily introduces subjectivity as we are required to understand these features by referring them to the experience of the agent. Moreover, these features require a focus on a temporal unit for analysis which extends beyond the basic action. Understanding meanings, motivation and the inner states of consciousness necessarily requires placing these features within the context of the whole history of the agent. Where the agent relies on faith-based arguments this may also require attention to the historical background of the tradition within which these arguments develop and take on their significance.

More specifically, three important modifications need to be made to incorporate these aspects. First, motivation, belief and the 'meaning' of practices take on a central rather than a peripheral role in this inquiry. Second, the conduct needs to be placed within the wider context of the experiences of the agent. This shift in focus means that the methods of neutrality and observation need to give way to techniques which focus on the data from the perspective of the agent. Objectivity will need to be supplemented by some attention to the viewpoint of the subject, as the theorist attempts to understand belief and conduct from this perspective. Third, the nature of these types of commitments sets important constraints on the degree of certainty and the type of understanding which the theorist should seek.

It is often assumed that understanding in these contexts requires reaching an agreement on shared values which can be endorsed by both – or all – relevant parties. However, this is not a helpful way of setting up the goal of analysis where the subject matter is faith-based belief or conduct. There is an alternative way of approaching study in this context which requires the theorist to proceed very differently. Rather than seeking agreement on absolute and neutral criteria, this alternative method suggests that 'understanding the other' is about making them – and their self-understanding – more intelligible.

Philosophical hermeneutics provides some of the resources necessary for making the experiences of agents amenable to analysis in this way.[17] This approach facilitates the understanding of a perspective that is different and alien. The 'interpretative turn in theory' is not free of its own difficulties and it has been the subject of powerful and well-rehearsed criticism. However, it has a number of clear advantages in the context of faith-based arguments.[18] It does not rely on the adoption of a 'neutral' starting point which, as we have seen, is inappropriate in analysing faith. Nor does it adopt a sceptical or relativist approach to the claims of value made by agents who rely on faith. Rather, this alternative approach seeks to mediate the tension between attention to the perspective of the subject relying on faith on the one hand, and the needs of a theorist who is seeking greater understanding and clarity on the other. Gadamer's work is particularly useful because of its explicit discussion of the problem of what constitutes understanding in these contexts. Gadamer's insight is that knowledge of the other – who is different and alien – is only possible if we use, rather than suspend, our pre-existing insights into the human condition: 'Only the support of familiar and common understanding makes possible the venture into the alien, the lifting out of something out of the alien, and thus the broadening and enrichment of our own experience of the world.'[19] For Gadamer, a pre-existing attitude towards experience is precisely what allows a meaningful experience of the new and different.

Emilio Betti's discussion of this alternative approach in legal theory is also illuminating for our present discussion concerning faith perspectives and political justice. For Betti, understanding the other requires attention to the 'representative value' which is implicit in their practical activity. The theorist needs to reflect upon this value and to make it explicit, and therefore uncover the 'marks of personality' of the subject. For Betti, this activity of making the 'representative value' explicit is a cognitive

---

[17] I am grateful to Dr Janet Martin Soskice for her Stanton Lectures (1998) (unpublished), especially her analysis of the work of F. Schleiermacher, which allowed me to appreciate the importance of philosophical hermeneutics as a resource for analysing faith-based arguments.

[18] The problems which are faced by 'interpretative approaches' to the human sciences are addressed by Taylor in his article, 'Interpretation and the Sciences of Man'. For a trenchant criticism see M. Moore, 'The Interpretative Turn in Modern Theory: A Turn for the Worse?', *Stanford Law Review* 41 (1989), p. 871.

[19] H. G. Gadamer, 'The Universality of the Hermeneutical Problem', in D. E. Linge, ed., *Philosophical Hermeneutics* (Berkeley: University of California Press, 1976). I would like to thank Sohail Nakhooda (Nottingham) for his assistance on this point.

act of interpretation: 'interpretation as action whose useful outcome is understanding.'[20] This method relies on a special relationship between the subject and object, which recognises the special nature of the phenomenon that is being studied: 'At one head of the process is the living and thinking spirit of the given interpreter. At another is some spark of the human spirit, objectivised in representative form . . .'[21] This method seeks to mediate a tension that does justice to the greater need for subjectivity, for understanding the experiences of the other, which may be important in the context of faith-based arguments. Betti states:

On the one hand, the interpreter must respond to the requirements of objectivity; his rethinking of the object, his reproduction of it, must be faithful and as close as possible to the expressive or characteristic value possessed by the representative form he seeks to understand . . . Two things are thus held in opposition: one, the subjectivity that is inseparable from the spontaneity of understanding; the second, the objectivity, or otherness so to speak, of the sense which interpretation seeks to elicit in the object. Upon it, one may construct a general theory of interpretation, which, in allowing critical reflection upon that process, can serve as the basis of an account of its ends and methods. This theory is hermeneutics.[22]

At first sight, it may seem that such a strategy will raise insurmountable problems when it comes to understanding faith under conditions of reasonable pluralism. How can such a range of diverse perspectives – many of which rely on beliefs radically different from, and often incompatible with, the normative 'home understanding'[23] – be studied in this way? Inner motivations will vary according to different subjects; they will be impossible to delineate with any degree of precision; and in the face of such diversity there is a danger of fragmentation and conflict rather than a better comprehension of the 'other'. Giving priority to the home perspective will mean that these divergent belief structures will be deemed to be wrong and erroneous, which will thereby invariably breach the requirements of the 'politics of recognition'.

Despite its inherent limit, such a reaction underestimates the potential for a shift in understanding when this alternative approach is used. Taylor has commented on the advantages of a hermeneutical method in the human sciences. He notes that a meaningful understanding of 'another' with radically different beliefs and practices requires placing these beliefs against analogous 'home' beliefs and practices. Understanding in this

[20] E Betti, 'On a General Theory of Interpretation: The *Raison D'Etre* of Hermeneutics', *The American Journal of Jurisprudence* 32 (1987), p. 245.
[21] Ibid., p. 248.   [22] Ibid., p. 249.
[23] I.e., from the perspective of the theorist's own beliefs and culture.

context necessarily requires a contrast. This may seem problematic. In analysing faith-based practices, the immediate outcome of this comparative process will be to notice that the faith is radically different from the home beliefs and practices with which the theorist is familiar. The theorist will apply his own home value system to judge the practice as clearly different and wrong. There will be a clear attribution of error to the beliefs and practices of the other, who will be seen as having missed some important feature of social reality. Bias and the application of external criteria will be explicit using this approach.[24]

However, the analysis does not end there. The fact that the theorist has been forced to make the contrast has consequences which go beyond the simple conclusion that the faith-based arguments are wrong. Understanding the very different practices of another through comparison takes a special form. By placing the very different faith practices against a home understanding, and, most importantly, by using a method that looks beyond merely external acts, the theorist is forced to notice a range of factors which often remain obscure when the 'neutrality' model is used. The theorist is forced to notice that the other person is acting out of inner beliefs, motivations and states of consciousness to advance what – from his perspective – is a social practice with value. The theorist uses, rather than neutralises, his own home understanding of his motivation, belief and conduct. This pre-existing knowledge acts as a modular frame within which faith-based practices are placed, contrasted and made more intelligible. In this way the act of making a comparison contains within it the seeds of its own success. Using this method, there is some possibility that the theorist will come to see and appreciate that the faith-based conduct is underpinned by motivation and belief; that it has point, value and meaning from the perspective of the agent; and that the agent will engage in a process of reflection which seeks to make sense of these features within the context of his whole personal history.

There are obvious limits to the extent of the agreement concerning values which we can expect using this method. However, once it is recognised that the task is to make the other more intelligible, it becomes meaningful to claim that the act of comparison has led to a shift in understanding the other. In Betti's terms, '[k]nowledge in this instance has a singular trait, not given or to be confused with knowledge of physical phenomena: it recognises and reconstructs a human spirit, communicating with the interpreter through

---

[24] C. Taylor, 'Comparison, Truth and History', in his *Philosophical Arguments* (Cambridge, MA: Harvard University Press, 1995), p. 146.

the forms of its objectivisation, and causing him to sense an affinity with it through their common humanity'.[25]

In this way, there is some potential for making sense of what seems to be irrational faith-based conduct. Rather than merely noticing that the action is different and alien, the theorist can attempt to comprehend the meaning of the action from the perspective of the subject. It is only from this perspective – from trying to grasp the significance of the external conduct for the agent – that the action can be made more intelligible. This does not mean that the action is now accepted as being valid or as meeting some objectively agreed criteria of what is rational. The action may still remain puzzling but it is now seen as one of a range of possibilities for human agents who are motivated to realise meaning, point and value in their lives. It is seen as a part of a stream of behaviour of an agent who will reflect upon it in order to make sense of his personal history.

There are limits to this type of inquiry. Of course, a method which is dependent for success on the starting 'home' understanding of the theorist will raise problems of subjectivity in an acute form. This approach is dependent on the theorist reviewing and re-examining his own perspective. Success in this enterprise will be dependent on the ability of the theorist to remain open to the possibility of a change and shift in his perspective. Self-understanding and the ability to analyse one's own 'home understanding' will be as important as the ability to describe and observe. The subjectivity of this approach, with the resulting lack of certainty, clarity and predictability, sits uneasily with methods of verifiable description and observation that are usually applied in these contexts. The obvious criticism will be that this approach leads us to a 'hermeneutical circle', which we cannot enter if we do not share the home understanding of the theorist, and which we cannot break out of if we lack objective criteria which we have discarded because of their 'ethnocentricity'. The accusation that this model is flawed because of its subjectivity, uncertainty and arbitrariness has some force and validity in this context.

Especially relevant to the present discussion, there may be cases where the faith-based conduct is so very different or irrational that it is not possible for the theorist to place it against any analogous 'home' practice. In these cases, the home understanding may operate as an absolute barrier to understanding and it is unlikely that the method will assist in understanding faith. The practices of the other will remain irrational and inexplicable, along with an absolute judgement that these are based on error. These may

---

[25] Betti, 'General Theory', p. 249.

be cases that fall within Rawls's classification of the 'irrational' which he states are 'unreasonable and irrational, and even mad, comprehensive doctrines. In their case the problem is to contain them so that they do not undermine the unity and justice of society.'[26] It could be argued that this approach will fail in exactly those cases where there is the most urgent need to make faith-based practices intelligible.

If the person seeking to understand the faith-based conduct or perspective of the 'other' from another tradition does not suspend his own evaluative criteria then he will be forced to the conclusion that the 'other' has missed an important aspect of truth and reality. Therefore, one obvious outcome of this method will be that this shift in understanding is necessarily accompanied by a judgement that the faith-based conduct of the other person is wrong. Is this equivalent to a lack of respect and recognition for that faith? Is this a fatal flaw for those who are seeking to communicate their faith perspective? These intractable difficulties and risks may suggest that a sterner response is preferable, one which openly acknowledges that it is not possible to do justice simultaneously to the ideal of reason that underpins liberal politics and the claims of those who rely on faith.

Both liberal institutions and faith perspectives have reasons to avoid the difficulties that are involved in understanding and accommodating faith in the contemporary context. In Part III of the essay I set out some of the reasons why liberal institutions can no longer avoid taking faith perspectives seriously, before moving to the final part of my argument in Part IV where I conclude that there are overwhelming reasons why those with a faith perspective should remain active participants in liberal politics.

PART III

Liberal institutions may conclude that rather than presenting itself as neutral between rational inquiry and faith, theory should resolve the tension by clearly advocating the former. On this view, faith-based arguments fail to meet the pre-requisite conditions of rationality that are the basis for organising public life and institutions. Although relevant in private life they should have nothing to do with the public sphere, and therefore they need not concern discussion about contemporary political and legal theory. In some cases liberal institutions may need to respond to the fact

[26] Rawls, *Political Liberalism*, p. xvii.

that its citizens base their comprehensive doctrines on faith perspectives. In these cases the motivation for such accommodation will be to ensure that the requirements of autonomy and respect for the individual are met. In these cases faith will be important not because of its absolute value as the truth but because of its importance in the life of the institutions. Once again, the critical issue here is understanding the faith perspective from the point of view of the insider/participant (i.e., from an agent-relative perspective), rather than because it is the absolute comprehensive truth.

There are good reasons why the liberal state should not insist that faith is only relevant in the private sphere. Pluralism, the 'here and now' of contemporary liberal politics, points us in the direction of why such a strategy is inappropriate. The resurgence of the 'politics of recognition' and 'identity politics' which has led to faith perspectives asking to be accommodated within the public sphere is a permanent aspect of our contemporary political culture. It confirms that relegating faith perspectives to the private sphere will not be seen as a sufficient response to the demands of these individuals and groups. In some cases this may be seen as an implicit dismissal of those individuals for whom faith is of great significance and value. In addition, it is a distinguishing characteristic of faith-based reasons that they have significant status for the relevant individual. One way in which they will operate on the reasoning of the individual is as a theoretical authority, and this will have important implications which go beyond the private realm. There is a potential for divergence and conflict. Where individuals are faced with conflicting demands – between the requirements of theoretical (faith-based) authority on the one hand and compliance with a liberal politics on the other – differing beliefs may lead to a barrier to understanding, creating a conflict and a refusal to act according to the requirements of law. In these circumstances it becomes necessary to overcome resistance and resolve this conflict. The agent's understanding of his situation will need to be replaced by a decision by an impartial third party (i.e., the legislator or the judge). Another option is to ensure that the prospect of these types of disputes is minimised, so that there is a greater convergence between all the various public institutions which provide the sources of normative guidance in the daily and practical lives of individuals. In order to fulfil these tasks adequately it will be important to ensure that the judge or legislator is in touch with, and has an accurate understanding of, the customs and practices of the individuals and sub-communities who rely on faith-based arguments. This will be especially important if the link between individual well-being, identity and recognition is accepted. In this context, minimising such conflicts is not just a matter of expediency and efficiency; it becomes an important part of the conditions necessary to allow individuals to flourish and lead fully autonomous lives.

A vision of liberal politics which sees it not only as a system for regulating conduct, but also as a source of creating and sustaining common meanings in a community, makes it especially important to take seriously the sincere feelings of those who rely on faith-based arguments. The self-perception of these individuals that their views have been considered and given some weight by public institutions becomes important in order to ensure their identification with the political system. This analysis suggests that where, as with prevailing conditions of reasonable pluralism, individuals draw their beliefs from a wide variety of sources, liberal politics needs not only to be factually comprehensible but also to 'speak' to people's beliefs and attitudes.[27] The prospect of a greater coalescence between the experience of individuals in their daily and practical lives and their experiences of normative political and legal institutions – and therefore of meaningful identification and a higher degree of willing co-operation with these institutions – would justify such an effort.

If one of the features of the contemporary political culture is the presence of faith as the justification for belief and conduct, then this has implications for our discussions of liberal political institutions. The challenge is not to justify these beliefs and attitudes as true or to seek absolute objective criteria on which to base a legal system. Nor that our reflections on politics should take the faith-based beliefs and attitudes of these insiders as the starting point for analysis or as true facts on which to build a political or legal system. This is not about coming up with a natural law theory out of which to build a true or perfect account of government and law based on objective moral facts. Rather, the challenge is that theorists must understand these facts about human agents accurately, treat them as serious and important matters, and where relevant take these participant beliefs into account. These are matters that are important not only for those 'insiders' who rely on faith, but also for all those concerned with understanding contemporary liberal politics.

PART IV

Earlier discussions set out the difficulties of using a method that communicates faith in a non-distorted and effective way. It was suggested that,

---

[27] For a discussion of the relevance of this issue in the specific context of criminal liability see R. A. Duff, 'Law, Language and Community: Some Preconditions of Criminal Liability', *Oxford Journal of Legal Studies* 18 (1998), p. 189.

rather than using a method that neutralises the particularity of any view-point, the particular starting point of the outsider seeking to understand the faith of another may be acknowledged as an invaluable resource. However, this method carries within it certain intrinsic risks. It will necessarily introduce the possibility that faith-based conduct which is radically different to the home understanding of the outsider will be deemed to be wrong and deluded in important respects. Those who are 'insiders' within a faith perspective may react to this risk and their contemporary situation by with-drawing from the public sphere. They may conclude that the challenges of accommodating themselves to liberalism and reasonable pluralism are too great. This may be a 'concession too far' for certain faith perspectives.[28] Shouldn't these faith perspectives be sceptical about a model that requires them to make concessions about the truth of their own doctrines? There are good reasons to suggest that such scepticism is misplaced. Faced with a choice between insisting that the absolute truth of their doctrine is acknowl-edged, and the prospect of communicating the value that their faith has for them to others, 'insiders' have good reason to prefer the latter. No one conception of the good, including a faith perspective, can insist on being the absolute truth around which to organise public life. This concession is the inevitable price that any faith-based doctrine must pay for intervening in a contemporary public sphere which maintains a distinction between the values that govern the private sphere (where faith can claim the truth) and the public sphere (where faith must be one of a number of possible comprehensive doctrines, all of which are equally valid).

The stark reality of politics in a contemporary liberal society is that reasonable pluralism will necessarily limit the role of faith in public life. Is this a cause of pessimism for faith-based doctrines? Well, 'yes' and 'no'. There will be something to regret by those who base their concept of the good on faith by the insistence that they maintain a dichotomy between their private and public life. Maintaining a dual identity in this way is notoriously difficult, especially for those who consider faith to be an integrating force that should in ideal circumstances pull them in the direction of integrating different facets of their life through their religious and spiritual beliefs. However, it is a mistake for those who rely on a faith perspective to think that they are unique in this respect. There are many individuals, not only

---

[28] Rawls discusses this in terms of the 'overlapping consensus' which will command the support of all reasonable comprehensive doctrines, and which will be the basis for organisation in the public sphere. See Rawls, *Political Liberalism*, p. xvi. A critique of Rawls's arguments in this context, which is also relevant to the present argument that the 'truth' of the faith-based arguments need not be the focus of the analysis for political theory, is J. Raz, 'Facing Diversity: The Case of Epistemic Abstinence', in his *Ethics in the Public Domain* (Oxford: Clarendon Press, 1994).

those who rely on faith, who are faced with a public order in the modern world that fails to reflect, and often contradicts, their deepest and most passionate beliefs. Reconciling private value and sentiment with public life, and so reducing this alienation, is an urgent task. I argued earlier that the State could accommodate faith in a way that reduces some aspects of this alienation.[29] Here I want to insist that despite the difficulties there are good reasons for those with a faith perspective to remain engaged in mainstream public life. Although they cannot insist on the truth of their own doctrines in the public sphere, those with a faith perspective can make a valuable and unique contribution in terms of *political advocacy*. The values of autonomy, self-development and freedom of expression that prevail in liberal political culture provide an unprecedented opportunity to understand their own situation with honesty and clarity and to convey this to others. In some contexts democratic politics is understood as a way of citizens exercising power: as the ability to influence decision making and 'trump' either the decision of others with whom they disagree or any collective action that threatens to interfere with individual rights. This model does not exclude citizen participation or control altogether but, rather, defines it in a specific way. The participation of citizens in the legal and political processes which affect their lives is ensured because of their ability to retrieve and rely upon the individual rights entrenched in a founding document, such as a constitution or human rights instrument. However, this 'instrumental' vision of politics needs to be supplemented by a vision that sees political participation as something of 'intrinsic' value. A very different vision of citizen participation informs the sovereigntist discourse with its greater focus on representative institutions. Within this model, citizen freedom and dignity do not lie in the ability to 'veto' collective decision making by reference to a set of individual rights or principles. Within this more 'republican' model, citizen power and freedom do not lie in blocking the decision of the community. Rather, participation in the political process is secured through coming together with others to form a consensus on substantive and controversial values.[30] One aspect of these contested values will be that they concern the provision of goods which an individual cannot secure individually and which require collective and

---

[29] For fuller discussion of the reasons why political and legal institutions should be concerned about faith perspectives see Malik, 'Faith and the State of Jurisprudence'.

[30] For a discussion of this vision of constitutional reform in the context of social democracy see K. D. Ewing, 'Human Rights, Social Democracy and Constitutional Reform', in C. Gearty and A. Tomkins, eds., *Understanding Human Rights* (London: Mansell, 1996), pp. 40–60.

co-ordinated action.[31] Debating ideas, building majorities, participating
in elections and seeking to ensure that the ruling party reflects decisions
relating to the common good become the focus of political activity. This
second vision of politics as an intrinsically important activity is at risk of
being nudged out of our contemporary consciousness by an instrumental
and consumer approach to our political life. This second, more 'republican'
and 'participatory', vision needs to be constantly nudged back into our view
of what constitutes valuable political activity.[32]

   Can intervening in the public sphere also allow a faith perspective to
address the question that Professor Oman posed in *Grace and Personality*:
'[C]an we, in the face of history and experience, maintain the conception
of God and man on which [the question of the infallibilities] rests?'[33] The
view of human nature that prevails in the contemporary public sphere takes
the fact of human agency as unproblematic. We are agents because we have
the power to exercise choice and plan strategically. This choice is exercised
in many forms but in the public sphere it is dominated by a system that
provides us with choice in two important areas: political choice as citizens
of a liberal democracy and consumer choice as participants in a free market
economy. The particular contribution of a faith perspective to this analysis
in the public sphere is to insist that there is a further aspect to human
agency that is relevant for analysis. We are human agents because certain
things matter to us: we are conscious that certain matters are qualitatively
more significant for our understanding of ourselves.[34] This may at times
seem like a modest contribution but it can provide a radically different
perspective to the concept of man as a rational maximiser and consumer
that prevails in contemporary public life.

   It would be wrong, however, to underestimate the very real and specific
difficulties that face faith perspectives in pursuing an agenda of political
advocacy and participation in the public sphere. There is one fundamental
problem that recurs and which is an intractable obstacle. As noted earlier,
one form of liberalism that relies on neutrality in support of its arguments
leaves very little space for alternative ways of presenting the social world.

---

[31] See for example J. Raz's discussion in *The Morality of Freedom* (Oxford: Oxford University Press, 1986). For other discussions of the common good see J. Finnis, *Natural Law, Natural Rights* (Oxford: Clarendon Press, 1979), ch. VI.

[32] For a more detailed discussion of these issues see M. Malik, 'Minorities and Human Rights', in T. Campbell, K. D. E. Ewing et al., eds., *Sceptical Approaches to the Human Rights Act* (Oxford: Oxford University Press, 2000).

[33] Oman, *Grace and Personality*.

[34] See the discussion in C. Taylor, 'The Concept of a Person', in *Human Agency and Language, Philosophical Papers*, vol. 1.

In presenting itself as a descriptive and empirical account of the social and political world it claims for itself a status of certainty and verification. Alternative methods that are more amenable to faith, which use techniques such as interpretation or non-literal methods, are at a significant disadvantage in this context. Neutrality in method claims for itself a degree of certainty, predictability and truth that puts rivals at a considerable disadvantage. This model is able to claim that it is neutral between different perspectives and therefore more appropriate than its rivals. One consequence is that this model will often claim all the space for defining social reality. This precludes a reading of our social reality and political life which is based on a different method and premises. The sense of reality that is presented through this neutral method claims to be absolutely true rather than just simply one version amongst a number of different interpretations. Alternative readings of social reality are presented as subjective and biased versions. In extreme cases there is likely to be a significant divergence between the description of social reality that a neutral descriptive method yields and a different interpretation. In these cases the alternative perspective or vision may be presented as not only tainted by bias but also irrational. In this way theory and practice do influence each other. The insistence on reading our social and political life by relying on facts and verification has real practical consequences. It makes it immensely more difficult for alternative versions to gain a fair hearing. That is the reason that those who seek to represent faith perspectives need to pay great attention to both levels of analysis – theory and practice.

To seek to intervene in the public sphere whilst still maintaining a faith perspective will for all these reasons be a considerable challenge. For the individual, this challenge requires skills rather like those of an alchemist: the ability to recognise and maintain fine distinctions between those precious activities and relations with which there should be engagement and struggle, and those areas of contemporary life which need to be rejected or endured in silence. Such a Herculean task invariably introduces the prospect of conflict, remorse and anguish. It is therefore easy to understand why a strategy of self-sufficiency and closure from the world seems preferable and why many people of faith develop a distaste for the times in which they live. The result is a state of disengagement with public life and disenchantment with the social world. Those with a faith perspective need to resist such pessimism. They will need to maintain a fine balance between optimistic intervention in support of their vision of the concept of man and the common good and a realism about the substantial obstacles that they face in this task of political advocacy.

It is also important to keep constantly in view two aspects of theory that we have discussed: first, a vision of politics as a participatory enterprise rather than a forum to pursue vested interests; second, our conclusions about the way in which faith can be understood and communicated. Theory can inform practice in these contexts. Our earlier discussion suggested that understanding faith perspectives requires using rather than suspending our 'home' understanding of human value. Often the goal of participation will be to gain concrete policy outcomes. At other times it may be equally important that an outcome of participation in the public sphere should be to facilitate a better understanding of the value that faith has in the lives of citizens *from their perspective as insiders/participants*.

For many political activists the prospect of intervening in the public sphere with little prospect of gaining substantial power or achieving outcomes will seem futile. However, political advocacy for those with faith perspectives need not set itself these goals. It will more often than not constitute an act of putting into the public sphere a unique vision of the nature of man or the common good. The validity of this act will not necessarily be predicated on the immediate effect it has on the conditions of an individual or a community. Despite its lack of practical effect such an intervention can be seen as a very special kind of response to the reality of the modern world. It presents a vision (an image almost) that sets itself up in opposition to others that often dominate in the public sphere. In this way faith perspectives can contribute to a pool of ideas in the public sphere which provide individuals with an alternative way of becoming conscious of their own sense of self, their choices and their predicament. A faith perspective provides a different type of public standard for evaluating the self and its actions. It can make a substantial contribution, and act as a redress, to the ideas and images that dominate our contemporary public sphere.[35] Political advocacy by those with a faith perspective may not always deliver spectacular policy outcomes but it has the potential to 'tilt the scales of reality towards a more transcendent equilibrium'.[36] This may seem a modest result for activists for whom contemporary politics is about power and immediate results. For those with a faith perspective it is a substantial victory.

[35] For a fuller discussion of these issues in the context of the function of poetry see Seamus Heaney, *The Redress of Poetry*, Oxford Lectures (London: Faber and Faber, 1995), esp. pp. 3–5.
[36] Ibid., p. 3.

Response

CHAPTER 13

Fields of faith: an experiment in the study of theology and the religions

Nicholas Adams, Oliver Davies and Ben Quash

INTRODUCTION

In the opening chapter of *The Beginning and the End of 'Religion'*, Nicholas Lash draws an analogy between (on the one hand) the academic thinker in the field of the study of theology and the religions, and (on the other) the figure of Arjuna in the thirteenth chapter of the *Bhagavadgita*, who finds himself in the middle of a field of battle, and who (with the help of Krishna) must try to find his way upon it: 'It is always on the field of battle, in the midst of action, that we are challenged to consider and to clarify, to cleanse the mind and heart and purify the springs of action.'[1] He also remarks that the field, or context of reflection, for any academic thinker will vary in an immense number of ways. Some of these variations will be obvious; some very subtle. Each person's context of thought and activity will have features that are entirely particular to it, because all our thought and activity is thought and activity that 'we do from somewhere, shaped by some set of memories and expectations, bearing some sense of duty borne and gifts that have been given. All sense, and truth, and goodness, are carried and constituted by some story, some pattern of experience, some tradition.'[2]

That the practice of studying theology and the religions has taken root in a wide variety of such 'fields' is something that this volume (including the title of the volume itself, *Fields of Faith*) wants to acknowledge. Those who study and teach theology and the religions will have intriguingly varied perspectives on the 'fields' they find themselves occupying. Participation in a particular religious tradition (a tradition of 'prayer and practice, thought and discipline and devotion'[3]) may constitute part of such a thinker's 'field', but so will the culture, the economics and the politics

---

[1] Nicholas Lash, *The Beginning and the End of 'Religion'* (Cambridge: Cambridge University Press, 1996), p. 18.
[2] Ibid., p. 19.   [3] Ibid., p. 15.

of the university system she works in, and of the society which fosters, but also almost certainly seeks to influence, that system. Other thinkers will occupy a 'field' defined aside from participative involvement in any of the religious traditions, though the very practice of Religious Studies as a 'non-performative' scholarly discipline has its own genealogy and its own traditioned character. And all thinkers, whether or not they identify themselves as religious, will be shaped in their work by their own personal histories and priorities.

Because the authors of this volume have different 'fields', the essays included in this volume inevitably form a complex unity, and the task of responding to them is not a straightforward one. They can be described as a set of attempts to 'find a way' upon the fields their authors variously find themselves in, and the respondents in turn must negotiate the terrain bequeathed by the authors. As the 'Introduction' to the volume makes clear (and a number of the authors remind us) the papers themselves were originally delivered at a conference in honour of Nicholas Lash who, at his retirement, concluded a period of some twenty-two years as a powerfully formative and creative presence in the Faculty of Divinity at the University of Cambridge and in the discipline of Theology and Religious Studies at large. Uppermost in the minds of the organisers was the desire to give the former Norris-Hulse Professor of Philosophical Theology an appropriate 'send-off' with a conference that reflected his diverse interests and achievements, not least in terms of his engagement with the nature of the academic study of Theology and Religious Studies and its possible futures in teaching and research at institutions in the UK and overseas. Inevitably the final shape of that conference was dictated as much by the exigencies of time and space and the availability of possible speakers as it was by an overall conceptual plan. But this was not viewed so much as a handicap as it was a generative necessity. Like Arjuna, both the conference organisers and the speakers were challenged to 'consider and clarify' their concerns without succumbing to the illusion that could step out of 'the midst of action'.

The construction of this volume reflects the same frank recognition of the particularity of the authors' various perspectives, and the unrealism of expecting total coverage, total representativeness, or a total overview when dealing with the hugely diverse areas that are of interest to scholars of Theology and Religious Studies. It is constructed 'from somewhere, shaped by some set of memories and expectations, bearing some sense of duty borne and gifts that have been given'. Our response to the set of papers brought together here will attempt as a consequence to be mindful of the particularities which characterised their first field of reception: the common life, the modes of dialogue and the practices of reasoning in the midst of which these papers were delivered, and by which they were shaped. But equally we shall have to show attentiveness to the reader of the volume, who may come to it with questions – perhaps challenging ones – about the nature and scope of the volume in its claim to suggest possible future directions of Theology and Religious Studies as a university discipline. To respond to such a volume, then, is to exercise a dual responsibility: to those who spoke and to those who did not speak.

But the first task in formulating our response has been to decide the method, or environment, of the answering. We are three authors with distinctive perspectives and backgrounds. Nicholas Adams teaches Philosophical and Political Theology at Edinburgh, which has a long tradition of Christian studies but more recently has developed an expanding emphasis on world religions. Oliver Davies until very recently taught Philosophical and Systematic Theology at University of Wales, Lampeter, which has a parallel emphasis upon Church History and Religious Studies, and is now Professor of Systematic Theology at King's College, London, with a strong legacy of teaching in Christian Theology and Biblical Studies. Ben Quash teaches Doctrine in the Faculty of Divinity at Cambridge, which retains great strengths in Christian Theology while also having expanded recently into the teaching of other world religions, specifically Judaism, Hinduism and Islam. In view of the different environments in which we teach and research, it seemed right to hold extensive discussions about our individual and common responses and then to select a primary author in whose presentation the voices of the other two would be fully present. This is a method of proceeding which focuses upon dialogue, time spent together, corrective readings of each other's work, and what can be termed 'envoicing', as an intensive and productive form of listening.

We have understood this method of working to be itself a reflection of the method of the organisational structure of the conference as a whole, with its implicit emphasis upon dialogue and debate. A number of the papers and discussions explicitly took up the themes of conviviality, debate, listening and conversation. As respondents we exercise a dual responsibility to the speakers at the conference and to those who were not themselves participants in the discussions, but who may feel themselves addressed by some of the issues raised and principles proposed. We have extended our own method of 'envoicing', therefore, to be one which should as far as possible include the many diverse voices of those who teach and research the subject in departments throughout the country and who have a vital contribution to make to the understanding of its possible futures.

ATTENTIVENESS TO THE AUTHORS

The open, critical engagement with ideas and texts which is evident in the essays included in this volume does not differ in kind from that pursued in the humanities in general. But there are emphases and kinds of contextualisation at work which do seem subtly to distinguish the subject of Theology and Religious Studies as represented here from the common strengths and practices of the humanities in general. There are also particular convergent tendencies in the various essays, to a degree both surprising and exciting given the range of their starting points and foci. These 'densities' of concern, and certain accompanying commonalities of approach, may be suggestive of where the study of theology and the religions can expect its energy to be released in the future.

In this section, our aim is to identify certain predominant themes in the essays, and also certain noticeable 'virtues' or 'values' that seem to characterise their approaches. This second task is in a certain sense a *qualitative* evaluation: an evaluation of the quality of the dialogues and practices of reasoning of which the essays here are distillations.

The theme of genealogy is repeatedly present in the papers, though in different ways. Michael J. Buckley exemplifies a particular genealogical approach, in his careful unearthing of the origins of modern Western conceptions of 'religion', and their attendant dangers. Eamon Duffy shows how some features of the modern Roman Catholic liturgy that are now virtually taken for granted have precise historical beginnings in the work of a single individual (they are 'carried and constituted by some story', to echo Lash) – and he also shows how some of the presuppositions held by the individual in question are open to judgement and re-assessment. Peter Ochs remarks that 'to seek models for the future is . . . to acknowledge that one's history is composed for the purpose of responding to the crises of the moment', and shows how (in a way that has relevance well beyond Judaism) the Torah received from Moses must therefore be understood as 'thick with its own internal history'.

The interest in genealogy evident in these and other authors in this volume is itself indicative of the extent to which the authors seek to locate themselves, for the greater part, within living communities of faith. This is not in any way to compromise independence of mind, but is rather an acknowledgement of the broader community-based context of creative and innovative thinking in Christianity, Judaism or Islam. This background sense of tradition itself fostered and deepened the dialogical ethos of the original conference, leading to creative encounters across traditions. It is a loss that it has not been possible for practical reasons to include in the final volume some of the vitality of the conference debates across Jewish, Christian and Islamic boundaries. But in the theme of genealogy we recognise a set of concerns that incorporate both a dispassionate inquiry into past tradition and a vital sense of the context of thinking within tradition-based communities of the present, whose beliefs and identity have been deeply shaped by inherited texts, rituals and practices.

In continuity with this, Gavin Flood's discussion of Religious Studies as *itself a tradition* enables him to suggest that it can learn from the tradition-internal readings, both corrective and pragmatic, which various religious traditions have themselves developed over time. As we will outline in the next section of the present chapter, Religious Studies was designed to meet certain needs, and drew on certain resources to do so (in Lash's words, 'some sense of duty borne and [of] gifts that have been given'). Those needs are changing continually, and so must the scholarly tradition adapted to them – neither presuming itself to be a wholly detached and value-neutral inquiry, nor going on to claim this to be its key difference from Theology. At the same time, religious traditions and those who articulate their theology can (and should) learn from the possibilities of reading and dialogue *across* traditions that Religious Studies can facilitate. Corrective readings of a tradition can come from beyond it; they may be as simple as requesting greater understanding of imprecise things in that tradition, highlighting contradictions or errors of fact, or challenging a 'mis-representation . . . due to certain presuppositions about the nature of [an]other community'.

These are suggestions whose implications, if taken seriously, could lead to a reconception of the relationship between Religious Studies and Theology (and the blurring of a dichotomy that many at the conference thought was not proving durable or fruitful in its present form, and was falling far short of doing justice to the actual 'best practice' found in university faculties). Theology and Religious Studies have a common concern with the disciplines of good description; that point emerges more consistently than any other in the essays gathered in this volume. It is admitted that both Religious Studies and Theology are vulnerable to mis-descriptions of each other, and the theology of any particular religious tradition is further vulnerable to mis-description of other religious traditions to the detriment of both. But the point can still persuasively be made: Religious Studies and Theology alike are engaged in a common pursuit of *good descriptions* of reality; descriptions of which genealogies are a crucial part; descriptions that do justice to the depth and complexity (in Geertz's terms, the 'thickness') of what they describe; descriptions that pay attention, acknowledge resistances and take seriously material that is unassimilable to 'high theory' (see Sarah Coakley's call to John Milbank to ensure that his 'meta-narrative' does not bypass 'close study of the messy realities of lived "religion"'). And both Theology and Religious Studies at their best recognise that poor descriptions can have deeply destructive consequences. In Maleiha Malik's words:

[With complex social practices, where a theoretical concept fails] there is a risk that it will distort the subject matter in a more fundamental way: it may influence the way in which the social practice is understood even by participants and those whose conduct and beliefs are being described. Where there is a failure of theory in relation to these types of beliefs, which fails to capture the full range of relevant data or uses methods of analysis which are likely to be distortive, this has serious consequences for the underlying subject matter.[4]

One of the strengths of this volume is the way that its contributors bring insights from a range of disciplines to bear on the question of how to describe responsibly and well. Insights from lawyers, historians, textual scholars, philosophers, ethicists, teachers of doctrine and so on (and simultaneously from Muslims, Christians and Jews) combine here to make the decisive point that good descriptions of the subject matter that concerns students of theology and the religions will require mixed economies of method, inquiry at various scales of ordering, and an eschewal of analytic oversimplification. Single hypotheses can be powerful, but brutally so, just as a certain sort of revisionist history (pointed to by Eamon Duffy) could be used 'not as a delicate scalpel, tracing the successive elaborations and accretions of tradition, but as a bulldozer, ripping away more than a millennium of development in pursuit of foundations'.

If an emphasis on getting the best possible descriptions of the subject matter is something that is potentially to draw theologians and religionists into close co-operation, then some of the essays here alert us to the fact that mere 'surface' phenomenology is not going to be good enough when it comes to what Coakley calls 'questions of God, "truth" and ultimacy'. Malik brings this point home, her argument emerging (as it should) from a specific context of reflection – in the case which formed the background to her chapter, the challenge of taking account of the beliefs of Muslim British citizens when formulating human rights legislation for a pluralist society (indeed, of *drawing* on those beliefs to good effect). The central challenge, she argues, is not to step back from these beliefs, as though the critical force of principles by which people live their lives can be bracketed.

---

[4] Maleiha Malik, delivering an earlier version of this paper to the conference on 'The Future of the Study of Theology and the Religions', Selwyn College, Cambridge (September 2000).

She is sharply critical of the way that a stance with pretensions to objectivity attributes the status of mere *opinion* to religious faith, thus evading the call to inquire seriously into any question of motivation, belief and the 'meaning' of religious practices. 'The usual methods of neutrality in the human and political sciences need to be reassessed,' she writes. Moreover, those same sciences habitually individualise religious faith (this is a consequence of eliding faith with opinion), so that religious meanings and beliefs are 'described' by merely 'noting their impact on or importance for individual agents', instead of seeing how they are 'embedded in and constitutive of the social and political culture'. In redressing these impoverished and sometimes deceptive accounts of the part that religious beliefs play in the world – and the claims religious beliefs make *about* the world – those working in the study of theology and the religions may find themselves leading the way in the development of better descriptive tools for the rich and complex constellations of thought and practice they attend to. The task has potentially massive implications for the contemporary geo-political order, not least in relation to Islam and its relationship to the West. In Malik's words: 'There are many individuals . . . who are faced with a public order in the modern world that fails to reflect, and often contradicts, their deepest and most passionate beliefs. Reconciling private value and sentiment with public life, and so reducing this alienation, is an urgent task . . . '

Accepting the fundamental importance of description both for Theology and for Religious Studies, and the common cause this may enable them to make in certain spheres, a number of authors in this volume nonetheless argue that a distinction needs to be maintained between them. While Religious Studies is descriptive in ways that have wide relevance and currency in the humanities, Theology, by contrast, is not just any other sort of description. It may benefit from many of the tools and methods of Religious Studies but, as Rowan Williams points out, it cannot be reduced to a 'gloss on a world that is already accurately described by secular reason'. Williams follows de Certeau in suggesting that Theology will talk about the same things as secular reason talks about, but it will retain a commitment to 'a language that points to and holds onto to what is "un-said" in the various regions of "scientific" language, the various analyses of the world's processes – not least by pondering out loud about the very nature of scientific process as always facing what is *not yet* thinkable in the terms already fashioned'. This is deeply convergent with Ochs's insight when he says that 'some of the most important questions raised by today's axiological crises' are not questions that can be answered on the basis of the empirical evidence currently available: 'In order to respond to these questions, scholars must either trespass beyond the limits of [what is counted as 'plain sense'], or else fall silent in the face of profound societal needs'. And yet, thorough training in the disciplines of good description will still be a vital method in the repertoire of the theologian, and a vital 'credential' in her search for inspiration to meet the needs of the present moment. For, as Ochs continues: '[W]ho is more qualified to peer beyond the plain sense than scholars disciplined by the rigours of empirical study?'

Consideration of the 'virtues' that manifest themselves in the essays collected here points one to the importance of taking account of the domain of values in the study of theology and the religions. Values can be distinguished from judgements in that they tend towards the communal and are constitutive of identity. In other words, the values we hold tend to bind us into particular elective communities amongst which religious communities are particularly prominent as corporate belief-systems in which strong values are encoded. In some important sense values precede judgements and form the ground within which evidence is weighed and organised, and positions adopted. Values are principles of action, or judgement, which are deeply embedded both in the will and in habitual actions, in a way that parallels the virtues. While judgements are individual, values are a sign that we are cognitively and experientially shaped by affinities and relations and that, as corporate forms of belief and action, these are the building blocks of our identity. In the case of religion, these values are often described as 'spirituality', and are principles of action which coinhere in a distinctive way of seeing the world, indeed of being in the world.

The language of values plays throughout a number of the essays included in this volume, and there is a subtle contestation here (in line with the argument in Malik's essay which we have touched on already) of the commonly held view that human cognitions are divorced from feelings and evaluative perceptions, or that awareness of the good – however diversely conceived – does not form part of our thinking selves. If critical thinking represents a 'horizontal' perspective, then the kind of thinking represented in this volume is one which also intersects with a 'vertical' trajectory – a trajectory not only of *depth* (acknowledging the creative role of the past in the construction of present concerns and communities in a way that is evident in the volume's emphasis on genealogy), but also of *height* (setting critical reasoning in the context of values and ideals).

To put it another way, description is not the only thing that does or should go on in the study of theology and the religions – at least not description for its own sake. The essays here contain reminders that practices or disciplines of description in Theology must take their place alongside other practices and disciplines – those of dialogue, for example (which will include practices and disciplines of *arguing* as well as of *friendship*), in a way that aspires to a 'common good' in some form. If they cannot contribute meaningfully to a common good then, as John de Gruchy points out, their future is genuinely in question. An evaluation of the papers given in this conference (and of the conference from which they emerged) would do well to note the remarkable way in which they often do not just talk about their themes, they enact them. Janet Soskice's careful listening to her 'friends' Buber and Rosenzweig is a case in point. She states: 'I have been trying in this essay not just to enunciate a position but to practise it.' If there are glimpses to be had here of a future for the study of theology and the religions, they are as much in the attentive, dialogical mode of engagement represented by these essays as in what they actually say. Many of the topics discussed are quite specific (a discussion of some contemporary human rights legislation rather than an attempt to say everything there is to be said about 'justice'; an engagement with very particular texts in the chapter on 'Scripture'), but the *methods* and the *manner* of engagement displayed are very widely applicable. What we see here are forms of imaginative sympathy, critical rigour, compassionate commitment, and concern with what Michael Welker (speaking at the conference) called 'the vibrancy and the stimulus of the contents of faith', all combining to make an intellectual enterprise that, like Aquinas's in his own day (in Nick Adams's analysis), should challenge Theology (and Religious Studies) when they are 'being taught boringly'.

ATTENTIVENESS TO THE READERS

The subject of Theology and Religious Studies as it exists on the ground in old and new universities, as well as in confessional institutions, up and down the country, is hugely diverse. As a relatively new discipline, Religious Studies shows a particular variety of styles and approaches. This is the result of the different historical trajectories which contributed to its formation, including the arrival in the United Kingdom of large numbers of Muslims, Hindus and Sikhs since the Second World War. There was a significant input in the formation of the subject from Christian theologians who were exasperated with what they felt was the insensitive exclusivism of their subject-area, as well as from specialists with a background in the various psycho-analytical, political or functional critiques of religion. But it is diverse also on account of its own nature as a discipline. Religious Studies needs to be concerned with general questions of religious life and habit as these exist across a number of religions, and yet many of the world religions with which it engages present formidable obstacles to serious study. The sacred languages of Buddhism, Hinduism or Islam are not easily learned and those who acquire such specialist skills may find that they have as much in common with colleagues in Oriental Studies departments as they do with those who specialise in general perspectives on religion. As has already been hinted, the image of Religious Studies as a 'neutral zone' from the perspective of religious subjectivity, in contrast with 'kerygmatic' Christianity, is something that is called into question by a clearer recognition of its *traditioned* character (Flood) – including its origins in population movements and globalisation. Many who attend courses in Religious Studies may have been born into a non-Christian world religion or, as often happens, may have been attracted as a practitioner to one or other Western adaptation of Eastern religious forms, such as meditation or yoga. It is by no means the case that Religious Studies students are driven by a dispassionate concern with understanding the principles of the religious character; indeed, many may well be engaged in some kind of personal quest for deeper values or a new life-orientation. If a lecturer in Christianity is likely on balance to prove to be either a believing Christian or a post-Christian, then a Religious Studies lecturer is as likely to be a committed practitioner of the religion he or she teaches, or an active participant in a religion he or she does not teach, as to have no religious affiliation at all.

Given the diversity and complexity of Religious Studies as it exists on the ground, it is perhaps inevitable that the appeal to hospitality, which is rooted in the particularity of tradition and which richly informs the papers given here, will appear to some to be a covert form of Christian hegemony: an attempt to recolonise the religious field in the name of a triumphalistic Christianity which sits astride our most ancient and well-resourced institutions and which, with a renewed self-confidence born of a post-modern relativism, now proclaims a second advent. Exercising our responsibility jointly to authors and readers, we recognise that this might be a real response in some quarters, particularly where Religious Studies perceives itself to be at a structural disadvantage to Theology. Christian Theology still dominates in many of the oldest and largest departments of Theology and Religious Studies, the Christian community in the country – broadly defined – still constitutes a substantial majority of religious believers, and postgraduate recruitment, of crucial importance to the financial well-being (and thus to the politics of appointments) of many university departments, is still heavily weighted in favour of students researching in areas of Christian interest.

And yet, while opening up this field of response, it is our view that the possible accusation of Christian triumphalism would be fundamentally misplaced. The practice of particularity that is conveyed in these papers is one which is thoroughly pluralistic in shape. Even though the papers by non-Christian contributors form a minority, the Christianity represented by the others is one which is commitedly ecumenical, and (as was emphasised in the previous section) dialogical. The ethos both of the conference and of its product is one which placed conversation with other religions at the centre of contemporary Christian identity and thought. Several of the theologians involved make the point that doing theology in the presence of representatives of other faiths (and in dialogue with the thought and practices of other faiths) made them better at inhabiting their own tradition. The same is almost certainly true when theologians do theology in the presence of Religious Studies scholars, and may even be true in reverse. Coakley puts it like this: '[T]he teaching of traditions other than Christianity, and the acute observation of religious traditions *as lived*, together provide the most creative dialectical context for the forging of systematic Christian positions (or indeed, the forging of Jewish, Hindu or Buddhist positions).'

The absence of an overarching universalism should not be taken to signify a disregard for the authenticity of non-Christian religions. Indeed, many would argue that such universalisms ignore the authenticity of all religions, which are incurably particularistic in their claims and practices. In terms of its outcomes, any dialogue between religions within the particularistic model will necessarily be difficult and subject to challenge at every stage (here the parallel with ecumenical dialogue between Christian denominations is instructive), but this is to define the broader ecumenism as a form of production rather than a process. Neither the conference nor the volume represent attempts to achieve ecumenical outcomes as such, but both signal a commitment to encounter between religions which can be conveyed by the theme of *conviviality*, which is a process of being-together, within a mutually hospitable space, as a project of living and conversing. The parallel with Christian ecumenism is again helpful, for it shows clearly that from the perspective of *rapprochement* within difficult historical narratives the desire to reach agreement on specific issues, which is founded on dimensions of a common life, is quite as important as the kind and structure of the arguments adduced.

But we do recognise that there are two aspects to this volume which will raise questions in the mind of a significant proportion of those engaged professionally in the teaching of Theology and Religious Studies. The volume as composed is predominantly christocentric, with eight out of twelve contributions engaging primarily with Christian material. Again, the accusation of triumphalism could be made, but we would answer that the model of hospitality across faiths which is proposed here *has to begin within a specific tradition.* Hospitality is generated from within religious difference and not from some perceived neutral and universalistic space. That the Christian tradition of belief and learning which supports this particular project of hospitality and conversation should be coloured by Anglicanism is, in the 'voice' of the non-Anglican respondent, a coherent part of that situatedness. Anglicanism has a long history of working from within the Higher Education institutions of the United Kingdom, in a combination of ecclesiastical and intellectual renewal. Again, from the perspective of that (Roman Catholic) respondent, the Anglicanism of the project seems a sign not of a narrow denominationalism but of a rootedness in tradition and determination to speak 'hospitably' to other communities in the name of a common experience of and commitment to religious situatedness. Understood in that light, the distinctive Anglican inheritance of an easy alliance with many of this country's institutions can be utilised in the service of a pluralistic vision of religion in close engagement with the most vigorous, deliberative ideals of critical reasoning.

The second problematic is, however, less easily addressed. The objection can be made that what is being offered here is a project based upon an insider relation with religion and that those many scholars who do not regard themselves as being in any sense a participant of the religion they teach are thereby excluded. This needs to be considered together with the fact that not all religious communities would feel equally at ease with the discourse of Western analytical reasoning which is used here. Furthermore, world religions are embedded in cultural forms which represent varying degrees of remoteness from Western norms. Not everyone can be a *nganga*, or a Jain, and any Western appropriations of these religious forms would entail complex processes of reflection and adaptation. There is an imperative here to expand the model of hospitality to include those who teach about a religious community without themselves being participant in it, in the ordinary sense of the term.

Concealed within the distinctions between those who teach a religion to which they have a personal commitment and those who do not are issues to do with the nature of representation. Undeniably those whose expertise lies within a particular religious tradition will seek representation of their field of interest on the syllabus and will feel that the community with whom they are linked through study deserves a place within the academic forum. A lecturer does not need to be, for instance, a practising Jain to feel that the history and beliefs of the Jain community have a right to representation where the world religions are being discussed and taught. Indeed, a specialist in Jain studies is likely to perform a key communicative and explanatory role with respect to the Jain community at large, whatever his or her individual beliefs may be. Thus that scholar can be said to be the 'voice' of the Jain community where academics are discussing religion. They can alert other scholars to the experience of that community, which has existed for well over two millennia and numbers over three million adherents. This is, admittedly, a very different kind of representation from that of the ordained Christian who counsels Archbishops or Popes, but it is one that has its own authenticity. The principle of hospitality functions beyond the limits of a conventional insiderness; it encompasses also the representative function of the trained scholar who becomes 'envoiced' by the people to whose beliefs and practices he or she has devoted years of study.

Authors and readers alike would be keen to stress that the critical thinking which defines the study of Theology and Religion is not different in kind from that of the other humanities. And yet certain of its contexts do seem to be different in ways that invite further comment. We see a greater awareness of the sociality of thought, and of the human subject who thinks, than is generally the case in the humanities. Religion is one of the most deeply communitarian forces to shape society, and it frequently carries with it pervasive memories of people from the past, who are to be imitated or revered. Religion, likewise, is a primary bearer of values and is thus the focus for the complex priorities of action and belief which define our social and cultural identities. It is inevitable that the scholar of religion, either working from within a religious community or in close association with religious communities and traditions, will be particularly aware of the communitarian frameworks which define human existence. There is little space here for the atomised and disembodied self who seems at times to haunt technological, goal-oriented intelligence. There is a discrete appeal in these pages for the operation of reason within such communitarian frameworks, which is to say dialogically, wisely and with conviviality. Secondly, the place of values, whose role is frequently to bind us into the various communities of which we are a part, receives here a greater and more explicit prioritisation. It is not, we would suggest, that other humanities lack such a base in values; indeed it is evident that the very opposite is the case. The best practice of

rigorous and conscientious analysis, and of thorough, well-founded, critique, entails commitment to a whole raft of values to do with obligations
to the pursuit of truth, openness and fairness. But there are nevertheless
distinctions to be made here. Many find for instance that best critical practice tends to isolate the scholar. By analysing a field of study dispassionately,
the individual researcher has to ask questions which set him or her apart
from the prejudices and fixed positions of others. In one sense this is of
course true also of the researcher in Theology and Religious Studies. It is
well known that the critical questioning of religion can alienate a scholar
from the community of those whose faith tends towards the uncritical.
But from another perspective, there is a clear alignment between critique
that is exercised with respect to a religious community or tradition and the
domain of values, since the communities which are the object of critical
reflection are themselves substantially constituted by shared values. The
understanding of such values is thus integral to the process of analysing
religion and the religious. This is not the claim that the theologian or
Religious Studies scholar must share the values of those whose beliefs they
study, but it does pose the question whether religious people and belief-
systems can be adequately reflected upon unless the scholar who does so
has some real empathetic understanding of the values in which they are
grounded. To understand the *values* of another seems a different kind of
engagement from merely understanding their reasoning or beliefs independently of the values that give these life. It is in this area, in reflection upon
the values which define a religious perspective, that the answerability of a
scholar before the tradition and community which they study is grounded.
Inevitably therefore the role of values will tend to be more explicit in the
work of theologians and Religious Studies scholars, inhabiting their work
more vigorously than is normally the case and providing a more overtly
communitarian context for it.

From the perspective of current debates in the field of Theology and
Religious Studies, the trajectory of 'pluralistic particularity' and of 'value-
awareness' that is evident here does constitute a new departure in a subject
which over recent years has shown a quite unusual degree of mobility.
Every initiative entails risk and trust, and this is no exception. There will
be those who see it as a retreat to old positions which they had thought were
long overcome. But the claims of this new paradigm, being foundationally
dialogical, cannot be hegemonic. And there is an attempt here, for all the risk
of the venture, to grasp deep issues of method whose influence may extend
beyond any one debate or set of problematics. What is at issue at this deeper
level is difference itself and the managing of difference. How should the

subject of Theology and Religious Studies, whose unity can at times seem a purely institutional one, relate to the differences which are germane to it: those between Arab and Jew, Catholic and Protestant, first world intellectual traditions and third world religions, between Christianity (Theology) and other world religions (Religious Studies), between insider and outsider perspectives, between Durkheim and Barth? How should departments of Theology and Religious Studies relate to the world outside the university, and to other university disciplines? The answer to such questions articulated here, albeit for the main part implicitly, is that there must not be an attempt to overwhelm or subjugate, grounded in inveterate hostility and suspicion. But there is an impulse here rather to re-envision the encounter with or in difference as being itself an invitation to a process of debate, openness and common living. This in turn should not be driven by a target list of outcomes but rather by a wise commitment to a certain way of shared living and thinking, constructed with attentiveness and critical discernment on intimations of blessing.

Index of names

Acosta, José de 9
Adams, Nicholas xiv, 49, 137–51, 209, 215
Adorno, Theodor 151
Aelred of Rievaulx 167–8, 170n. 7, 173, 175n. 19
Alison, James 83
Ambrose of Milan 167, 172
Aristotle 19, 32, 33, 168, 173
Auden, W. H. 87
Augustine of Hippo, St 7, 167, 172
Austin, John 187n. 10

Baierl, Joseph J. 21
Barth, Karl 44n. 15, 60–1, 69n. 37, 81, 138, 139, 141–3, 144, 145, 150, 160, 161
Bauerschmidt, F. C. 82
Beeck, Frans Josef van 45
Benjamin, Walter 56, 57, 66, 72, 151
Berger, Gaston 63
Betti, Emilio 193–4, 195–6
Bianchi, Ugo 11n. 34
Bonhoeffer, Dietrich 156, 161
Bossy, John 128, 129
Botha, P. W. 155
Brerewood, Edward 9
Brueggemann, Walter 139, 140, 142
Buber, Martin 148, 151, 174, 175–9, 180, 181, 215
Buckley, Michael J. 3–24, 44, 94n. 7, 210
Burgess, Clive 128
Burrell, David 77, 88

Cain, Seymour 14n. 45
Calvin, John 7–8, 10
Carter, Stephen L. 186n. 8
Cavanaugh, William T. 5
Certeau, Michel de 56, 80, 81, 82–4, 85, 88, 213
Chopp, Rebecca 51
Cicero 6, 167–9, 170, 172, 173, 175n. 19, 180
Cimabue, Giovanni 132
Clark, Elizabeth A. 50n. 33
Clement of Alexandria 9
Coakley, Sarah 39–55, 95n. 9, 212–13, 217

Cohen, Hermann 148, 151, 178
Comte, Auguste 13

Darwin, Charles 18, 20
Davies, Martin 56n. 1
Davies, Oliver 209
Davis, R. 71
Denney, James 160
Derrida, Jacques 32, 64
Descartes, René 9n. 25
Dewey, John 3
Dix, Gregory 123
Donne, John 56, 57, 72
Duccio, Augostino di 133
Duffy, Eamon xiv, 119–34, 210, 212
Duffy, Regis 124n. 7
Durkheim, Émile 3, 6, 10, 11, 12–13, 14, 15, 21

Eck, D. 71
Eichrodt, Walther 139n. 8
Eliade, Mircea 3–4, 6, 10, 14, 21

Farley, Edward 43, 53
Faure, B. 71
Feuerbach, Ludwig A. 36
Fiorenza, Francis Schüssler 47, 48n. 27
Fishbane, Michael 108–9, 111
Flood, Gavin 56–72, 94n. 6, 98, 211, 216
Ford, David F. xiii–xvii, 41, 49
Foucault, Michel 67, 151
Frazer, George 17
Frei, Hans 76
Freud, Sigmund 3, 10, 11, 15, 56
Frymer-Kennedy, Tikvah 109n. 5

Gadamer, H. G. 193
Geertz, Clifford 49, 101n. 14, 211
Gilpin, Clark 48
Giotto 132
Gregory of Nyssa 181
Griffiths, P. 66

222

Subject index